TENTH EDITION

THE COLLECTOR'S ENCYCLOPEDIA OF

DEPRESSION GLASS

BY GENE FLORENCE

COLLECTOR BOOKS

A Division of Schroeder Publishing Co., Inc.

The current values in this book should be used only as a guide. They are not intended to set prices, which vary from one section of the country to another. Auction prices as well as dealer prices vary greatly and are affected by condition as well as demand. Neither the Author nor the Publisher assumes responsibility for any losses that might be incurred as a result of consulting this guide.

ACKNOWLEDGMENTS

Writing this tenth book in Kentucky has given me time to look back at my 20 years of writing for Collector Books. I said in Kentucky because this is the last book that I am planning on writing here. My sons are now in college and we have a home in Florida that beckons me during the winter. Since my writing is done at the time of the year I will be there, it only seems natural to write a little, fish a little or maybe write a little, fish a lot! There are additional advantages such as a phone not ringing every five minutes interrupting trains of thought (as just happened in the middle of this sentence). Where was I? My Florida office overlooks a canal, where the alligators and the fish play. There is no way to adequately compare it to the wall I am facing as I write now!

The Macintosh II computer is working out fine now that I have my special computer bifocals in use. They arrived two days after I finished the ninth edition. Of course it took six or seven months to prove to the optometrist that his non-glare finish could not be cleaned without streaking so badly that I couldn't see out of them. They work fine after that wonderful finish was removed! Unfortunately, the computer only does about fifty percent of what I was told it would. Now that everything has been entered manually instead of scanned, it does about 90% of what's needed. If I could only get it to *write* without my help, I could eat more fish!

There have been over one hundred measurements corrected in this book. These corrections have occurred due to original catalogue errors, typing mistakes and errors in measurement in the past. Realize, too, that the same plate or tumbler **can** vary in each pattern, especially if it were made for a long time. Be sure to read about measurements on page 4.

Even after 20 years, there have been approximately *75 newly discovered pieces added to the listings* since the ninth edition! By the same token, there have been 14 deletions from the book of pieces that have never been found that were listed in catalogues or had mysteriously appeared in my listings. Computer people explain it as the "cosmic ray" theory. If you can not find out why it happened, place the blame on something else! Those of you who feel that nothing new is ever found had better look closely at your favorite pattern!

A special thanks to all you readers and collectors at shows who keep me inspired with your letters, cards and reports of new information! Thanks for the measurements and the photographs confirming new discoveries! Those photographs are invaluable when confirming a new piece. If you have trouble photographing glass, take it outside in natural light, place the glass on a neutral surface and forget the camera has a flash attachment. A cloudy bright day works best. Please enclose a *SASE* (self addressed stamped envelope) that is *large* enough to send back your pictures, if you wish them returned!

Thanks to all the Depression Glass Clubs and show promoters who invited me as a guest at their shows. I have enjoyed them, gained knowledge from them, and hopefully contributed to them.

Cathy, my wife, has become chief editor, critic and non-typist. She continues to try to make sense out of my run-on or "non" sentences so you will understand what I meant to say when I first "pecked it" out.

A special thanks to "Grannie Bear," my Mom, who spent hours wrapping and packing glass for the numerous photography sessions we had for this book. She, along with my Dad, have kept records since the last book on measurements and new listings as well as prices that items sold for in the shop. All of this makes my writing much easier.

Thanks, too, to Cathy's Mom, Sibyl, who helped Cathy sort and pack glass for days and days! My gratitude to Dad, Charles and Sibyl who kept everything under control at home while we travelled. Thanks to Marc for keeping the house in one piece and helping us at shows so I could study prices and visit. Since Chad started college and Marc is now enrolled this summer, my help in loading and unloading all the glass for photography and shows is suddenly gone!

Glass and information for this book were furnished by Earl and Beverly Hines, Dick and Pat Spencer, Sam and Becky Collings, Dan Tucker and Lorrie Kitchen, Dot and Jim Kimball, Gladys Florence and numerous readers from across the U.S.A., Puerto Rico, Canada, England, New Zealand and Australia!

Photographs for this book were made at Curtis and Mays Studio in Paducah by Tom Clouser. Glass arranging, unpacking, sorting, carting and repacking for a dozen photography sessions over two years was accomplished by Steve Quertermous, Jane White, Sherry Kraus, Lisa Stroup and Cathy Florence. There is no way anyone could believe what we have to do to get you these photographs short of being there. A new helper remarked that she *still* didn't believe it after four days of working last December! I've heard, "It certainly makes you appreciate the books," more than once, believe me.

Thanks to the special people in the Editing Department at Collector Books: Lisa Stroup who is working as Editor and Della Maze who transferred all my files into a book and caught some mistakes that Cathy and I missed!

As we go to press with the Tenth Edition, I wish to thank my readers for making this America's #1 Best Selling Glass Book! I hope you find something wonderful or rare!

FOREWORD

Depression Glass as defined in this book is the colored glassware made primarily during the Depression years in the colors of amber, blue, black, crystal, green, pink, red, yellow and white. There are other colors and some glass made before, as well as after, this time period; but primarily, the glass within this book was made from the 1920's through the end of the 1930's. This book is mostly concerned with the inexpensively made dinnerware turned out by machine in quantity and sold through the smaller stores or given away as promotional or premium items for other products of that time. Depression glass was often packed in cereal boxes, flour bags or given as gifts at the local movie theaters, gasoline stations and grocery stores.

There have been changes in the collecting of Depression Glass since my first book was sold in 1972. Prices have soared; seemingly plentiful patterns have been gathered into vast collections and removed from the market. Smaller Depression patterns and previously ignored crystal colors have picked up buyers; in fact, *anything* that is Depression Glass, whether it is a known pattern or not, suddenly has added value and collectability. Collectors have become more knowledgeable and sophisticated in their collecting. Many collectors are enhancing their collections of "A to W" (Adam to Windsor) with patterns of hand-made glassware made during the same time period. This broadening interest of collectors prompted me to research and write four more books in the field of Depression Glass, one on ELEGANT glassware of the time, one on the glass KITCHENWARE items of the Depression and two others on the VERY RARE glassware of the Depression era. Additionally, collectors have been buying later made patterns encompassing the 1950's and even the early 1960's that has led to my newest book *Collectible Glassware from the 40's, 50's, 60's.* In order to correctly handle glassware from that time period, it was necessary to move some patterns heretofore exclusive to this book into the newer book's time frame. However, one last time, I have allowed overlapping of patterns between the two books, hoping to circumvent the ire of loyal collectors. A separate section (pages 198-213) giving updated prices and listings for patterns being eliminated from this time frame is included! This should create additional "room" in this book to expand the next edition within the Depression time frame for which it was originally intended.

Information for this book comes via research, experience, fellow dealers, collectors and over 900,000 miles of travel pursuant to glassware. Too, some of the most interesting information has come from readers who were kind enough to share catalogues, magazines, photographs of glass and their special knowledge with me. These gestures I especially value.

PRICING

All prices in this book are retail prices for mint condition glassware. This book is intended to be only a guide to prices as there are some regional price differences which cannot reasonably be dealt with herein!

You may expect dealers to pay from 30% to 50% less than the prices quoted. Glass that is in less than mint condition, i. e. chipped, cracked, scratched or poorly molded, will bring only a small percentage of the price of glass that is in mint condition.

Prices have become pretty well standardized due to national advertising by dealers and the Depression Glass Shows which are held from coast to coast. Several nationally known dealers have assisted in pricing updates for this book. However, *there are still some regional differences in prices due partly to glass being more readily available in some areas than in others.* Too, companies distributed certain pieces in some areas that they did not in others. Generally speaking, however, prices are about the same among dealers from coast to coast.

Prices tend to increase dramatically on rare items and, in general, they have increased as a whole due to more and more collectors entering the field and people becoming more aware of the worth of Depression Glass. I receive letters daily from new collectors who have just "discovered" Depression Glass!

One of the more important aspects of this book is the attempt made to illustrate as well as realistically price those items which are in demand. The desire was to give you the most accurate guide to collectible patterns of Depression Glass available.

MEASUREMENTS

To illustrate why there are discrepancies in measurements, I offer the following sample from just two years of Hocking's catalogue references:

Year		Ounces		Ounces		Ounces
1935	Pitcher	37,58,80	Flat Tumbler	5,9,13½	Footed Tumbler	10,13
1935	Pitcher	37,60,80	Flat Tumbler	5,9,10,15	Footed Tumbler	10,13
1936	Pitcher	37,65,90	Flat Tumbler	5,9,13½	Footed Tumbler	10,15
1935	Pitcher	37,60,90	Flat Tumbler	5,9,13½	Footed Tumbler	10,15

All measurements in this book are exact as to some manufacturer's listing or to actual measurement. You may expect variance of up to ½" or 1-5 ounces. This may be due to mould variations or changes by the manufacturer as well as rounding off measurements for catalogue listings.

INDEX

ADAM JEANNETTE GLASS COMPANY, 1932-1934

Colors: Pink, green, crystal, yellow, some Delphite blue. *(See Reproduction Section)*

Pink Adam continues to be collected at a more vigorous pace than the green. Green Adam is less plentiful, but numerous collectors of pink Adam are causing prices of the pink to increase faster than the green. Many pink prices have a long way to go to catch those same items in green; but several, including the tumblers and serving pieces, are selling for as much as the green items. Of course, the pink vase remains the most elusive piece of Adam unless you consider the Adam/Sierra butter dish. Some pink vases are very lopsided. Many collectors are not willing to pay the high price for these. You may find a bargain if you decide to accept a "leaner."

That Adam/Sierra butter dish is shown on the left in the picture. If you look closely you can see the Sierra design on the top along with the Adam design. In other words, the top has both designs. Adam is on the outside of the top and Sierra is on the inside of the top only. You can find these tops on either the Adam or Sierra butter bottoms. The bottoms contain only one pattern. To be this combination butter it has to have both patterns and just not a top of the Adam butter on a Sierra butter bottom or vice versa as I have seen on numerous occasions priced as the rare butter. An explanation of how this combination could happen has been discussed in earlier books.

Although a fair number of Floral lamps have been found, most notably on the Northwest coast, very few Adam lamps have been found. In the Floral pattern, you can see lamps which are designed the same as Adam. A sherbet was frosted to hide the wiring and a notch was cut into the top edge to accommodate a switch. A metal cover was applied to the top of the frosted sherbet holding a tall bulb that was connected to a switch which fits through the notch. The prices below are for working lamps. It is the bulb assembly that is hard to find. Notched, frosted sherbets can be found.

As with several other Jeannette patterns, the sugar and candy lids are interchangeable.

As I said above, green Adam is much harder to find than the pink. Yet, prices have been rather steady in green for quite a while. They seem ripe for an increase. The butter dish, candy, candlesticks and shakers have all but disappeared. If you start collecting green Adam, buy those pieces first!

The butter dish is the only piece that has been reproduced! Do not use the information given in the Reproduction Section in the back of the book for any other pieces in a pattern. You can not apply the directions of the arrows on the butter to any other pieces in Adam. It only applies to the butter. This goes for all reproductions I have listed in the back. Only apply the telltale clues I have listed for the piece I am describing. Transferring information to some other item will not work!

Inner rims of cereal bowls and other Adam pieces need to be checked carefully. They became damaged from usage as well as stacking over the years. It is fine to purchase these as long as you do not pay mint condition prices. Damaged glass is becoming more and more of a problem in collecting. You will have to decide if you are willing to accept less than perfect glass. When it comes time to resell, I guarantee you will be happier with the prices obtained for mint glassware. Prices in this book are for mint (like new) condition glass. Some damaged glass can be repaired by competent workmen (but should be so labeled). I might add that not all glass grinders and glass repairmen are competent!

For new collectors I point out the green candy dish shown in back of the candle on the left. If you find one of these without a lid, It is not a "rare" lady's cuspidor – merely a topless candy!

	Pink	Green		Pink	Green
Ash tray, ¾"	25.00	20.00	** Cup	20.00	18.00
Bowl, 4¾" dessert	12.50	12.50	Lamp	230.00	250.00
Bowl, 5¾" cereal	35.00	35.00	Pitcher, 8", 32 oz.	32.50	37.50
Bowl, 7¾"	17.50	19.50	Pitcher, 32 oz. round base	45.00	
Bowl, 9", no cover	23.00	37.50	Plate, 6" sherbet	5.00	5.00
Bowl, cover, 9"	20.00	37.50	*** Plate, 7¾" square salad	9.50	10.00
Bowl, 9" covered	47.50	77.50	Plate, 9" square dinner	20.00	18.00
Bowl, 10" oval	20.00	20.00	Plate, 9" grill	16.00	15.00
Butter dish bottom	17.50	60.00	Platter, 11¾"	16.50	18.00
Butter dish top	47.50	215.00	Relish dish, 8" divided	15.00	18.00
Butter dish & cover	65.00	275.00	Salt & pepper, 4" footed	55.00	87.50
Butter dish combination			****Saucer, 6" square	5.00	6.00
with Sierra Pattern	750.00		Sherbet, 3"	22.50	33.00
Cake plate, 10" footed	17.50	20.00	Sugar	14.00	16.00
* Candlesticks, 4" pr.	70.00	85.00	Sugar/candy cover	18.50	33.50
Candy jar & cover, 2½"	67.50	85.00	Tumbler, 4½"	22.50	20.00
Coaster, 3¼"	17.50	15.00	Tumbler, 5½" iced tea	50.00	39.50
Creamer	15.00	17.50	Vase, 7½"	200.00	42.50

* Delphite $200.00   ** Yellow $85.00   *** Round pink $50.00; yellow $85.00   **** Round pink $50.00; yellow $65.00

Please refer to Foreword for pricing information

6

AMERICAN PIONEER LIBERTY WORKS, 1931-1934

Colors: Pink, green, amber and crystal.

Newly discovered pieces continue to make American Pioneer a pattern that keeps longtime collectors searching! Cocktails in two different sizes have now been found! One holds 3 oz. and stands 3¹³/₁₆" while the other holds 3½ oz. and stands 3¹⁵/₁₆". Also, a pink dresser set was found in Ohio! You can see it pictured here, but an American Pioneer collector in Texas now owns it.

That dresser set has become the most valuable item in the set. Only that one has been found in pink! This set has become a hot property due, in part, to the many perfume and cologne bottle collectors searching for those collectibles. Many times a piece in a Depression glass pattern becomes more valuable because collectors from another collecting field start searching for that particular item also. It makes for heated competition, and sometimes, frustration, if you are looking for such an item for your collection.

Green is still the most prized color, but be aware that there are three distinct shades of green available. You can see two in the lower picture; color variances do not seem to bother collectors of American Pioneer as much as in some other Depression glass patterns. They are just happy to acquire any new piece. I have met only a few collectors of crystal and even fewer for amber, the color that is truly rare!

Collectors of amber pieces have told me that there is little being found except basic luncheon pieces. To date, only one set of amber covered pitchers (urns) has ever been found! The liners for the pitchers are the regular 6" and 8" plates. That ought to make finding liners easy except for the 6" pink plate, which is also rare.

There are two styles of American Pioneer cups being found. Some cups have more rim flair than others which makes one style have a 4" diameter being 2¼" tall while the other has a 3⅝" diameter and is 2⅜" tall.

There still may be additional items in American Pioneer which I do not have listed; so if you find one, be sure to let me know. I do appreciate the information that you take time to share with me; and I'm making a point to pass that information along to readers.

	Crystal, Pink	Green		Crystal, Pink	Green
*Bowl, 5" handled	13.50	16.00	Lamp, 5½" round, ball		
Bowl, 8¾" covered	85.00	105.00	shape (amber $80.00)	65.00	
Bowl, 9" handled	17.50	22.50	Lamp, 8½" tall	80.00	95.00
Bowl, 9¼" covered	85.00	105.00	Mayonnaise, 4¼"	52.50	85.00
Bowl, 10¾" console	45.00	55.00	Pilsner, 5¾", 11 oz.	90.00	90.00
Candlesticks, 6½" pr.	57.50	77.50	**Pitcher, 5" covered urn	125.00	195.00
Candy jar and cover, 1 lb	75.00	90.00	***Pitcher, 7" covered urn	145.00	200.00
Candy jar and cover, 1½ lb.	80.00	105.00	Plate, 6"	11.50	14.00
Cheese and cracker set (in-			*Plate, 6" handled	11.50	14.00
dented platter and comport)	45.00	55.00	*Plate, 8"	7.50	10.00
Coaster, 3½"	22.50	25.00	*Plate, 11½" handled	14.00	17.00
Creamer, 2¾"	16.50	19.00	*Saucer	4.00	5.00
*Creamer, 3½"	17.50	20.00	Sherbet, 3½"	14.00	17.00
*Cup	9.00	11.00	Sherbet, 4¾"	23.00	30.00
Dresser set (2 cologne, powder			Sugar, 2¾"	17.00	20.00
jar, on indented 7½" tray)	300.00	285.00	*Sugar, 3½"	17.50	20.00
Goblet, 3¹³/₁₆", 3 oz., cocktail	30.00	35.00	Tumbler, 5 oz. juice	23.00	30.00
Goblet, 3¹⁵/₁₆", 3½ oz., cocktail	30.00	35.00	Tumbler, 4", 8 oz.	23.00	30.00
Goblet, 4", 3 oz. wine	32.50	42.50	Tumbler, 5", 12 oz.	32.50	42.50
Goblet, 6", 8 oz. water	32.50	37.50	Vase, 7", 4 styles	67.50	87.50
Ice bucket, 6"	40.00	50.00	Vase, 9", round		185.00
Lamp, 1¾", w/metal pole 9½"		50.00	Whiskey, 2¼", 2 oz.	40.00	

*Amber - Triple the price of pink unless noted
**Amber $250.00
***Amber $300.00

Please refer to Foreword for pricing information.

AMERICAN SWEETHEART MacBETH-EVANS GLASS COMPANY, 1930-1936

Colors: Pink, Monax, red, blue; some Cremax and color trimmed Monax.

American Sweetheart continues to rise in price. There are many reasons for this, but availability is a major asset for this pattern. Beginning collectors see the numerous colors and learn that it has not been reproduced. Then, too, there is an abundant supply of Monax (white color) in basic pieces such as cups, saucers, plates, sugar and creamers that can be found at reasonable prices. Monax plates were widely distributed, and can be found in almost all parts of the country which gives a good starting point for new collectors. Too, the additional rare pieces offer a challenge to collectors who have already bought all the basic pieces. Black and white color schemes are presently in vogue, further enhancing this sixty-year-old glassware's charm in today's market place.

Monax soups, both cream and flat, have become difficult to find. For the novice, a cream soup is two handled and was used for consomme or creamed soups. A pink cream soup can be seen in the right foreground of the top picture. Neither soup was a part of basic sets. Today, that means that there are fewer of these to be found. The sugar lid and shakers in monax are finally beginning to move up in price. Lid prices had leveled for several years, but additional new collectors have finally caused this price to creep upward. Shakers have just begun to be in short supply for the same reasons, but their price rise seems to be slower. I can remember the "early days" when $15.00 for a pair of **rare** Depression shakers seemed like a fortune! Of course, I was a Kentucky school teacher and that $15.00 was about 10% of a week's wages. Now, $100.00 each, seems like a fair price for many hard to find shakers.

Pink pitchers, tumblers and shakers continue to be an albatross for collectors of that color. Many collectors settle for the water sized tumbler without adding juice and iced tea tumblers. The smaller pitcher, shown on the left, is not as plentiful as its larger counterpart; however, not all collectors try to find two pitchers. Please note that there are pitchers **shaped like** American Sweetheart that do not have the moulded design of American Sweetheart. These are not American Sweetheart (or even Dogwood which has to have the silk screened Dogwood design), but are the blanks made by MacBeth-Evans to go with the plain, no design tumblers they made. The **pattern** has to be **moulded** into the pitcher for it to be American Sweetheart.

Complete sets of pink and Monax can still be accumulated with patience and money. Both colors have tid-bit sets, with a two tier set being shown in the photo in Monax. The origin of many of these sets has been questioned over the years. Although a few of these were made at the factory, others were newly made by someone in the St. Louis area in the early 1970's. If you wish to buy a tid-bit, remember that it can be almost impossible to tell newly made from old. Because of this, I do not list a price for tid-bits unless they are made up of hard to find plate sizes. Most original tid-bits sell in the $50.00 range.

There are two sizes of sherbets. Although the sherbet on the left in the top picture looks much larger than the one on the right, there is only ½" difference in diameter. The smaller, 3¾", is more difficult to find than the larger; but many collectors only buy one size, making prices closer than rarity indicates. Rarity does not always determine price nearly as much as demand does! Simply put, if few collectors desire a rarely found item, then the price remains reasonable.

	Pink	Monax		Pink	Monax
Bowl, 3¾" flat berry	30.00		Plate, 15½" server		175.00
Bowl, 4½" cream soup	40.00	50.00	Platter, 13" oval	28.00	47.50
Bowl, 6" cereal	11.50	9.50	Pitcher, 7½", 60 oz.	475.00	
Bowl, 9" round berry	30.00	50.00	Pitcher, 8", 80 oz.	425.00	
Bowl, 9½" flat soup	35.00	47.50	Salt and pepper, footed	325.00	225.00
Bowl, 11" oval vegetable	37.50	55.00	Saucer	3.50	2.50
Bowl, 18" console		325.00	Sherbet, 3¾" footed	15.00	
Creamer, footed	9.50	8.50	Sherbet, 4¼" footed		
Cup	13.50	9.00	(design inside or outside)	11.00	15.00
Lamp shade		425.00	Sherbet in metal holder		
Plate, 6" or 6½" bread & butter	3.50	3.00	(crystal only)	3.00	
Plate, 8" salad	8.50	7.00	Sugar, open, footed	9.00	6.00
Plate, 9" luncheon		9.00	*Sugar lid		175.00
Plate, 9¾" dinner	25.00	16.00	Tid-bit, 2 tier, 8" & 12"	50.00	50.00
Plate, 10¼" dinner		16.00	Tid-bit, 3 tier, 8", 12" & 15½"		200.00
Plate, 11" chop plate		10.00	Tumbler, 3½", 5 oz.	55.00	
Plate, 12" salver	12.00	11.00	Tumbler, 4¼", 9 oz.	50.00	
			Tumbler, 4¾", 10 oz.	70.00	

*Two style knobs.

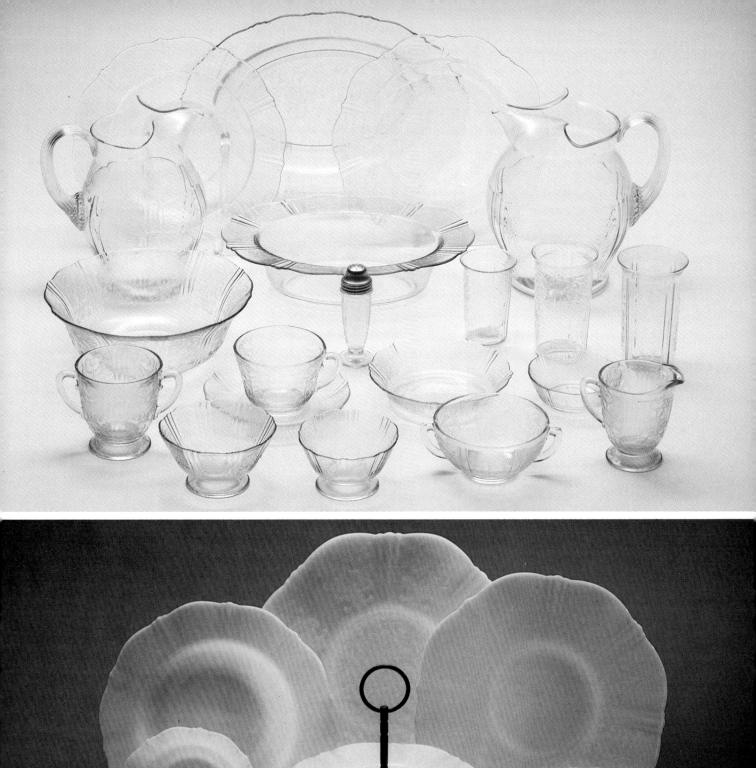

AMERICAN SWEETHEART (Cont.)

Mostly, red and blue American Sweetheart was sold in fifteen piece settings consisting of four each cups, saucers and 8" plates with a creamer, sugar and 12" salver. The additional pieces found in these colors were **very limited** in distribution.

For those who are not familiar with terminology, Cremax is the beige-like color illustrated by the 8" bowl turned upside down on the left in the top picture. Compare that color to the Monax 15½" server next to the bowl. That server is missing the heart shaped handle and is on a lazy susan (ball bearing) base. These lazy susans keep turning up in the Midwest!

Blue American Sweetheart still attracts more attention than red. Several reasons for that include the abundance of red found in comparison to blue which intrigues the avid collector. Also, more people seem to prefer blue glass to red. Over the years that has remained true in all patterns that have a blue color.

Note the red sherbet shown on the left in the top picture. This sherbet was made from the mould shape of American Sweetheart, but does not carry the design as we know it. As with the pink pitchers discussed on page 10, these are not considered to be American Sweetheart but are only **shaped** like American sweetheart. You can also find 8" plates and 6" cereal bowls without the design in both red and blue.

Monax with colored trims (shown in previous books) turns up infrequently. Many collectors try to find a piece or two, but there is not enough around for many collectors to have complete sets of the colored trims. You will find pieces trimmed in pink, green, yellow or black. The black trimmed American Sweetheart has a bluish/gray panel extending to the black edge and is called "Smoke" by collectors. Much of Monax American Sweetheart has a bluish cast to its edges, but to be "Smoke" it will always have a black trim at the edge. This black trimmed Monax seems to turn up more in the Midwest than any place, although I did find a platter at an antique show in Atlanta last year.

Real 22K gold is also found as a trim on Monax. This was often used as a glass "trim" at the time. Unfortunately, there is no premium for the gold trim; in fact, many dealers have difficulty selling it because it is hard to find a full set with gold that is not worn. The gold, and only the gold, can be removed by using a pencil eraser on it. Don't try to use a scouring pad since you may damage the glass!

The 8" Monax plate with the "Indian Trail" advertisement is the only one I have owned, but I have heard of other ads on these plates. No one has contacted me to tell me **what** other ads, however. So, if you have another one of these advertising plates, let me know. The pattern shot below shows a green trimmed lamp shade found on a floor lamp by a California collector.

	Red	Blue	Cremax	Smoke & Other Trims
Bowl, 6" cereal			8.00	35.00
Bowl, 9" round berry			30.00	95.00
Bowl, 18" console	700.00	850.00		
Creamer, footed	75.00	95.00		75.00
Cup	65.00	95.00		65.00
Lamp shade			425.00	
Lamp (floor with brass base)			650.00	
Plate, 6" bread and butter				15.00
Plate, 8" salad	40.00	65.00		25.00
Plate, 9" luncheon				35.00
Plate, 9¾" dinner				60.00
Plate, 12" salver	115.00	145.00		85.00
Plate, 15½" server	225.00	300.00		
Platter, 13" oval				135.00
Saucer	18.00	22.50		15.00
Sherbet, 4¼" footed (design inside or outside)				65.00
Sugar, open footed	75.00	95.00		75.00
Tid-bit, 2 tier, 8" & 12"	175.00	225.00		
Tid-bit, 3 tier, 8", 12" & 15½"	450.00	550.00		

Please refer to Foreword for pricing information

13

AUNT POLLY U.S. GLASS COMPANY, Late 1920's

Colors: Blue, green and iridescent.

Aunt Polly pattern, unfortunately, has no cups or saucers which affects the collectability of this pattern. Prices would soar if any were ever found. That lack of cup and saucers causes problems with the other U. S. Glass patterns such as Strawberry and Cherryberry.

It has now been fifteen years since I discovered that U. S. Glass was the manufacturer of Aunt Polly and her sister patterns mentioned above. In all that time, not one additional piece has been discovered. Surely, there are additional pieces awaiting unveiling!

There is an Aunt Polly "look-alike" shown in both pictures. At least they are assumed to be "look-alikes," but they may be variations of the the tumbler mould. The blue tumbler on the outside left and the vaseline colored tumbler in the bottom photo are slightly different than the normally found tumblers. The panelled lines are wider and there is no design in the bottom. The ground bottoms on these items may indicate early prototypes that were reworked, because the vaseline colored tumbler is a typical U. S. Glass color of the late 1920's. In any case, they make interesting additions to any collection!

By the same token, there are two variations of the creamer shown. One has a more pronounced lip than the other. Originally these lips were formed by hand using a wooden tool; so that probably accounts for those abnormalities.

Aunt Polly collectors are still finding several pieces extremely difficult to obtain. The oval vegetable, sugar lid, shakers and butter dish have always been a problem in blue. The blue butter top or bottom creates a headache; on the other hand, the bottoms in green or iridescent are plentiful. This occurs because all of the U.S. Glass butter bottoms are interchangeable. The bottom is plain and fits Cherryberry, Strawberry and U. S. Swirl as well as Aunt Polly. That is one reason that the butter top prices are so much more than the bottoms in the green and iridescent. There is no blue color in the other patterns, however; so there were always less bottoms available in blue.

Many collectors are having trouble finding mint sherbet plates. This pattern is very prone to mould imperfections such as roughly made seams on almost all pieces. For collectors who are adamant about mint condition, I suggest you look for some other pattern.

Blue is still the number one color collected, but there are a few collectors of the iridized and green. The major difficulty in collecting green is the varying shades of green. Some green is almost yellow in appearance as you can see in the photograph on the next page. Note the green two handled candy in the foreground. The lid for that candy is the same as the sugar. These candy dishes have only been found in green and iridescent colors.

	Green, Iridescent	Blue		Green, Iridescent	Blue
Bowl, 4¾" berry	7.00	12.00	Creamer	25.00	40.00
Bowl, 4¾", 2" high	9.00	16.00	Pitcher, 8" 48 oz.		150.00
Bowl, 5½" one handle	13.00	18.00	Plate, 6" sherbet	5.00	10.00
Bowl, 7¼" oval, handled pickle	10.00	30.00	Plate, 8" luncheon		16.00
Bowl, 7⅞" large berry	16.00	25.00	Salt and pepper		185.00
Bowl, 8⅜" oval	35.00	75.00	Sherbet	7.50	10.00
Butter dish and cover	210.00	175.00	Sugar	20.00	27.50
Butter dish bottom	75.00	75.00	Sugar cover	42.50	90.00
Butter dish top	135.00	100.00	Tumbler, 3⅝", 8 oz.		22.50
Candy, cover, 2-handled	57.50		Vase, 6½" footed	25.00	37.50

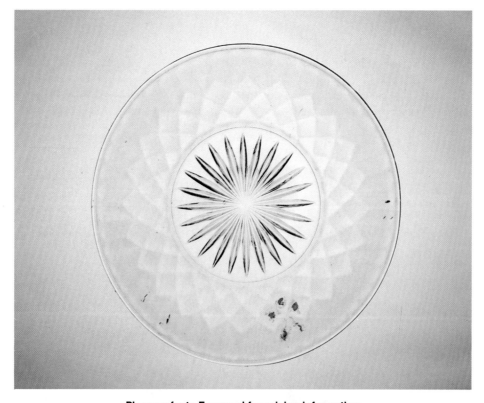

Please refer to Foreword for pricing information

"AURORA" HAZEL ATLAS GLASS COMPANY, Late 1930's

Colors: Cobalt blue, pink, green and crystal.

As soon as I said that "Aurora was a nice addition to any collection that will not completely drain your budget," the little 4½" deep bowl went skyrocketing in price! No matter how many of those I have found, not one has lasted in my booth beyond the first three hours of a show! Of course, cobalt blue attracts collectors in a way no other color seems to do. Even with the price of the little bowl now fetching $25.00, an eight place setting would not involve thousands of dollars as other cobalt blue sets will; so, if this is the color you like, here is a smaller pattern to check out!

Several readers have suggested that patterns which have only a tall creamer and no sugar should have the creamer listed as a milk pitcher. If you prefer calling it that, do so.

Not all pieces have been found in pink, but those found command as high a price as the blue due to scarcity of the pink.

Green cereal bowls, cups and saucers have been found, but so far only collectors of cup and saucers have been very excited over that find! Cereal bowls have also turned up in crystal. The green and crystal may be rare or maybe they have merely been overlooked. Only time will tell; if you find any other Aurora pieces in these (or other) colors, please let me know.

	Cobalt, Pink		Cobalt, Pink
Bowl, 4½" deep	25.00	Plate, 6½"	8.00
* Bowl, 5⅜" cereal	12.50	*** Saucer	4.00
Creamer, 4½"	15.00	Tumbler, 4¾", 10 oz.	16.00
** Cup	9.50		

*Green $7.00 or crystal $5.00   **Green $7.50   ***Green $2.50

"AVOCADO," NO. 601 INDIANA GLASS COMPANY, 1923-1933

Colors: Pink, green, crystal, white. *(See Reproduction Section)*

All sixteen pieces made in Avocado are pictured this time. Avocado is expensive, and in my experience, usually sells in large size lots rather than a piece here and there. Unless someone breaks up a collection, finding it is the problem. The only green pitcher I have had in the last year sold in Missouri. After that show, I had several calls wanting to buy it after friends of collectors had seen it at the show!

Green is still the predominant color collected. Notice some big price jumps in pitchers and tumblers as well as some bowls that have just about disappeared from the market. Tumblers are rapidly approaching the $200.00 mark. Reproduced green items are much darker than the original green shown here. I have preached since 1974 about the reproductions and how to tell the differences so that you will not be taken in by a fake. (On the positive side are reports that that particular glass selling scheme is finally collapsing).

Pink reproduced items have an orange cast to the color, but this does vary. Buyer beware! Know your dealer and his reputation for integrity. Pink has almost recovered from those reproduced pitchers and tumblers that were introduced in 1974.

There are beginning to be a few collectors of crystal, but not all pieces are found in this color. The only pieces I have seen sell in crystal are the deep bowl at $25.00 and the two-handled bowl for $8.50. I have only had one collector of crystal write since the last edition when I said I would work on a price listing for crystal. Help me if you will!

	Pink	Green		Pink	Green
Bowl, 5¼" 2-handled	23.00	28.00	*Pitcher, 64 oz.	625.00	785.00
Bowl, 6" footed relish	20.00	23.00	***Plate, 6⅜" sherbet	12.00	14.00
Bowl, 7" 1 handle preserve	16.00	23.00	**Plate, 8¼" luncheon	15.00	17.00
Bowl, 7½" salad	30.00	45.00	Plate, 10¼" 2-handled cake	30.00	45.00
Bowl, 8" 2-handled oval	18.00	24.00	Saucer, 6⅜"	22.50	25.00
Bowl, 9½", 3¼" deep	80.00	100.00	***Sherbet	47.50	50.00
***Creamer, footed	27.50	30.00	***Sugar, footed	27.50	30.00
Cup, footed, 2 styles	27.50	28.00	*Tumbler	125.00	195.00

*Caution on pink. The orange-pink is new!

**Apple design $10.00. Amber has been newly made.

***Remade in dark shade of green.

Please refer to Foreword for pricing information

BEADED BLOCK IMPERIAL GLASS COMPANY, 1927-1930's

Colors: Pink, green, crystal, ice blue, vaseline, iridescent, amber, red, opalescent and milk white.

A pink Beaded Block pitcher has finally been found! It was found in an antique mall in Florida last year and is pictured on the next page. I have had reports of five white pitchers now, but this is the only known pink one!

Beaded Block is a pattern that is also acquired by collectors of other patterns who wish an additional serving or display piece of Depression glass. The array of colors found in Beaded Block is matched by only a few other patterns in this book. It is one pattern that gets priced by unknowledgeable antique dealers as "Carnival," "Vaseline" or "Pattern" glass. It was originally made in the late 1920's and early 1930's. I say "originally" because Imperial had a reissue of the pink and pink iridized in the late 1970's and early 1980's. This is easily spotted since it is marked IG in the bottom. The only other marked piece that I know is the white lily bowl shown in the bottom photograph. When I visited the factory in 1981, I was told that the white was made in the early 1950's and the IG mark (for Imperial Glass) was first used about that time.

There are an abundance of square plates, but most of the round plates must have been turned into bowls, which was how bowls were made in Beaded Block. The edges of plates were turned up to make a bowl. That makes the size variances in this pattern a major headache for collectors. Sizes listed in the Imperial catalogues vary greatly as to actual sizes found today. The sizes listed here were all obtained from actual measurements and not from the catalogue. You may find some differences in your measurements, so don't get too alarmed. The 2-handled jelly which most companies called a cream soup measures from 4¾" to 5". Be sure to read the section on measurements at the bottom of page 4!

Red lily bowls are still being found in the central Ohio area and that seems to be the only place they were distributed. In fact, no other pieces in red appear to be available except that 4½" lily bowl.

The 6" vases shown in cobalt and pink are not Beaded Block, but are often sold as such. Note that they have no beading and no scalloped edge as do all the other pieces except the white lily bowl previously discussed. Imperial called these tall pieces "footed jellies." These were attained at groceries with a product inside. One found with the original label still attached reads "Good Taste Mustard Seed, 3½ oz., Frank Tea & Spice Co., Cin., O." I imagine the edge had to be smooth to take a lid, but why change the sides to a "zipper-like" design? Remember, these are a "go-with" piece and not truly Beaded Block.

	*Crystal, Pink, Green, Amber	Other Colors
Bowl, 4⅞"-5" 2-handled jelly	7.00	15.00
**Bowl, 4½" round lily	9.00	18.00
Bowl, 5½" square	7.00	9.50
Bowl, 5½" 1 handle	7.00	11.00
Bowl, 6" deep round	10.00	17.50
Bowl, 6¼" round	7.00	15.00
Bowl, 6½" round	7.00	15.00
Bowl, 6½" 2-handled pickle	12.00	17.50
Bowl, 6¾" round, unflared	11.00	15.00
Bowl, 7¼" round, flared	11.00	17.50
Bowl, 7½" round, fluted edges	20.00	22.00
Bowl, 7½" round, plain edge	18.00	22.00
Bowl, 8¼" celery	12.00	17.50
Creamer	15.00	25.00
***Pitcher, 5¼", pint jug	90.00	
Plate, 7¾" square	6.50	9.00
Plate, 8¾" round	15.00	18.00
Stemmed jelly, 4½"	9.00	17.00
Stemmed jelly, 4½", flared top	10.00	18.00
Sugar	14.00	23.00
Vase, 6" bouquet	11.00	20.00

* All pieces 25% to 40% lower.
** Red $100.00
*** White $160.00, pink $150.00

BLOCK OPTIC, "BLOCK" HOCKING GLASS COMPANY, 1929-1933

Colors: Green, pink, yellow, crystal and some blue.

Block Optic is the pattern that gets many new collectors started since it was widely distributed and a piece or two seems to be lingering in everyone's family. I used to recommend Block Optic to new collectors because it was economically priced and a beginner could afford to start with it. Today, the price is no longer as economical as it once was! Of course, nothing else is either! As far as collectability goes, Block remains high on the list of collector demand. There is an abundant supply of most of the basic pieces, and rarely found items are not yet "out of sight" as is the case of many of the most desirable green Depression patterns.

Add to the five styles of cups shown the fact that there are three different shapes of creamer and sugars. Looking at the bottom of page 21 mentally number the cup and saucers from one to five starting on the left. Number 1 and 3 are the rounded cups which come with plain or fancy handles as do the cups in Cameo. Number 1, which has the fancy handle, fits the 6⅛" saucer with cup ring. Number 2 is the only cup that will fit the 5¾" saucer with cup ring. Number 4 is a flat bottomed cup that fits on a combination saucer/sherbet plate. Number 5 has a pointed handle. I will not make price distinctions now; but pricing patterns are beginning to emerge on the different styles of cups!

There are variations in handles and slight differences in style to also make a total of five different creamers and sugars that can be collected in this set. In yellow, only the fancy handled, rounded type shown on page 23 has been found. There are three styles of pink creamer/sugar sets, flat bottomed and two styles of cone shaped pairs. One of the cone shaped styles has a base that is plain whereas the other type has a rayed base. (This is true of many of Hocking's patterns. Some tumblers or stems will show these variations of plain and ribbed bases.) In green creamers/sugars, there are the two cone shaped styles with one of these having pointed handles, the flat bottomed variety, and the rounded with plain handles evidenced by the frosted pair in the top photo. I have never seen a green fancy handled set. Let me know if you have such a pair!

Regarding the frosted green creamer and sugar shown in the top picture, Hocking, as well as other companies, satinized (frosted by using camphoric acid) many of their dinnerware lines. Evidently, these were special orders or special promotions since many were hand decorated with flowers or fruit. Today, collectors shy away from these pieces for some reason. Frosted items only bring a fraction of the price of their unfrosted counterparts. Even though these pieces are much more rare, there is so little demand that the price is lessened. That is one of the lessons beginners need to learn as soon as possible about collectibles. Rarity does not always determine price! Demand is the major determining factor of price!

A tumble-up set has been found that explains how they were sold. A stopper in a bottle was marked "Baree' Fragrant Bath Salts Paris, New York." That is how the decanter in Mayfair was also sold years ago. It, too, contained bath salts and the stopper was used as a measuring device!

Dinner plates received heavy usage and mint ones are premium items today.

There has been a dramatic jump in some of the prices of pink. Collectors of this color are finding that the supply is well short of that of the green. Stemware has turned out to be almost non existent. Add to that the lack of serving pieces and you have a set that will take time and patience to put together.

You will find some green Block with a black foot or stem. There is not enough of this available to collect a set unless you find it all at one time. Popularity of this is limited. As far as I can determine, that black is fired-on and can not be removed! Few pieces of crystal Block can be found. Only the butter dish has a premium value. Other pieces in crystal sell for about half the prices of green if a buyer can be found.

A reader in California sent some interesting information about the green butter dish top. In the twenty years I have been buying Depression glass, I have seen 15 to 20 green Block butter tops for every bottom. I had assumed that the heavy top had destroyed many of the bottoms over the years since it is difficult to grasp when trying to pick it up. It seems that the tops were also sold as a butter holder for ice boxes. This top slid into a metal holder eliminating the need for a glass bottom! It is amazing the ideas that glass companies had to market their glass.

I assume that you noticed the amber pair of candlesticks shown on page 23. I had never seen a pair until last June and since then I have seen four! Time will tell us their desirability. These seem to be selling in the price range of the green.

BLOCK OPTIC, "BLOCK" (Cont.)

	Green	Yellow	Pink		Green	Yellow	Pink
Bowl, 4¼" diam., 1⅜" tall	6.50		6.00	Plate, 9" dinner	15.00	35.00	22.00
Bowl, 4½" diam., 1½" tall	25.00			Plate, 9" grill	10.00	35.00	15.00
Bowl, 5¼" cereal	10.00		17.50	Plate, 10¼" sandwich	20.00		17.50
Bowl, 7" salad	20.00			Salt and pepper, footed	30.00	65.00	65.00
Bowl, 8½" large berry	21.00		18.00	Salt and pepper, squatty	75.00		
*Butter dish and cover, 3" x 5"	40.00			Sandwich server, center handle	47.50		42.50
Butter dish bottom	24.00			Saucer, 5¾", with cup ring	8.50		6.00
Butter dish top	16.00			Saucer, 6⅛", with cup ring	8.00		5.00
**Candlesticks, 1¾" pr.	90.00		65.00	Sherbet, non-stemmed (cone)	3.50		
Candy jar & cover, 2¼" tall	40.00	50.00	40.00	Sherbet, 3¼", 5½ oz.	5.00	8.00	7.00
Candy jar & cover, 6¼" tall	45.00		100.00	Sherbet, 4¾", 6 oz.	12.00	14.00	12.00
Comport, 4" wide mayonnaise	25.00		55.00	Sugar, 3 styles: as creamer	10.00	10.00	9.00
Creamer, 3 styles: cone shaped,				Tumbler, 2⅝", 3 oz.	17.50		20.00
round, rayed-foot & flat (5 kinds)	11.50	11.50	10.50	Tumbler, 3½", 5 oz. flat	17.50		20.00
Cup, four styles	6.00	7.50	6.00	Tumbler, 9½ oz. flat, 3¹³⁄₁₆" flat	12.00		12.00
Goblet, 3½" short wine			250.00	Tumbler, 10 or 11 oz., 5" flat	15.00		12.00
Goblet, 4" cocktail	30.00		28.00	Tumbler, 12 oz., 4⅞" flat	22.50		20.00
Goblet, 4½" wine	30.00		28.00	Tumbler, 15 oz., flat, 5¼",	30.00		28.00
Goblet, 5¾", 9 oz.	19.00		25.00	Tumbler, 3¼", 3 oz. footed	20.00		17.00
Goblet, 7¼", 9 oz. thin		30.00		Tumbler, 9 oz. footed	15.00	19.00	12.00
Ice bucket	30.00		35.00	Tumbler, 6", 10 oz. footed	22.50		22.00
Ice tub or butter tub, open	35.00		80.00	Tumble-up night set	55.00		
Mug	30.00			Tumbler, 3" only	40.00		
Pitcher, 7⅝", 54 oz., bulbous	65.00		60.00	Bottle only	15.00		
Pitcher, 8½", 54 oz.	30.00		30.00	Vase, 5¾" blown	180.00		
Pitcher, 8", 80 oz.	55.00		60.00	Whiskey, 1⅝", 1 oz.			35.00
Plate, 6" sherbet	2.00	2.50	2.00	Whiskey, 2¼", 2 oz.	22.50		22.50
Plate, 8" luncheon	4.00	4.00	3.00				

* Green clambroth $150.00 - blue $375.00 - crystal $85.00

**Amber $100.00

"BOWKNOT" MANUFACTURER UNKNOWN, Probably late 1920's

Color: Green

Bowknot still remains a mystery pattern. The mystery is the manufacturer and the exact dates it was made. Add to that a cup with no saucer and two different style tumblers with no pitcher and you have a real "who-done-it?"

At last you can see the cereal bowl, which I have had a devil of a time finding! Many dealers do not carry small patterns such as Bowknot to shows. It's a mistake since every time I take Bowknot to shows (when Cathy has extra pieces that she does not need), they are some of the first pieces to leave with collectors. My wife still thinks this is a neat pattern. Evidently, she is not the only one. It is beginning to sell to other collectors besides her.

I still get letters from novice collectors who feel that they have found the first creamer and sugar. The Fostoria pattern "June" has a bow also but does not come in green. If you find a green Bowknot creamer or sugar, run, don't walk to the nearest phone and give me a call.

	Green		Green
Bowl, 4½" berry	12.00	Sherbet, low footed	12.00
Bowl, 5½" cereal	15.00	Tumbler, 5", 10 oz.	15.00
Cup	6.00	Tumbler, 5", 10 oz. footed	15.00
Plate, 7" salad	9.00		

Please refer to Foreword for pricing information

CAMEO, "BALLERINA" or "DANCING GIRL" HOCKING GLASS COMPANY, 1930-1934

Colors: Green, yellow, pink and crystal w/platinum rim. (*See Reproduction Section*)

Yellow Cameo has not traditionally attracted collectors in the quantities that the green does; however, there is some evidence in my shop that that trend may be changing. Many pieces in yellow are quite difficult to obtain. The butter dish shown on the next page is one of the few known. There are a few extra butter bottoms floating around, but only four or five tops. (Strangely, a butter bottom in green is the more difficult piece to find.) Yellow Cameo cups, saucer/sherbet plates, grill and dinner plates were heavily promoted by Hocking. These four yellow pieces are still plentiful today. In fact, until recently, they were difficult to sell. While the trend for Cameo's prices in general has been upward, prices on commonly found yellow pieces have remained steady. It's an attractive yellow pattern; so if you like it, now may be the time to get your basic set!

I receive letters or calls about yellow saucers in Cameo each year. The real Cameo saucer has an indented cup ring, but it has never been seen in yellow. Hocking made few indented saucers. They made a dual purpose saucer/sherbet plate for most patterns. If you will look on the bottom of page 27, the difference can be seen in green. The saucer on the right has a distinct indented ring (1¾" center) while the saucer/sherbet plate (2¾" center) on the left does not.

Green Cameo remains one of Depression glass's most desirable patterns. There are enough easily found pieces to obtain a set without having all the rare accessory items. However, if you want an eight or twelve place setting with all the serving pieces, then be prepared to dig deep into your savings or equity account. Many collectors can not afford everything; so they do not try to find every stem and every tumbler; instead they purchase only one or two different size tumblers or stems.

Pink Cameo is rarely found, but it is also expensive as you can tell by looking at the prices. Few new collectors try to start this color because of the price and the difficulty in obtaining it.

All of the miniature pieces in Cameo are new! No small size Cameo was ever made during the Depression era. See the Reproduction Section in the back of the book for information on this and the reproduced Cameo shakers. A new importer is making a sometimes weakly patterned shaker in pink, cobalt blue and a darker shade of green than the original color. If new tops are the first thing you notice — beware!

The short 3½" and 4" wines can be seen on the closed handled plate between the saucers discussed above. Many collectors are desirous of these!

Another question that needs to be addressed is the difference between grill plates. A grill plate is a sectioned or divided plate which keeps the food separated. They were used mostly in restaurants and "grills" of that day. In the picture of yellow Cameo, both styles are shown. One has tab handles and one does not. Both are common in yellow. In green, however, the grill with the tab or closed handles is harder to find. The 10½" rimmed dinner plate is just like the heavy edged grill plate only without the dividers! You can see the difference easily in the photograph of yellow.

For novice collectors I need to reiterate some basic information shown in the pictures on page 27. In the top picture there are two vases shown in the back right. The 8" vase is the bulbous one. The smaller 5¾" is shown in front of it. This smaller vase is often confused with the tall candy bottom. There is no Cameo "rope" design at the top of the vase. There is on the candy. The two handled bowl on the left is a cream soup bowl; and the tray on which the creamer is sitting is called a Domino sugar tray. This one is indented for the creamer although some are not.

In the bottom picture please note the plates in the back. The dinner plate with a large center area is on the right. The plate on the left with the smaller center is called a sandwich plate. I also should point out the color variations in the cups as well as the handle styles. The cups on the right have plain handles (abbreviated "ph" in ads) and the cup on the left has a fancy handle (abbreviated "fh" in ads). The darker green bottle is marked "Whitehouse Vinegar" on the bottom. These originally came from the grocery with vinegar — and a cork.

Shown at right are the rare center handled sandwich server (see pricing) and the only known goblet style oil lamp base.

	Green	Yellow	Pink	Crystal, Plat		Green	Yellow	Pink	Crystal, Plat
Bowl, 4¼" sauce				5.00	Cake plate, 10", 3 legs	17.50			
Bowl, 4¾" cream soup	55.00				Cake plate, 10½" flat	85.00		115.00	
Bowl, 5½" cereal	26.00	25.00	50.00	6.00	Candlesticks, 4" pr.	90.00			
Bowl, 7¼" salad	45.00				Candy jar, 4" low				
Bowl, 8¼" large berry	30.00		125.00		and cover	60.00	65.00	425.00	
Bowl, 9" rimmed soup	35.00		85.00		Candy jar, 6½" tall				
Bowl, 10" oval vegetable	17.50	35.00			and cover	115.00			
Bowl, 11", 3-legged					Cocktail shaker (metal				
console	57.50	75.00	35.00		lid) appears in				
Butter dish and cover	165.00	1,300.00			crystal only				450.00
Butter dish bottom	95.00	425.00			Comport, 5" wide				
Butter dish top	70.00	875.00			mayonnaise	25.00		175.00	

Please refer to Foreword for pricing information

CAMEO, "BALLERINA" or "DANCING GIRL" (Cont.)

	Green	Yellow	Pink	Crystal, Plat
Cookie jar and cover	42.50			
Creamer, 3¼"	18.00	15.00		
Creamer, 4¼"	20.00		95.00	
Cup, 2 styles	13.00	7.00	65.00	5.00
Decanter, 10" with stopper	120.00			175.00
Decanter, 10" with stopper, frosted (stopper represents ⅓ value of decanter)	25.00			
Domino tray, 7" with 3" indentation	95.00			
Domino tray, 7" with no indentation			175.00	100.00
Goblet, 3½" wine	550.00		600.00	
Goblet, 4" wine	55.00		195.00	
Goblet, 6" water	45.00		155.00	
Ice bowl or open butter, 3" tall x 5½" wide	135.00		450.00	225.00
Jam jar, 2" and cover	135.00			150.00
Pitcher, 5¾", 20 oz. syrup or milk	165.00	455.00		
Pitcher, 6", 36 oz. juice	50.00			
Pitcher, 8½", 56 oz. water	42.50		1,250.00	450.00
Plate, 6" sherbet	3.00	3.00	80.00	1.75
Plate, 7" salad				3.00
Plate, 8" luncheon	8.50	9.00	25.00	3.50
Plate, 8½" square	32.50	125.00		
Plate, 9½" dinner	14.00	6.00	60.00	
Plate, 10" sandwich	12.00		35.00	
Plate, 10½" rimmed dinner	85.00		125.00	
Plate, 10½" grill	7.50	5.00	42.50	
Plate, 10½" grill with closed handles	60.00	5.00		
Plate, 10½" with closed handles	10.00	10.00		
Platter, 12", closed handles	16.00	35.00		
Relish, 7½" footed, 3 part	24.00	150.00		125.00
* Salt and pepper, footed pr.	60.00		600.00	
Sandwich server, center handle	3,250.00			
Saucer with cup ring	145.00			
Saucer, 6" (sherbet plate)	3.00	3.00	75.00	
Sherbet, 3⅛" molded	11.50	35.00	60.00	
Sherbet, 3⅛" blown	13.00		60.00	
Sherbet, 4⅞"	30.00	37.50	85.00	
Sugar, 3¼"	15.00	12.00		
Sugar, 4¼"	19.50		95.00	
Tumbler, 3¾", 5 oz. juice	24.50		75.00	
Tumbler, 4", 9 oz. water	20.00		70.00	8.00
Tumbler, 4¾", 10 oz. flat	22.00		85.00	
Tumbler, 5", 11 oz. flat	23.00	40.00	80.00	
Tumbler, 5¼", 15 oz.	55.00		110.00	
Tumbler, 3 oz. footed juice	50.00		110.00	
Tumbler, 5", 9 oz. footed	22.00	13.50	95.00	
Tumbler, 5¾", 11 oz. footed	50.00		110.00	
Tumbler, 6⅜", 15 oz. footed	400.00			
Vase, 5¾"	140.00			
Vase, 8"	22.50			
Water bottle (dark green) Whitehouse vinegar	15.00			

* Beware Reproductions

Please refer to Foreword for pricing information

CHERRY BLOSSOM JEANNETTE GLASS COMPANY, 1930-1939

Colors: Pink, green, Delphite (opaque blue), crystal, Jadite (opaque green) and red. *(See Reproduction Section)*

I have been amazed at the change in attitudes that collectors have made in purchasing Cherry Blossom. A few years ago the reproductions had dealers refusing to stock this pattern since you couldn't give it away. Education about the differences in old and new has brought back collecting Cherry Blossom with a vengeance. Almost all prices have increased since the last book with the notable exception of the Delphite color. (That color is an opaque light blue if you are not familiar with it.) I might mention that the Delphite pitcher and tumbler prices were out of place in the last list. I have cleared that up this time. My wife finds the Delphite attractive.

Prices have risen to ante-repro days except for the shakers which still have a long way to go. The problem with the shakers concerns not only the large number of reproductions made, but the fact that many collectors are willing to purchase these fakes in order to have a pair of shakers for their set and not have to pay the high price of the rarely found older ones. I still get many calls and letters on the pink shakers. Only two pair of original pink shakers were ever found; so the likelihood of your finding another old pair is fairly remote, at best, particularly at a bargain price. I've learned never to say "never," however.

A 11" platter finally surfaced in green! Measure this platter outside edge to outside edge. The 13" platter measures 11" on the inside rims. Other pieces of Cherry are becoming harder and harder to find. The aforementioned platter, soup and cereal bowls and the 10" green grill plate have all been difficult for collectors to obtain, especially in mint condition. Now the three footed bowl and flat iced teas have joined the list. Be sure to check the inner rims of Cherry Blossom pieces since there is a tendency for them to have chips and nicks.

You will find crystal Cherry Blossom at times. Usually it is the two handled bowl which sells in the $12.50 range. It is scarce, but there is not enough crystal found to be collectible. A few red pieces have been found, but the reproduction red wiped out the demand for those.

The letters AOP stand for "all over pattern" on the footed tumblers and pitcher shown on the right in the pictures. The footed large tumblers and the AOP pitcher come in two styles. One style has a scalloped or indented foot while the other is round with no indentations. PAT stands for "pattern at the top" illustrated by the flat bottomed tumblers on the left in the pictures.

There are some known experimental pieces of Cherry such as a pink cookie jar, pink five-part relish, orange with green trim slag bowl and amber children's pieces. Pricing on these is difficult to determine; but keep your eye out for these pieces, and don't pass them up!

	Pink	Green	Delphite		Pink	Green	Delphite
Bowl, 4¾" berry	12.00	14.50	12.00	Sugar cover	12.00	15.00	
Bowl, 5¾" cereal	25.00	28.00		Tray, 10½" sandwich	15.00	16.00	16.00
Bowl, 7¾" flat soup	45.00	45.00		Tumbler, 3¾", 4 oz.			
*Bowl, 8½" round berry	37.50	37.50	35.00	footed AOP	13.00	16.00	17.00
Bowl, 9" oval vegetable	27.50	28.00	42.50	Tumbler, 4½", 9 oz. round			
Bowl, 9" 2-handled	25.00	27.50	20.00	foot AOP	25.00	28.00	16.00
**Bowl, 10½", 3 leg fruit	65.00	65.00		Tumbler, 4½", 8 oz.			
Butter dish and cover	60.00	75.00		scalloped foot AOP	25.00	28.00	16.00
Butter dish bottom	15.00	20.00		Tumbler, 3½", 4 oz.			
Butter dish top	45.00	55.00		flat PAT	15.00	24.00	
Cake plate (3 legs) 10¼"	22.50	23.00		Tumbler, 4¼", 9 oz.			
Coaster	12.00	10.00		flat PAT	15.00	19.00	
Creamer	15.00	16.00	16.00	Tumbler, 5", 12 oz.			
Cup	15.00	17.00	14.00	flat PAT	45.00	60.00	
Mug, 7 oz.	175.00	150.00					
*** Pitcher, 6¾" AOP, 36 oz.							
scalloped or round bottom	40.00	45.00	70.00				
Pitcher, 8" PAT, 42 oz. flat	45.00	45.00					
Pitcher, 8" PAT, 36 oz.							
footed	47.50	47.50					
Plate, 6" sherbet	6.00	6.00	8.50				
Plate, 7" salad	15.00	17.00					
****Plate, 9" dinner	18.00	20.00	15.00				
Plate, 9" grill	20.00	22.00					
Plate, 10" grill		60.00					
Platter, 9" oval	725.00	775.00					
Platter, 11" oval	25.00	28.00	38.00				
Platter, 13" and 13" divided	50.00	50.00					
Salt and pepper							
(scalloped bottom)	1,200.00	800.00					
Saucer	4.00	4.00	4.00				
Sherbet	12.00	15.00	12.00				
Sugar	11.00	13.00	16.00				

*Yellow - $350.00   **Jadite - $275.00   ***Jadite - $300.00
****Translucent green - $175.00   Jadite - $40.00

CHERRY BLOSSOM - CHILD'S JUNIOR DINNER SET

	Pink	Delphite
Creamer	37.50	40.00
Sugar	37.50	40.00
Plate, 6"	8.00	10.00 (design on bottom)
Cup	30.00	30.00
Saucer	3.50	5.00
14 Piece set	250.00	260.00

Original box sells for $15.00 extra with pink sets.

Please refer to Foreword for pricing information

CHERRYBERRY U.S. GLASS COMPANY, Early 1930's

Colors: Pink, green, crystal; some iridized.

Cherryberry collecting has evolved from searching for Strawberry. Very few collectors took notice of this pattern for years, except those who were buying Strawberry. Now Cherryberry has become a viable Depression glass pattern with a few "Carnival" glass collectors raiding our ranks to grab the iridescent pitchers, tumblers and butter dishes. Butter dishes and pitchers are the most desirable iridized pieces. Not only do Cherryberry collectors search for these, but collectors of butters and pitchers seek them, also.

Crystal and iridescent are much rarer than pink or green, but there are fewer collectors for these colors.

This is another of the U.S. Glass patterns that has no cup or saucer and has a plain butter base. If all these U.S. Glass patterns are "sister" patterns, then Strawberry and Cherryberry are twins. You can only tell them apart by the fruit.

	Crystal, Iridescent	Pink, Green		Crystal, Iridescent	Pink, Green
Bowl, 4" berry	6.00	8.00	Olive dish, 5" one-handled	7.50	13.00
Bowl, 6¼", 2" deep	35.00	47.50	Pickle dish, 8¼" oval	8.00	13.00
Bowl, 6½" deep salad	15.00	17.50	Pitcher, 7¾"	150.00	140.00
Bowl, 7½" deep berry	16.00	18.00	Plate, 6" sherbet	5.00	8.00
Butter dish and cover	140.00	150.00	Plate, 7½" salad	7.00	12.00
Butter dish bottom	75.00	85.00	Sherbet	6.00	8.00
Butter dish top	65.00	65.00	Sugar, small open	11.00	15.00
Comport, 5¾"	15.00	20.00	Sugar, large	14.00	22.00
Creamer, small	11.00	15.00	Sugar cover	27.00	45.00
Creamer, 4⅝" large	14.00	30.00	Tumbler, 3⅝", 9 oz.	16.00	27.50

CHINEX CLASSIC MacBETH-EVANS DIVISION OF CORNING GLASS WORKS, Late 1930's - Early 1940's

Colors: Ivory, ivory w/decal decoration.

I will show you more Chinex than I have before. This pattern "grows" on you. I have had fun finding the many pieces shown on the opposite page and on page 33. Eliminating the 1950's patterns from this book will allow me to expand the amount of space I can use on some of the patterns that can be collected, but are not as popular as some of the others. My personal Chinex preference is the blue trimmed castle decal, but the blue rimmed pieces with the red flower run a close second. I am not as fond of the brown trimmed castle scenes, but other collectors are. That is what makes collecting so interesting. If everyone liked the same pattern, then it wouldn't take long for that one pattern to disappear from the marketplace.

Some collectors got upset with me for exposing the beauty of the floral pattern in an earlier book. I have been blamed for higher prices having been caused by new collectors buying it before the long time collectors can find it. They are right in that more collectors did start to search and it disappeared quickly into new collections. Collecting the blue or pink trimmed floral is a challenge. More of this is being found in western Pennsylvania area. Since it was made in that area, that makes sense.

The plainer, undecorated beige pieces are still awaiting collectors to notice them. So far, not many have taken on this challenge. This undecorated Chinex is great in the microwave according to a Midwestern collector. I must admit that I have never tried it in the microwave, so remember to test it out first by putting it in for a short period of time and checking for "hot" spots just as you would any other dish not designed specifically for the microwave.

Castle decal decorated items are the most desirable, but the darker trimmed blue is more popular than the lighter blue or the brown trimmed.

Remember, the butter bottoms look like Cremax instead of Chinex. The butter tops have the "scroll like" design that distinguishes this pattern, but this scroll design is missing from the bottoms. The bottom has a plainer pie crust edge. The floral or castle designs will be inside the base of the butter. See the butter bottom on the right hand side of the castle decorated picture. I have never found a top to this butter; so I do not know if there is a castle scene on the top as there is with the floral decorated top shown at the left bottom on page 33.

Please refer to Foreword for pricing information

	Browntone or Plain Ivory	Decal Decorated	Castle Decal
Bowl, 5¾" cereal	4.50	7.00	14.00
Bowl, 7" vegetable	13.00	18.00	30.00
Bowl, 7¾" soup	12.00	16.00	27.50
Bowl, 9" vegetable	10.00	20.00	30.00
Bowl, 11"	16.00	30.00	40.00
Butter dish	50.00	70.00	110.00
Butter dish bottom	10.00	25.00	40.00
Butter dish top	40.00	45.00	70.00
Creamer	5.00	9.00	17.00
Cup	4.00	6.00	12.50
Plate, 6¼" sherbet	2.00	3.00	6.00
Plate, 9¾" dinner	4.00	8.00	15.00
Plate, 11½" sandwich or cake	7.00	12.50	20.00
Saucer	2.00	4.00	6.00
Sherbet, low footed	6.50	10.00	20.00
Sugar, open	5.00	8.50	15.00

CIRCLE HOCKING GLASS COMPANY, 1930's

Colors: Green, pink and crystal.

Circle patten has two style cups. The flat bottomed style fits a saucer/sherbet plate while the rounded cup takes an indented saucer. I still have not found the indented saucer for my cup, but I did find the pink saucer/sherbet plate this time. At this time I believe only a luncheon set was made in the pink. I have never heard of tumblers, pitchers or bowls in pink. Pink, although rarely collected, is not abundant.

Circle is more noticed by kitchenware collectors (especially reamer collectors) than it is by Depression glass enthusiasts because the pitcher (80 oz.) with a reamer top is collected. (Hocking made a reamer top that fits this pitcher.) The major problem with that fact is color variations in the pitchers make it difficult to find a reamer that matches the green shade of the pitchers. Notice how yellow looking the pitcher is compared to the other green pieces. (Hopefully, that yellowish tint will show when the book is printed.)

The only new listing for this pattern is a flat 15 oz. tumbler.

Both of the bowls, 9⅜" and 5¼", have ground bottoms.

You can find green colored stems with crystal tops easier than you can find plain green stems; however, no one seems to want the crystal stemmed items.

I said I doubted the existence of the 9½" dinner plate, but here is a 10" sandwich plate.

	Green, Pink		Green, Pink
Bowl, 4½"	5.00	Plate, 6" sherbet/saucer	1.50
Bowl, 5¼"	6.00	Plate, 8¼" luncheon	4.00
Bowl, 5½" flared	6.00	Plate, 10" sandwich	12.00
Bowl, 8"	11.00	Saucer w/cup ring	1.50
Bowl, 9⅜"	14.00	Sherbet, 3⅛"	4.00
Creamer	8.00	Sherbet, 4¾"	6.00
Cup (2 styles)	4.00	Sugar	7.00
Decanter, handled	35.00	Tumbler, 3½", 4 oz. juice	8.00
Goblet, 4½" wine	10.00	Tumbler, 4", 8 oz. water	9.00
Goblet, 8 oz. water	9.00	Tumbler, 5", 10 oz. tea	16.00
Pitcher, 60 oz.	27.50	Tumbler, 15 oz. flat	18.00
Pitcher, 80 oz.	25.00		

CLOVERLEAF HAZEL ATLAS GLASS COMPANY, 1930-1936

Colors: Pink, green, yellow, crystal and black.

Cloverleaf collecting has been fairly well spread out among the yellow, black, and green colors. Since there are so few pieces in crystal and pink, those colors have little to offer collectors except the challenge of putting together a luncheon set. There is a pink flared 10 oz. tumbler to go with the basic luncheon pieces, but that is all. That tumbler is quite sparsely distributed I might add. Crystal makes a nice table display with colored accoutrements. In crystal the tumbler is missing.

Other Cloverleaf colors are selling well with yellow leading the way. In yellow, the candy dish, shakers and bowls do not seem to be available at any price. In green, the 8" bowl and the tumblers are selling briskly.

Black Cloverleaf has seen a surge in collecting recently with only the ash trays being ignored. I have noticed that this is true in many patterns. Evidently, the non-smokers are being heard for a change or the smokers are finally "wising up"; and it is affecting the sale of smokers' items even in the glassware business. Some black pieces in the photograph on page 37 are gold decorated. The Cloverleaf design was highlighted in gold probably for a special promotion. I have included samples of these hoping the Cloverleaf pattern will show better in the picture. Years ago we highlighted the designs with Bon Ami, but that made for unnatural white cloverleaves.

Actually, Cloverleaf was fairly limited in distribution nationally. About ten years ago, I bought a large collection of Cloverleaf in Ohio. It had been gathered from dealers all over the country, but major portions of the accumulation had come from Ohio and Pennsylvania. One of my favorite buys was a yellow candy bottom marked "large sherbet – $2.00". Because the collector had kept that sales tag on it, I enjoyed the same chuckle the original collector did when he bought it at a flea market years earlier.

I have been asked to point out that the Cloverleaf pattern comes on both the inside and outside of the pieces. That does not seem to make a difference in value or collectability. In order for the black to show the pattern, moulds had to be designed with the pattern on the outside. On transparent pieces the pattern could be on the bottom or the inside and it would still show. In black, the pattern on the bottom of a plate makes it look like a plain black plate; so it was moved to the top. Over the years, transparent pieces also were made using the moulds designed for the black; so, you now find these pieces made with designs on both sides.

The black sherbet plate and saucer are the same size. The saucer has no "Cloverleaf" pattern in the center. These sherbet plates still turn up as saucers occasionally; so keep your eyes open!

Please refer to Foreword for pricing information

CLOVERLEAF HAZEL ATLAS GLASS COMPANY, 1930-1936 (Cont.)

	Pink	Green	Yellow	Black
Ash tray, 4", match holder in center				65.00
Ash tray, 5¾", match holder in center				75.00
Bowl, 4" dessert	10.00	16.00	22.00	
Bowl, 5" cereal		22.00	25.00	
Bowl, 7" deep salad		35.00	45.00	
Bowl, 8"		47.50		
Candy dish and cover		45.00	95.00	
Creamer, 3⅝" footed		8.50	14.00	15.00
Cup	6.00	7.00	9.00	14.00
Plate, 6" sherbet		4.00	6.00	30.00
Plate, 8" luncheon	6.00	6.00	12.00	13.00
Plate, 10¼" grill		16.00	18.00	
Salt and pepper, pr.		25.00	95.00	75.00
Saucer	3.00	3.00	4.00	5.00
Sherbet, 3" footed	5.00	6.00	9.50	17.50
Sugar, 3⅝" footed		8.50	14.00	15.00
Tumbler, 4", 9 oz. flat		35.00		
Tumbler, 3¾", 10 oz. flat flared	17.00	30.00		
Tumbler, 5¾", 10 oz. footed		19.00	25.00	

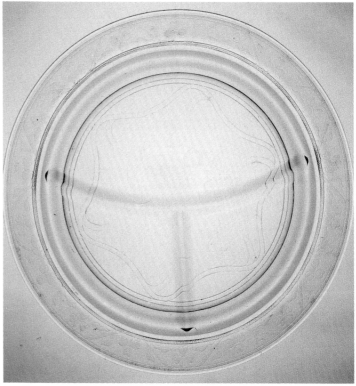

COLONIAL, "KNIFE AND FORK" HOCKING GLASS COMPANY, 1934-1936

Colors: Pink, green, crystal and opaque white.

Since Colonial pink and crystal sales have picked up considerably, I am showing those colors this time. After buying two collections with sets in each of the three colors, I found that the green took the longest to sell! Pink seems to be the color everyone now wants.

Demand for green Colonial stemware has finally slowed. Prices on crystal stems are rapidly approaching prices of their green counterparts. There is a true scarcity of crystal stems. There are no stems in pink.

The 10 oz. tumbler measures 2¾" across the top while the 12 oz. measures exactly 3" across the top. The spooner stands 5½" tall while the sugar without lid is only 4½". I bought the last pink spooner I saw at a large flea market as a $15.00 sugar bowl!

The 15 oz. lemonade turns up regularly in green but rarely in pink or crystal. Lately an abundance (compared to the last few years) of green lemonade tumblers have cropped up.

Occasionally, mugs are found in pink; but only three have turned up in green. These were found in Washington Court House, Ohio, for $1.00 each. A few bargains still turn up, so keep looking. I get letters every week of bargain "finds" somewhere in the world.

The cheese dish lid is ¼" shorter than the butter top. The butter top is 4" tall and the cheese top is only 3¾" tall. It took a level and some ingenuity to discover that there was not the ½" difference that I have previously recorded. The cheese top has a more flattened look when you have the two tops together. So far, the cheese has only been found in green; but the pink butter is already impossible to find without looking for a cheese dish also! The 3" pink sherbet is more than twice as difficult to find as the normally found 3⅜" sherbert, but it only sells for twice as much. So far, no 3" green or crystal sherbets have surfaced.

Soups, both cream and regular, cereals, shakers and dinners are still difficult to discover in all colors of Colonial. Cereal bowls in green may be the most difficult to obtain in all of Depression glass.

A white sugar and creamer have now been found to go with the other white luncheon pieces previously reported.

	Pink	Green	Crystal		Pink	Green	Crystal
Bowl, 3¾" berry	40.00			Plate, 6" sherbet	4.00	5.00	3.00
Bowl, 4½" berry	10.00	12.00	6.00	Plate, 8½" luncheon	8.00	8.00	4.00
Bowl, 5½" cereal	45.00	75.00	20.00	Plate, 10" dinner	40.00	52.00	20.00
Bowl, 4½" cream soup	52.50	52.50	55.00	Plate, 10" grill	20.00	20.00	12.00
Bowl, 7" low soup	47.50	47.50	20.00	Platter, 12" oval	25.00	19.00	14.00
Bowl, 9" large berry	20.00	25.00	15.00	Salt and pepper, pr.	120.00	120.00	50.00
Bowl, 10" oval vegetable	25.00	28.00	16.00	Saucer/sherbet plate (white 3.00)	4.00	4.00	3.00
Butter dish and cover	550.00	50.00	35.00	Sherbet, 3"	17.50		
Butter dish bottom	375.00	30.00	22.50	Sherbet, 3⅜"	9.00	12.00	6.00
Butter dish top	175.00	20.00	12.50	Spoon holder or celery	110.00	100.00	65.00
Cheese dish		150.00		Sugar, 5"	20.00	12.00	8.00
Creamer/milk pitcher, 5", 16 oz.	35.00	18.50	12.00	Sugar cover	40.00	17.00	12.00
Cup (white 7.00)	10.00	10.00	7.00	Tumbler, 3", 5 oz. juice	15.00	23.00	12.00
Goblet, 3¾", 1 oz. cordial		26.00	17.00	**Tumbler, 4", 9 oz. water	18.00	18.00	12.00
Goblet, 4", 3 oz. cocktail		23.00	14.00	Tumbler, 5⅛" high, 11 oz.,	33.00	38.00	16.00
Goblet, 4½", 2½ oz. wine		23.00	14.00	Tumbler, 12 oz. iced tea	40.00	45.00	23.00
Goblet, 5¼", 4 oz. claret		23.00	15.00	Tumbler, 15 oz. lemonade	55.00	65.00	35.00
Goblet, 5¾", 8½ oz. water	35.00	26.00	15.00	Tumbler, 3¼", 3 oz. footed	13.00	20.00	11.00
Mug, 4½", 12 oz.	425.00	725.00		Tumbler, 4", 5 oz. footed	26.00	35.00	15.00
+ Pitcher, 7", 54 oz.	40.00	45.00	25.00	***Tumbler, 5¼", 10 oz. footed	40.00	40.00	22.00
+* Pitcher, 7¾", 68 oz.	55.00	60.00	27.50	Whiskey, 2½", 1½ oz.	9.50	12.00	7.50

*Beaded top in pink $1,000.00 **Royal ruby $95.00 ***Royal ruby $150.00 +With or without ice lip

COLONIAL BLOCK HAZEL ATLAS GLASS COMPANY, Early 1930's

Colors: Green, crystal, black and pink; white in 1950's.

I have had several readers send pictures of black and frosted green powder jars in Colonial Block. However, all I have been able to find is the black lid! Other black pieces may exist. Let me hear what you find. The white creamer, sugar and lid are the only white pieces available to date. I had reports of a white butter, but it was never verified. By the way, notice the other new listing, a sherbet! A few of these have been found recently. How a piece like that can go undiscovered all these years is one of those astounding things that keep me writing about glass!

The green candy dish, butter tub (shown in the foreground) and pitcher are the most sought after items. The few pink Colonial Block collectors report that they never seen a pink pitcher or goblet. That goblet by the pitcher is Colonial Block and not Block Optic as I see it often mislabeled. Many Block Optic collectors use these goblets with their sets since they are less costly. The heavier Colonial Block goblets are definitely more durable when compared to the thinner Block Optic.

I haven't had one letter in four years about round Block Optic butter dishes! Until I put Colonial Block in the book, I received fifty or sixty letters a year about a round Block Optic butter dish even though the bottom of that piece is marked H A (Hazel Atlas symbol). Most pieces of Colonial Block are marked HA , but not all are so marked. The H and A are on top of each other confusing some novice collectors into believing that this is the symbol for Anchor Hocking. The anchor is a symbol used by Anchor Hocking and that was not used until after the 1930's.

U.S. Glass made a similar pitcher to the one shown here. There is little difference in them except most Hazel Atlas pitchers are marked. Collectors today are not as rigid in collecting as they once were. Many collectors will buy either pitcher to go with their set. That is why I call items that are similar to a pattern but not actually a part of it, "go-with" or "look-alike" pieces. Usually, these items are more reasonably priced.

	Pink, Green	White		Pink, Green	White
Bowl, 4"	6.00		Creamer	9.50	6.00
Bowl, 7"	15.00		Goblet	9.50	
Butter dish	40.00		Pitcher	35.00	
Butter dish bottom	10.00		*Powder jar with lid	15.00	
Butter dish top	30.00		Sherbet	7.50	
Butter tub	35.00		Sugar	9.50	5.00
Candy jar w/cover	32.50		Sugar lid	9.00	4.00

*Black $22.50

COLONIAL FLUTED, "ROPE" FEDERAL GLASS COMPANY, 1928-1933

Colors: Green and crystal.

Colonial Fluted is another set of Depression glass that is usually a starter set for beginning collectors. There is no dinner plate in Colonial Fluted; but there is a dinner sized plate having the roping effect around the outside of the plate (without the fluting) made by Federal which goes very well with this if you are willing to overlook the missing flutes. It is shown in the back of the photograph.

The "F" in a shield found in middle of many Colonial Fluted pieces is the trademark used by the Federal Glass Company. Not all pieces are marked.

Colonial Fluted can be blended with other sets or used for occasions such as card parties or small gatherings. In fact, much of the original advertising for this pattern was for bridge sets. Crystal is seldom collected, but there is a demand for the crystal decal pieces with hearts, spades, diamonds and clubs which make up a bridge set.

It is a pattern that was used extensively originally; so you will find many pieces with heavy wear marks. It is still priced moderately enough that it can be used today without fear of a piece or two being broken by guests. My experiences have shown me that most guests recognize this old glass as "antique" and treat it very gently.

Although listed in an early catalogue as being made in pink, I have never seen nor received reports of any of this being found in that color! Let me know if you get lucky and find some!

	Green		Green
Bowl, 4" berry	4.50	Plate, 6" sherbet	2.00
Bowl, 6" cereal	7.50	Plate, 8" luncheon	4.00
Bowl, 6½", deep (2½") salad	15.00	Saucer	1.50
Bowl, 7½" large berry	14.00	Sherbet	5.00
Creamer	5.00	Sugar	4.00
Cup	4.00	Sugar cover	12.00

Please refer to Foreword for pricing information

COLUMBIA FEDERAL GLASS COMPANY, 1938-1942

Colors: Crystal, some pink.

The newly recognized Columbia tumblers come in two sizes. The juice and water are all I am sure about at this time. Both are pictured. I have had several reports of other sizes and have had several other sizes shown to me at Depression Glass shows. So far these have all turned out to be Duncan and Miller pieces and not Columbia. Some of the water tumblers are being found with advertisements of dairy products on them. Keep watching!

Price continues to increase for the bowls, tumblers and any of the harder to find items.

One piece of Columbia that was abundantly produced was the butter dish. You can find these with all sorts of multicolored flashed decorations and floral decals. Federal must have tried everything to sell these and it must have worked since there are so many found today!

You will find many pieces decorated besides the butter dish. Luncheon sets have been found with pastel bands and floral decals. These are difficult to sell today unless you find a complete matching set. It is nearly impossible to find these sets piece by piece.

I hope you can see the elusive snack tray shown behind the juice on the right. It looks a little more hidden now than it did in the photography studio. Many collectors have not known what to look for since it is an unusual piece and shaped differently than most Columbia. These were found with Columbia cups in a boxed set about fifteen years ago in northern Ohio. The box was labeled "Snack Sets" by Federal Glass Company. The trays are also being found with cups other than Columbia. I have been told that they turn up regularly in the Denver area.

Pink Columbia sells very well! That is surprising since there are only four different pieces to be found and they are in very short supply.

	Crystal	Pink		Crystal	Pink
Bowl, 5" cereal	13.50		Cup	7.00	16.00
Bowl, 8" low soup	15.00		Plate, 6" bread & butter	2.50	10.00
Bowl, 8½" salad	14.00		Plate, 9½" luncheon	7.50	22.00
Bowl, 10½" ruffled edge	17.00		Plate, 11" chop	8.00	
Butter dish and cover	15.00		Saucer	2.50	7.50
Ruby flashed (17.50)			Snack plate	32.50	
Other flashed (16.00)			Tumbler, 2⅞", 4 oz., juice	16.00	
Butter dish bottom	5.00		Tumbler, 9 oz., water	18.00	
Butter dish top	10.00				

CREMAX MacBETH-EVANS DIVISION OF CORNING GLASS WORKS, Late 1930's-Early 1940's

Colors: Cremax, Cremax with fired-on color trim.

The green castle decal threw me off stride when I first found it. I had never seen that decal in green, but I would not mind finding a complete set. Besides the red floral decorations, it is the first decoration on Cremax that I have actually liked!

Cremax continues to be an orphan that few collectors want. Its sister pattern, Chinex, has many collectors, while Cremax goes virtually unnoticed. It has never been given the credit it is due. It is not easily found. There are several different floral patterned decals that can be collected. Maybe it is the scarcity which keeps collectors from buying Cremax the way they do Chinex. Often the bottom to the butter in Chinex is thought to be Cremax. The scalloped edges of the butter bottom are just like the edges on Cremax plates; however, the only tops to the butter ever found have the Chinex scroll-like pattern. If you find only the bottom of a butter, it is a Chinex bottom and not Cremax!

Another confusing problem concerns the name Cremax. The beige-like color made by MacBeth-Evans is also called cremax so you have to be aware of that. Usually the pattern name uses the capital "C".

Demitasse sets are being found in sets of eight. Some have been found on a wire rack. The usual make-up of these sets has been two sets each of four colors: pink, yellow, blue and green. I have had a problem finding these sets to photograph for recent books. They were shown in earlier editions.

	Cremax	Decal Decorated		Cremax	Decal Decorated
Bowl, 5¾" cereal	3.00	6.50	Plate, 9¾" dinner	4.00	8.50
Bowl, 9" vegetable	6.00	12.00	Plate, 11½" sandwich	4.00	9.50
Creamer	4.00	7.00	Saucer	1.50	3.00
Cup	3.50	4.00	Saucer, demitasse	4.00	8.00
Cup, demitasse	12.00	20.00	Sugar, open	4.00	7.00
Plate, 6¼" bread and butter	1.50	3.00			

Please refer to Foreword for pricing information

CORONATION, "BANDED RIB," "SAXON" HOCKING GLASS COMPANY, 1936-1940

Colors: Pink, green, crystal and Royal Ruby.

It has been eight years since I first showed green Coronation. Now you can see the small berry bowl without handles that I mentioned last time. Notice that the handles on the Royal Ruby bowls are open; handles on the pink are closed and handles on the green are nonexistent. If you find another style of handle on a different color than these, let me know.

I have to laugh every time I see a big price on those commonly found red handled berry bowls. They have always been plentiful and some years ago a large accumulation was discovered still sitting in an old warehouse. They are hard to sell; yet, I see them in my travels priced by unknowing dealers for two to three times their worth. They are usually marked "rare" or "old" or "pigeon blood." That "pigeon blood" terminology comes from old time collectors who used that term to describe dark red glass. Royal Ruby is darker than the red glass that was made using gold ore.

Coronation tumblers have always received most of the notoriety for this pattern since they have been regularly confused with the rarely found "Lace Edge" tumblers. Note the fine ribs above the middle of the Coronation tumbler. These ribs are missing on a "Lace Edge" glass. Look on the bottom of page 93 or in the store display photographs following to see the differences. (I might point out here that the real name of the pattern we have called "Lace Edge" is shown in those store displays as OLD COLONY. Until December of 1990 this true name had remained hidden in Anchor Hocking's old files. I was surprised to make that discovery, but it made my trip!)

Many collectors buy Coronation tumblers and use them with Lace Edge since they cost a third as much. Both are the same shape and color since both were made by Hocking. Just don't confuse the two since there is quite a price discrepancy!

There are many red cups found but no red saucer/sherbet plates have ever been seen. I would not go so far as to say that red saucers were never made. If I have learned anything in the last 20 years, it is never to say some piece of glass was never made. I do know the red cups were marketed on crystal saucers. In fact, those crystal saucer/sherbet plates are the only crystal pieces that I have seen in this pattern.

The larger green tumbler in the lower photograph is 5⁷⁄₁₆" tall and holds 14¼ oz. For new readers the lower photo was taken by Anchor-Hocking of glassware from their morgue. The morgue is so called since it has examples of past (dead production) patterns made by the Company. Unfortunately, this was not well kept. Many examples have "walked out" over the years. It is now under lock, but the disappearance of items began long ago. Who knew Depression glass was going to be so important?

	Pink	Royal Ruby	Green
Bowl, 4¼" berry	4.00	6.00	
Bowl, 4¼", no handles			20.00
Bowl, 6½" nappy	4.00	10.00	
Bowl, 8" large berry, handled	8.00	14.00	
Bowl, 8" no handles			100.00
Cup	4.00	5.00	
Pitcher, 7¾", 68 oz.	200.00		
Plate, 6" sherbet	1.50		
Plate, 8½" luncheon	4.00	7.00	30.00
* Saucer (same as 6" plate)	1.50		
Sherbet	4.00		50.00
Tumbler, 5", 10 oz. footed	18.00		100.00

*Crystal $.50

CUBE, "CUBIST" JEANNETTE GLASS COMPANY, 1929-1933

Colors: Pink, green, crystal, amber, white, ultramarine, canary yellow and blue.

Green Cube is harder to find than the pink, but there are more collectors of the pink. The major difficulty in collecting pink is not in finding it, but in finding it with the right shade of pink. The pink varies from a light pink to an orange-pink. This only shows how difficult it was for glass factories to consistently produce the same quality of glassware in the Depression era. As the glass tanks got hotter, the color got lighter. The orange shade of pink is difficult to sell. I have a beautiful pitcher in my shop that has been there longer than normal because it has an orange cast to the pink. I have also shown two distinct shades of green using the butter dish as an example. The darker shade of green is not as sought after as the normally found green. Both colors of Cube make for difficulties when ordering by mail if you want your glass to match. That is why it is preferable to attend shows and see what you are getting. You might even be willing to pay a little more for that convenience!

Prices for the pitcher and tumblers continue to rise. Both colors are hard to find, but green seems to be disappearing faster than pink. Because most collectors are looking for four, six or eight tumblers, it usually takes longer to find these than the pitcher. Be sure to check the sides of tumblers and pitchers since they damaged on the sides before the heavy rims did!

Cube is a pattern that catches the eye of non-collectors. The cubed design catches the light and makes it stand out in the crowd. Fostoria's American pattern is also recognized by non-collectors of that pattern. Cube is often mistaken for American by beginning collectors, but it is easily corrected when the two patterns are compared in quality. The large crystal 3⁹⁄₁₆" creamer and sugar on the 7½" round tray are the most often confused pieces. Cube is very dull and wavy in appearance when compared to the bright, clearer quality of Fostoria's American pattern.

Many pieces of pink and a darker shade of green are now being marketed under the name Whitehall by Indiana. If you have a pitcher or some other colored piece with a cubed pattern in a shape not shown here, you likely have Whitehall.

The powder jar is three legged and shown directly behind the green creamer in the picture. Occasionally, the jars are found with celluloid or another similar lid. Powder jars were not made with those lids at the factory. These were possibly replacements when tops were broken. Another possibility is that powder bottoms were bought from Jeannette and non-glass lids were made up elsewhere to fit the bottoms. In any case, prices below are for intact, original glass lids. The powder jars with other types of lids sell for half or less.

Lack of a dinner size plate is one drawback of collecting this pattern. At least Cube has a pitcher for the tumblers (and all the other basic pieces including cups and saucers)!

	Pink	Green
Bowl, 4½" dessert	5.00	6.00
* Bowl, 4½" deep	6.00	
Bowl, 6½" salad	8.00	12.00
Butter dish and cover	50.00	50.00
Butter dish bottom	15.00	15.00
Butter dish top	35.00	35.00
Candy jar and cover, 6½"	25.00	28.00
Coaster, 3¼"	5.00	6.00
** Creamer, 2⅝"	2.00	
Creamer, 3⁹⁄₁₆"	5.00	7.00
Cup	6.00	8.00
Pitcher, 8¾", 45 oz.	175.00	200.00
Plate, 6" sherbet	2.50	3.00
Plate, 8" luncheon	4.50	5.00
Powder jar and cover 3 legs	20.00	20.00
Salt and pepper, pr.	30.00	30.00
Saucer	2.00	2.00
Sherbet, footed	5.00	6.50
** Sugar, 2⅜"	2.00	
Sugar, 3"	6.00	7.00
Sugar/candy cover	10.00	11.00
Tray for 3⁹⁄₁₆" creamer and sugar, 7½" (crystal only)	4.00	
Tumbler, 4", 9 oz.	50.00	55.00

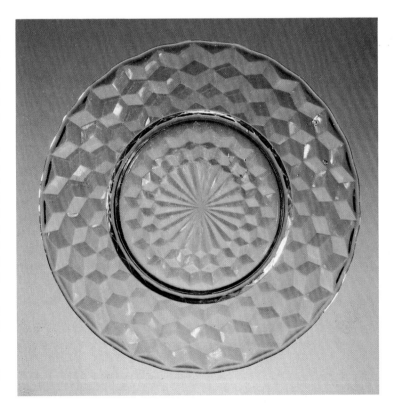

*Ultramarine - $20.00
**Amber or white - $3.00; crystal $1.00

Please refer to Foreword for pricing information

"CUPID" PADEN CITY GLASS COMPANY, 1930's

Colors: Pink, green, light blue, peacock blue, black, canary yellow, amber and crystal.

Cupid discoveries continue to be made. An unusual cobalt vase with silver overlay was brought to me in Miami last year. It was the wrong color and shape to be Cupid, so I looked at the bottom and saw the words "Made in Germany" there. The collector was shocked when I showed him since he had never noticed those words. Hold on! This is not the only piece. Cathy and I have found two other vases since then. One is yet a different shaped cobalt vase and the other is a stately lavender. They both have silver overlays of the exact Cupid pattern found on the Paden City pieces. The cobalt lamp with silver overlay reported from Arizona is probably German also. How this happened is beyond me, but with Europe's doors opening wider, we may see some other mysteries unveiled in the future. If anyone has an explanation, let me hear from you.

The only piece of black Cupid known is the covered casserole shown previously in the ninth edition. The silver decorated edges give this an elegance all its own. Now, I wonder if that, too, were made in Germany.

Samovars are rarely found, but are fetching "big bucks" when they are! So far, these have only been reported in green and blue. There should be other colors available. I received a letter just today from collectors in Texas who found a blue samovar in a "Antique Mall" at a reasonable price. The Cupid samovar glass insert is shown in the lower left photo on this page.

Paden City is a company where new discoveries are the norm rather than unusual! Most pieces are shown in catalogues with no etchings; and until a piece shows up with a Paden City etching, there is no way to know that it does exist in that pattern.

After photographing our pink for this book, I found a 5" footed candy in Oregon. Oh well, it gives us another piece for next time! The only new green piece we have added to our collection is the rolled edge console bowl.

Prices on this Paden City pattern continue to soar. People have been known to buy a piece of Cupid just to own a pretty piece of glass. After a while this one little purchase creates a Cupid collector. You do not have to own a large number of Cupid pieces to enjoy using what you have!

Those center-handled pieces were called sandwich trays and the odd, center-handled bowls of Paden City were called candy trays.

I wish someone else would report a piece of blue. Surely, the blue plate used for a pattern shot is not an experimental piece or color. I certainly hope that there are other pieces in this lovely color! Let me know what you find in Cupid!

	Green/Pink		Green/Pink
Bowl, 8½" oval-footed	125.00	Creamer, 5" footed	75.00
Bowl, 9¼" footed fruit	135.00	Ice bucket, 6"	125.00
Bowl, 9¼" center-handled	100.00	Ice tub, 4¾"	135.00
Bowl, 10¼", fruit	100.00	* Lamp, silver overlay	300.00
Bowl, 10½", rolled edge	95.00	Mayonnaise, 6" diameter,	
Bowl, 11" console	95.00	fits on 8" plate	100.00
Cake plate, 11¾"	125.00	Plate, 10½"	75.00
Cake stand, 2" high, footed	125.00	Samovar	750.00
Candlestick, 5" wide, pr.	125.00	Sugar, 4¼" footed	75.00
Candy w/lid, footed, 5¼" high	150.00	Sugar, 5" footed	75.00
Candy w/lid, 3 part	135.00	Tray, 10¾" center-handled	80.00
Casserole, covered (black) silver overlay	300.00	Tray, 10⅞" oval-footed	100.00
Comport, 6¼"	65.00	Vase, 8¼" elliptical	250.00
Creamer, 4½" footed	75.00	Vase, fan-shaped	150.00

* possibly German

Please refer to Foreword for pricing information

DIAMOND QUILTED, "FLAT DIAMOND" IMPERIAL GLASS COMPANY, Late 1920's-Early 1930's

Colors: Pink, blue, green, crystal, black; some red and amber.

The darker green candle is shown in the catalogue ad at the bottom of the page. I have sometimes seen these candlesticks mistaken as Windsor Diamond. Console sets at 65¢ and a dozen candy dishes in assorted colors for $6.95 would be quite a bargain today. No, I do not have any for sale at that price. This ad is from a 1930's catalogue and not my store. I mention that since I get several letters a year from people trying to order glass from these old catalogue ads placed throughout the book!

Diamond Quilted punch bowls are still **the** pieces to own in this pattern. I have not seen one at a show since both pink and green sets were in Chicago two years ago. I had never before seen both sets at the same show. As more and more of the harder to find pieces are disappearing into collections, there are fewer rare pieces being offered for sale. Until these collections are sold, those rarely found items are not seen again. Believe me, they're just becoming more and more valuable as they remain in those collections, too!

Pink and green Diamond Quilted are the only colors that can be collected in large sets. Unfortunately, the largest plate is the 8" luncheon. Lack of a larger serving plate stops some collectors from pursuing this pattern further. I have always said that you should collect what you like to look at and don't let the missing dinner plate stop you from putting the rest of the set together.

Black pieces have the design on the bottom. Thus, the design on the plate can only be seen if it is turned over. A black creamer is shown satinized with painted flowers. It is the only piece I have seen with such treatment.

Blue is the color many people would like to collect, but there is very little of that color being found. Amber and red are found even less often.

There is a Hazel Atlas quilted diamond pitcher and tumbler set made in pink, green, cobalt blue and a blue similar to the blue shown here that is confused with Imperial's Diamond Quilted. The quilting on Hazel Atlas pieces ends in a straight line around the top of each piece. Notice this *Imperial* Diamond Quilted pattern ends unevenly in points. You may also notice that the diamond designs on Diamond Quilted pieces are flat as opposed to those others that are curved.

	Pink, Green	Blue, Black		Pink, Green	Blue, Black
Bowl, 4¾" cream soup	7.00	16.00	Pitcher, 64 oz.	42.50	
Bowl, 5" cereal	6.00	12.00	Plate, 6" sherbet	3.00	4.00
Bowl, 5½" one handle	6.00	14.00	Plate, 7" salad	5.00	8.00
Bowl, 7" crimped edge	6.50	14.00	Plate, 8" luncheon	5.00	11.00
Bowl, 10½", rolled edge console	16.00	45.00	Punch bowl and stand	375.00	
Cake salver, tall 10" diameter	47.50		Plate, 14" sandwich	10.00	
Candlesticks (2 styles), pr.	22.00	45.00	Sandwich server, center handle	20.00	42.00
Candy jar and cover, footed	55.00		Saucer	2.50	4.00
Compote, 6" tall, 7¼" wide	37.50		Sherbet	4.50	13.00
Compote and cover, 11½"	62.50		Sugar	7.00	14.00
Creamer	7.00	15.00	Tumbler, 9 oz. water	8.00	
Cup	9.00	14.00	Tumbler, 12 oz. iced tea	8.50	
Goblet, 1 oz. cordial	9.00		Tumbler, 6 oz. footed	8.50	
Goblet, 2 oz. wine	9.00		Tumbler, 9 oz. footed	11.00	
Goblet, 3 oz. wine	9.00		Tumbler, 12 oz. footed	14.00	
Goblet, 6", 9 oz. champagne	9.00		Vase, fan, dolphin handles	45.00	65.00
Ice bucket	42.50	80.00	Whiskey, 1½ oz.	7.50	
Mayonnaise set: ladle, plate, comport	35.00	55.00			

Covered Bowl—6⅜ in. diam., deep round shape with 3 artistic feet, dome cover, fine quality brilliant finish **pot glass,** allover block diamond design, transparent Rose Marie and emerald green. **I C5603**—Asstd. ½ doz. in carton, 20 lbs.
Doz $6.95

I C989—3 piece set, 2 transparent colors (rose and green), good quality, 10½ in. rolled rim bowl, TWO 3½ in. wide base candlesticks. Asstd. 6 sets in case, 30 lbs. . . . . SET (3 pcs) **65**c

Please refer to Foreword for pricing information

DIANA FEDERAL GLASS COMPANY, 1937-1941

Colors: Pink, amber and crystal.

Pink Diana has made some of the biggest price leaps of any pattern since the last book. I should qualify that by saying price jumps percentage wise. Many other patterns have increased dramatically, but this was one of the used-to-be less expensive patterns! It is not as available as it once was and collectors have been paying through the nose to finish sets that they have started. Of course that goes for many other Depression glass patterns as well. The prices listed below are actual selling prices and not advertised prices. There is a major difference between an advertised price for an item and the price it may actually bring. Rarely have I heard of something selling for more than advertised, but often I've heard of less! Not only does my shop, Grannie Bear, sell a lot of glass; but dealers coast to coast are willing to share prices obtained on glassware with me. I thank them for that!

No, I do not use auction results either. Pieces at auctions rarely sell for realistic figures. Rare items will bring small prices if only one person knows it is rare. Common items will fetch astronomical prices if two people want it or two "bidders" try to keep each other from owning it. My personal feeling is that dealer lists and auction results are the two worst indicators of true prices.

Crystal Diana collectors have found out what collectors of the other colors found out years ago. There are very few tumblers available. Besides the tumblers, there are fewer candy dishes, shakers, sherbets and even platters being found. This is true for all colors of Diana. Only pink has made the big price jumps recently, but that is usually an indicator that other colors are soon to follow suit.

New collectors confuse Diana with some of the other swirled patterns such as Swirl and Twisted Optic. The centers of Diana's pieces are swirled where the centers of the other patterns are plain. The elusive sherbet is shown in amber behind the sugar. The spirals on this sherbet are often mistaken for Spiral by Hocking. This is the only sherbet shown in original advertisements for this pattern.

There are very few pink demitasse sets being found. Sets in crystal seem to be more plentiful as well as the cranberry or red sprayed-on sets. These flashed red sets are selling in the $10.00 to $12.00 range. So far, there is little demand for the frosted or satinized pieces that have shown up in crystal or pink. Some crystal frosted pieces have been trimmed in colors, predominantly red.

	Crystal	Pink	Amber
* Ash tray, 3½"	2.00	3.00	
Bowl, 5" cereal	3.50	7.50	10.00
Bowl, 5½" cream soup	2.50	18.00	12.00
Bowl, 9" salad	5.00	18.00	
Bowl, 11" console fruit	5.00	22.50	12.00
Bowl, 12" scalloped edge	6.50	22.50	15.00
Candy jar and cover, round	12.00	25.00	30.00
Coaster, 3½"	2.00	4.00	
Creamer, oval	3.00	10.00	8.00
Cup	2.50	11.00	6.00
Cup, 2 oz. demitasse and 4½" saucer set	12.50	40.00	
Plate, 6" bread & butter	1.00	1.50	1.50
Plate, 9½"	4.00	12.00	8.00
Plate, 11¾" sandwich	4.50	20.00	9.00
Platter, 12" oval	5.00	20.00	12.00
Salt and pepper, pr.	22.50	60.00	90.00
Saucer	1.00	4.00	1.50
Sherbet	2.50	10.00	8.00
Sugar, open oval	2.50	10.00	7.00
Tumbler, 4⅛", 9 oz.	20.00	30.00	23.00
Junior set: 6 cups and saucers with round rack	85.00	250.00	

* Green $3.00

DOGWOOD, "APPLE BLOSSOM," "WILD ROSE" MacBETH-EVANS GLASS COMPANY, 1929-1932

Colors: Pink, green, some crystal, Monax, Cremax and yellow.

Pink Dogwood is selling faster than I can find it. I haven't owned a large bowl or platter in over a year. The set of green I purchased over a year ago is long gone. There are plenty of pitchers and most size tumblers to go around in both colors. Only the pink juice tumbler is rarely found, but the price has gotten so high on that piece that few collectors are willing to buy more than one.

Please note that there are pitchers shaped like Dogwood that do not have the silk screen design of Dogwood. These are not Dogwood, but are the blanks made by MacBeth-Evans to go with the plain, no design tumblers they made. The pattern has to be silk screened onto the pitcher to be Dogwood. (In the case of the fat pitcher on the left, it is also not American Sweetheart if it has no pattern moulded into it!)

Few pieces of yellow are being found, but there is not much demand for it either. Years ago, a blank yellow pitcher turned up at Washington Court House, Ohio. A dealer from Pittsburgh bought it and took it back where he hand decorated it himself. As a joke he brought it back and sold it for a substantial price. Later, he told the dealer who bought it what he had done and gave the dealer's money back. I've often wondered what became of that pitcher. It was well done!

Cremax is another rare color of Dogwood which does not excite many collectors. The Monax salver (12" plate) was once thought of as hard to find; but, over the years it has turned out to be more of a novelty than rare. In fact, you can buy them today for less than you could fifteen years ago. I used to sell them in the $25.00 range, but have had a couple in my shop recently at $15.00.

The pink sugar and creamer on the left represent the thick footed style while the pink sugar in the middle and the green creamer and sugar show the thin, flat style. Pink is found in both styles, but the green is only found in the thin variety. The thin creamers were made by adding a spout to the cups. Some of these thin creamers have a very undefined spout. Although there are thick and thin pink cups, the saucers for both style cups are the same.

Grill plates come in two styles. Some of these have the Dogwood pattern all over the plate and others have only the pattern around the rim of the plate. Sherbets, grill plates (rim pattern only), and the large fruit bowl are also difficult to accumulate in green Dogwood.

Sherbets come in two styles. Some have a Dogwood blossom etched on the bottom; some do not. I have been told that this gives mail order dealers a problem. Please be sure to specify which style you are trying to match if that is important to you. It really makes no difference in price since they are only from different moulds.

Be aware that there are stemmed pieces with a "Dogwood-like" pattern on them. These come in several sizes and many collectors buy them to go with their sets.

See the *Very Rare Glassware of the Depression Years, Second Series* for a picture of the only known Dogwood coaster!

	Pink	Green	Monax Cremax		Pink	Green	Monax Cremax
*Bowl, 5½" cereal	20.00	20.00	4.00	Plate, 9¼" dinner	22.00		
Bowl, 8½" berry	45.00	90.00	35.00	Plate, 10½" grill AOP or			
Bowl, 10¼" fruit	275.00	175.00	65.00	border design only	16.00	16.00	
Cake plate, 11" heavy				Plate, 12" salver	22.00		15.00
solid foot	200.00			Platter, 12" oval (rare)	325.00		
Cake plate, 13" heavy				Saucer	5.00	6.00	15.00
solid foot	75.00	70.00	150.00	Sherbet, low footed	25.00	85.00	
Coaster, 3¼"	450.00			Sugar, 2½" thin, flat	14.00	40.00	
Creamer, 2½" thin, flat	15.00	40.00		Sugar, 3¼" thick, footed	14.00		
Creamer, 3¼" thick, footed	16.00			Tumbler, 3½", 5 oz.			
Cup, thin or thick	12.00	22.00	35.00	decorated	235.00		
Pitcher, 8", 80 oz. decorated	140.00	450.00		Tumbler, 4", 10 oz. decorated	30.00	70.00	
Pitcher, 8", 80 oz. (American				Tumbler, 4¾", 11 oz.			
Sweetheart Style)	500.00			decorated	35.00	80.00	
Plate, 6" bread and butter	6.00	7.00	20.00	Tumbler, 5", 12 oz. decorated	45.00	90.00	
* Plate, 8" luncheon	6.00	7.00		Tumbler, moulded band	14.00		

*Yellow - $50.00

DORIC JEANNETTE GLASS COMPANY, 1935-1938

Colors: Pink, green, some Delphite and yellow.

Doric tumblers, especially the footed ones, cereal and cream soup bowls, and pitchers have all become key pieces to own in Doric. Green is more scarce and has more collectors than pink; therefore, the price for green is higher than the pink. Green Doric collecting is a challenge. It probably will not break you at one time since you will need years to complete a large set unless you get extremely lucky!

One of the major problems for Doric collectors are the mould seams on the footed tumblers and the cereals. This stops many collectors who are searching for perfection. Some collectors have not seen either piece! In other words, don't let a little roughness keep you from owning these if you see them for sale!

Having spent a lot of time in Florida the last few years, I have noticed more green Doric there than any place I have travelled. One of the major difficulties in buying glass in Florida is cloudy glass. Evidently, well water creates cloudiness with deposits on the glass. Nothing will remove this and you could make a fortune if you can figure out a way to remove these deposits. In any case, most of the tumblers I've seen in Florida are cloudy or "sick" as most dealers call this condition. Don't get roped into buying cloudy glass unless it is very inexpensive.

The yellow pitcher in the bottom photo is still the only one known. Pay attention to its price! Speaking of the pitchers, the large footed ones come with or without an ice lip as shown in the pink. All Doric footed pitchers are difficult to find, with the green nearly impossible. The candy and sugar lids in this pattern are not interchangeable. The candy is taller and more domed. See the pictures on the right with a green candy and pink sugar.

I still get a lot of letters about rare Delphite (opaque blue) pieces. Actually, the sherbet and the cloverleaf candy are common in Delphite. All other Delphite pieces are rare in Doric; however, there are few collectors; and so the price is still reasonable for so rare a color.

The three part candy can be found in a metal holder. One of these is shown in earlier editions.

An iridized three part candy was made in the 1970's and sold for 79 cents in our local dish barn. All other colors of the three part candy are old.

The lids on the pink shakers are original old nickel plated tops; those on the green are newly made aluminum tops. Original lids are preferable when available, but there are alternatives to having no lids at all.

	Pink	Green	Delphite		Pink	Green	Delphite
Bowl, 4½" berry	6.00	7.00	35.00	Plate, 6" sherbet	3.00	4.00	
Bowl, 5" cream soup		225.00		Plate, 7" salad	14.00	15.00	
Bowl, 5½" cereal	37.50	55.00		Plate, 9" dinner			
Bowl, 8¼" large berry	12.00	15.00	100.00	(serrated 50.00)	10.00	14.00	
Bowl, 9" 2-handled	11.00	12.00		Plate, 9" grill	11.00	15.00	
Bowl, 9" oval vegetable	20.00	25.00		Platter, 12" oval	18.00	20.00	
Butter dish and cover	60.00	75.00		Relish tray, 4" x 4"	8.00	7.50	
Butter dish bottom	20.00	27.50		Relish tray, 4" x 8"	10.00	12.00	
Butter dish top	40.00	47.50		Salt and pepper, pr.	27.50	30.00	
Cake plate, 10", 3 legs	20.00	20.00		Saucer	3.00	3.50	
Candy dish and				Sherbet, footed	9.50	11.00	5.00
cover, 8"	27.50	30.00		Sugar	10.00	11.00	
* Candy dish, 3-part	5.00	6.00	5.00	Sugar cover	12.00	19.00	
Coaster, 3"	11.00	13.00		Tray, 10" handled	10.00	12.00	
Creamer, 4"	9.00	10.00		Tray, 8" x 8" serving	15.00	15.00	
Cup	7.00	8.00		Tumbler, 4½", 9 oz.	40.00	65.00	
Pitcher, 6", 36 oz. flat	30.00	35.00	950.00	Tumbler, 4", 10 oz.			
Pitcher, 7½", 48 oz.				footed	40.00	65.00	
footed	400.00	750.00		Tumbler, 5", 12 oz.,			
(Also in yellow				footed	55.00	85.00	
at $1,500.00)							

*Candy in metal holder - $40.00. Iridescent made recently. Ultramarine $15.00.

Please refer to Foreword for pricing information

DORIC AND PANSY JEANNETTE GLASS COMPANY, 1937-1938

Colors: Ultramarine; some crystal and pink.

   I received a call from England a few months ago from a school teacher who had found two boxed sets of ultramarine Doric and Pansy. She was wanting to know what the current values for this glassware were since she had a ten-year-old book of mine. I do not think she believed the prices that I quoted her. I think she found it impossible to believe that the glassware was worth less now than it was then. I wasn't "putting her on" and I hope she picks up a later edition to see the price drops.

   Discoveries of large quantities of Doric and Pansy continue to be made in Canada and England. No wonder we always thought Doric and Pansy was rare. It is in the continental United States, but not so outside these boundaries! I have now heard of at least twenty butter dishes found in England in the last five years. Those are just the ones that I have heard from and I am sure there are others. The price on the butter dish has continued to slide with so many butters on the market.

   Watch out for the weak patterned shakers. These should fetch less by 20 or 25 percent than the price listed. If the only way you can tell that the shaker is Doric and Pansy comes from color and shape instead of pattern, then leave it alone. Sugars and creamers are also being found along with those butter dishes; however, their price has not been as dramatically affected since they were not so highly priced as the butters. Tumblers and large and small berry bowls are not being found as often in the accumulations abroad. There have also been no reported findings of the children's sets in England or Canada!

   The only other major problem facing ultramarine collectors of Doric and Pansy is color variations. Many pieces have a distinct green cast instead of blue. Few collectors buy the green shade of ultramarine, so it is hard for dealers to sell. Unless you are able to buy the green cast as a large lot, you may have trouble if you ever go to resell it. However, there is the plus side to this greener shade if you like it. Oft times you can purchase it at a bargain price!

   Only berry and children's sets have been found in pink. Crystal creamer and sugar sets can be found, but there are few collectors. These sets are purchased by collectors of sugar and creamers rather than Doric and Pansy collectors.

I suppose you may have noticed the newly found odd shaped tumbler in the center of the picture. Two of these were found in Pittsburgh and sold in California to a Michigan dealer. Sadly only one of these has survived!

	Green, Teal	Pink, Crystal		Green, Teal	Pink, Crystal
Bowl, 4½" berry	12.00	7.00	Plate, 6" sherbet	8.50	7.00
Bowl, 8" large berry	67.50	18.00	Plate, 7" salad	27.50	
Bowl, 9" handled	27.50	12.00	Plate, 9" dinner	22.00	6.00
Butter dish and cover	395.00		Salt and pepper, pr.	350.00	
Butter dish bottom	70.00		Saucer	4.00	3.00
Butter dish top	325.00		Sugar, open	105.00	60.00
Cup	16.00	8.00	Tray, 10" handled	17.50	
Creamer	110.00	65.00	Tumbler, 4½", 9 oz.	50.00	

DORIC AND PANSY
"PRETTY POLLY PARTY DISHES"

	Teal	Pink		Teal	Pink
Cup	35.00	25.00	Creamer	35.00	25.00
Saucer	5.00	4.00	Sugar	35.00	25.00
Plate	8.00	6.00	14-Piece set	265.00	190.00

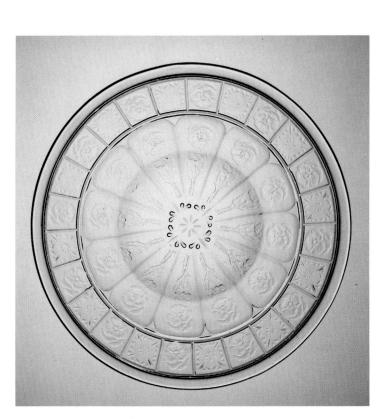

59

ENGLISH HOBNAIL WESTMORELAND GLASS COMPANY, 1920's-1970's

Colors: Crystal, pink, amber, turquoise, cobalt, green, blue and red.

Collecting a complete set of English Hobnail is difficult. This, too, is a pattern that has many color variances. Pink is the easiest color to find, but there are two distinct shades of pink. There are also two distinct shades of amber. One of these is a light yellow amber while the other is dark, and even that varies from piece to piece. There are three different greens, from a light yellow green to a deep, dark green. Many collectors mix shades of color, but others can not abide mixing them. That only becomes a problem when you have searched for eons for a particular piece, and when you find it, the color shading is wrong.

English Hobnail collectors have begun to make their voices heard in the collecting world. The demise of Westmoreland has spurred many new collectors of blue, pink and green. I have only seen a little activity begun in collecting crystal, but I suspect that collectors will soon spring up for crystal, also. (I may be able to use the crystal as an addition to my 1950's book.) There have been many rumors of reproduction Westmoreland glass being made. Rumors are facts when it comes to some of the old reamer moulds being used, but to my knowledge, as of now (June 1991), no new pieces of English Hobnail have been made since the factory closed.

Cobalt blue pieces of English Hobnail are found very rarely. The turquoise blue has more collectors than the cobalt because so many more pieces can be found in that shade of blue. The turquoise blue vase is particularly nice as an accessory piece.

There is a story behind the 15" candy shown in green at the back of the upper photo. The one in the photograph sold a couple of years ago in Houston for $250.00. Originally there were a pair of these on a mantle in Cincinnati, Ohio, bought as urns for family ashes I'm told. The new owner will probably not put candy in it since I told him about the intended usage when I sold it.

For beginning collectors, I offer the following observations to distinguish English Hobnail from Miss America. The centers of English Hobnail pieces have centered rays of varying distances. Notice the upright pieces in the photographs for this six point star effect. In Miss America, shown on page 113, the center rays all end equidistant from the center. The hobs on English Hobnail are more rounded and "feel" smoother to the touch; goblets flair and the hobs go directly into a plain rim area. On Miss America the hobs are sharper to touch and the goblets do not flair at the rim with both goblets and tumblers having three sets of rings above the hobs before entering a plain glass rim.

	Cobalt, Amber, Turquoise, Pink, Green			Cobalt, Amber, Turquoise, Pink, Green
* Ash tray, several shapes	19.50	** Goblet, 6¼ oz.		22.50
Bowls, 4½", 5" square and round	10.00	Grapefruit, 6½" flange rim		16.00
Bowl, cream soup	14.00	Lamp, 6¼" electric		45.00
Bowls, 6" several styles	11.00	** Lamp, 9¼"		95.00
Bowls, 8" several styles	22.00	Lamp shade, 17" diameter (crystal)		125.00
** Bowls, 8" footed and 2-handled	47.50	Marmalade and cover		35.00
** Bowls, 11" and 12" nappies	40.00	Pitcher, 23 oz.		145.00
Bowls, 8", 9" oval relish	18.00	Pitcher, 39 oz.		175.00
Bowl, 12" oval relish	20.00	Pitcher, 60 oz.		210.00
Candlesticks, 3½" pr.	32.00	Pitcher, ½ gal. straight sides		235.00
Candlesticks, 8½" pr.	52.00	** Plate, 5½", 6½" sherbet		4.00
Candy dish, ½ lb. cone-shaped	47.50	Plate, 7¼" pie		5.00
Candy dish and cover, three feet	70.00	** Plate, 8" round or square		8.00
Candy dish and cover, 15" high	275.00	Plate, 10" dinner		22.00
Celery dish, 9"	20.00	Salt and pepper, pr., round or square bases		77.50
Celery dish, 12"	25.00	Salt dip, 2" footed and with place card holder		22.00
** Cigarette box	30.00	Saucer		4.00
** Cologne bottle	30.00	** Sherbet		14.00
Creamer, footed or flat	22.00	Sugar, footed or flat		24.00
Cup	16.00	Tumbler, 3¾", 5 oz. or 9 oz.		14.00
Decanter, 20 oz. with stopper	98.00	Tumbler, 4", 10 oz. iced tea		16.00
Demitasse cup and saucer	50.00	Tumbler, 5", 12 oz. iced tea		24.00
Egg cup	36.00	Tumbler, 7 oz. footed		15.00
Goblet, 1 oz. cordial	25.00	Tumbler, 9 oz. footed		16.00
** Goblet, 2 oz. wine	22.00	Tumbler, 12½ oz. footed		22.00
Goblet, 3 oz. cocktail	17.00	Vase		135.00
Goblet, 5 oz. claret	20.00	Whiskey, 1½ oz. and 3 oz.		24.00

*Add about 50% more for turquoise
** Cobalt double price listed

Please refer to Foreword for pricing information

FIRE-KING DINNERWARE "PHILBE" HOCKING GLASS COMPANY, 1937-1938

Colors: Blue, green, pink and crystal.

I have only found a few pieces including a pink sandwich plate in Fire-King dinnerware since the last edition two years ago. This is a pattern that everyone looks for, but few are successful in finding. You can see additional pieces pictured in my *Very Rare Glassware of the Depression Years, Second Series* including the blue candy dish, tall water goblet and green cookie jar. The green cookie is the one I first owned in the early 1970's. I bought it in Washington Court House, Ohio, for $10.00 and sold it for $10.00 to a friend who was "collecting" this pattern. She was "collecting" for a few months, that is, until she sold it for $300.00 to a collector in California! After all these years I was able to purchase that same cookie jar in January. Of course, it had been through a couple of dealers inventories and the price was a lot more than the $10.00 I had paid for it originally. It is now in a collection in Oregon!

Fire-King dinnerware is one of the rarest patterns in Depression Glass, but also one of the most desirable. Some people only collect one piece of each pattern and this is one pattern missing from their collection. The blue is very similar to Mayfair's blue, but many pieces have an added platinum trim as can be seen in the photograph.

On my first trip to Anchor Hocking in 1972, there was a large set of this glassware in a window display in the showroom. Until then all I knew was that it had the same shape as Cameo and the color of blue Mayfair. I discovered then that the footed tumblers and the goblet even had the same shape as Mayfair. Only once did I ever see several pieces for sale at one time and they are all shown here in the photograph of the blue. All of the platinum banded blue pieces, except the pitcher, turned up in 1975 at the same flea market that the green cookie jar had.

Many of the pieces shown on the right are the only ones ever found. Of the four pitchers shown on the right, only one other pink juice and a blue water without platinum band have been found. The blue cup is still the only one ever found in any color.

The more commonly found items include the blue footed tumblers of which the footed tea is the more easily found. Finally, you can see the footed blue tumblers which have missed the two previous photography sessions although they were there. One of the ladies who is kind enough to loan her rare glass for photographing has an organization of packing by size and not pattern. Sometimes a piece or two turns up after the photograph for that pattern has already been made. It happened twice to the blue footed tumblers! But not this time as I waited until they turned up before we got the rest of the pattern together!

The photography sessions for this and other books are major productions. Organizing the multitude of glass for these pictures is quite a process. Ask those collectors who have helped! They have a hard time believing what we do year after year - even after going through a session with us. Hopefully, you will find everyone's effort worthwhile.

Pink oval vegetable bowls are the only common pink piece although that same bowl is also common in green and crystal. Green grill plates or luncheon plates might end up in your collection with more ease than anything else in "Philbe."

	Crystal	Pink, Green	Blue
Bowl, 5½" cereal	17.50	35.00	45.00
Bowl, 7¼" salad	25.00	4500	65.00
Bowl, 10" oval Vegetable	25.00	50.00	95.00
Candy jar, 4" low, with cover	200.00	600.00	750.00
Cookie jar with cover	500.00	900.00	1,000.00
Creamer, 3¼" footed	35.00	100.00	125.00
Cup	35.00	80.00	130.00
Goblet, 7¼", 9 oz. thin	55.00	125.00	165.00
Pitcher, 6", 36 oz. juice	250.00	600.00	850.00
Pitcher, 8½", 56 oz.	350.00	850.00	1,000.00
Plate, 6" sherbet	15.00	30.00	50.00
Plate, 8" luncheon	18.00	25.00	35.00
Plate, 10" heavy sandwich	20.00	60.00	85.00
Plate, 10½" salver	20.00	45.00	65.00
Plate, 10½" grill	20.00	40.00	55.00
Plate, 11⅝" salver	20.00	60.00	85.00
Platter, 12" closed handles	25.00	75.00	125.00
Saucer, 6" (same as sherbet plate)	15.00	30.00	50.00
Sugar, 3¼" footed	35.00	100.00	125.00
Tumbler, 4", 9 oz. flat water	30.00	100.00	125.00
Tumbler, 3½" footed juice	30.00	100.00	135.00

	Crystal	Pink, Green	Blue
Tumbler, 5¼", 10 oz. footed	25.00	65.00	60.00
Tumbler, 6½", 15 oz. footed iced tea	30.00	65.00	45.00

FLORAL, "POINSETTIA" JEANNETTE GLASS COMPANY, 1931-1935

Colors: Pink, green, Delphite, Jadite, crystal, amber, red and yellow.

The latest "news" in this pattern is that Floral *reproduction shakers* are now being found in pink, cobalt blue and a dark green color. Cobalt blue and the dark green Floral shakers are of little concern since they were never made in these colors originally. The green is darker than the original green shown here but not as deep a color as Forest Green. The new pink shakers, however, are not only a very good pink, but they are also a fairly good copy! There are lots of minor variations in design and leaf detail to someone who knows glassware well, but I have always tried to pick out a point that anyone can use to determine validity whether he be a novice or professional. There is one easy way to tell the Floral reproductions. Take off the top and look at the threads where the lid screws onto the shaker. On the old there are a PAIR of parallel threads on each side or at least a pair on one side which end right before the mould seams down each side. The new Floral has ONE CONTINUOUS LINE thread which starts on one side and continues around the shaker until it ends above the beginning line on the other side. There is approximately one inch of overlapped thread making two lines for that inch; but the whole thread is ONE CONTINUOUS LINE and not two separate ones as on the old. No other Floral reproductions have been made as of June 1991.

Unusual Floral green pieces continue to be found in England and Canada. As with Doric and Pansy, it is the more unusual and thought to be rare pieces which are being found. They were rare in our country until collectors in Canada discovered Depression glass and started digging in the nooks and crannies up there. Many Canadians have ancestry in England who continued the search over there. The green Floral flat bottomed pitchers and flat bottomed tumblers are blossoming and the prices are moderating because of the many discoveries. Much of this Floral found in Canada and England is a slightly lighter color green, and the flat pieces all have ground bottoms. This Floral is also panelled to the extent that it stands out from normally found Floral. I just purchased a green cup in Florida with a ground bottom. The saucer is the normally found one and the cup, which is slightly footed, will not fit this saucer's indentation! You can see this style cup in the foreground at the top of page 65!

Rose bowls, and vases in all sizes have been found in England; so if you vacation in Europe, remember to try England for Depression glass. Also, I frequently visit the English furniture importer's shops since you can never tell what they will have shipped over here.

Floral lemonade pitchers are still being found in the Northwest, but the pink substantially outnumber the green. I just came back from a show in Oregon and there were only two lemonade pitchers at the show this year. There had been six last year! There are more collectors for green than pink; so these two factors cause the price differences.

There are several pieces of the dresser set being found (shown on page 65). Few of these are complete, even though there are quantities of the 9¼" tray used by the set. The powder jars are not available.

Floral is one of Jeannette's patterns in which the sugar and candy lids are interchangeable.

There are two distinct varieties of pink platters. One has a normal flat edge as shown in the back left of the photo; and the other has a scalloped edge like the platter in Cherry Blossom.

Unusual items in Floral (so far) include the following:
- a) an entire set of *Delphite Floral*
- b) a *yellow* two-part relish dish
- c) *amber and red* plate, cup and saucer
- d) green and crystal juice pitchers w/ground flat bottoms (shown)
- e) footed vases in green and crystal, flared at the rim (shown); some hold flower frogs with *the Floral pattern on the frogs* (shown)
- f) a crystal lemonade pitcher
- g) lamps (shown in green and pink)
- h) a green *grill* plate
- i) an octagonal vase with patterned, octagonal foot (shown)
- j) a *ruffled edge* berry and master berry bowl
- k) pink and green Floral *ice tubs* (shown)
- l) oval vegetable with cover
- m) *rose bowl* and *three footed vase* (shown)
- n) two styles of *9" comports* in pink and green (shown)
- o) 9 oz. flat tumblers in green (shown)
- p) 3 oz. footed tumblers in green (shown)
- q) 8" round bowl in beige and opaque red
- r) *caramel* colored dinner plate
- s) *cream soups* (shown in pink)
- t) beige creamer and sugar
- u) green *dresser set* (shown)
- v) Cremax, 8½" bowl (like Cherry Blossom)

FLORAL, "POINSETTIA" JEANNETTE GLASS COMPANY, 1931-1935 (Cont.)

	Pink	Green	Delphite	Jadite
Bowl, 4" berry (ruffled $55.00)	13.50	14.00	30.00	
Bowl, 5½" cream soup	675.00	675.00		
* Bowl, 7½" salad (ruffled $95.00)	12.00	14.00	47.50	
Bowl, 8" covered vegetable	27.50	37.50	40.00 (no cover)	
Bowl, 9" oval vegetable	12.00	14.00		
Butter dish and cover	75.00	80.00		
Butter dish bottom	20.00	22.50		
Butter dish top	55.00	57.50		
Canister set: coffee, tea, cereal sugar, 5¼" tall, each				32.00
Candlesticks, 4" pr.	60.00	70.00		
Candy jar and cover	30.00	35.00		
Creamer, flat (cremax $75.00)	11.00	12.00	70.00	
Coaster, 3¼"	12.00	8.00		
Comport, 9"	62500	725.00		
*** Cup	9.00	10.00		
Dresser set (as shown)		1000.00		
Frog for vase (also crystal $500.00)		650.00		
Ice tub, 3½" high oval	625.00	675.00		
Lamp	230.00	250.00		
Pitcher, 5½", 23 or 24 oz.		425.00		
Pitcher, 8", 32 oz. footed cone	25.00	30.00		
Pitcher, 10¼", 48 oz. lemonade	185.00	205.00		
Plate, 6" sherbet	4.50	6.00		
Plate, 8" salad	8.00	9.00		
** Plate, 9" dinner	1300	15.00	120.00	
Plate, 9" grill		155.00		
Platter, 10¾" oval	12.00	14.50	130.00	
Platter, 11" (like Cherry Blossom)	60.00			
Refrigerator dish and cover, 5" square		57.50		18.00
*** Relish dish, 2-part oval	12.00	13.00	250.00	
**** Salt and pepper, 4" footed pair	39.00	45.00		
Salt and pepper, 6" flat	42.50			
*** Saucer	8.00	9.00		
Sherbet	1300	15.00	77.50	
Sugar (cremax $75.00)	8.00	9.00	60.00 (open)	
Sugar/candy cover	11.00	15.00		
Tray, 6" square, closed handles	12.00	14.00		
Tray, 9¼", oval for dresser set		155.00		
Tumbler, 4½", 9 oz. flat		155.00		
Tumbler, 3½", 3 oz. footed		97.50		
Tumbler, 4", 5 oz. footed juice	15.00	18.00		
Tumbler, 4¾", 7 oz. footed water	15.00	18.00	175.00	
Tumbler, 5¼", 9 oz. footed femonade	35.00	4000		
Vase, 3 legged rose bowl		425.00		
Vase, 3 legged flared (also in crystal)		425.00		
Vase, 6⅞" tall (8 sided)		400.00		

*Cremax $125.00
**These have now been found in amber and red.
***This has been found in yellow.
****Beware reproductions!

FLORAL AND DIAMOND BAND U.S. GLASS COMPANY, Late 1920's

Colors: Pink, green; some iridescent, black and crystal.

Floral and Diamond iridescent pitchers with good solid color fetch higher prices from "Carnival" glass collectors as a pattern named "Mayflower" than they do with Depression glass collectors. Several dealers who sell both Depression and Carnival glass have been buying these pitchers at Depression glass shows and reselling them at Carnival conventions or auctions. Sometimes glassware that fits into two different categories, as does Floral and Diamond, receives more respect from one group of collectors than it does the other. It happens all the time. Prices for toys "Made in Occupied Japan" sell for higher prices to toy collectors than to collectors of "Occupied Japan" or "advertising" collectors will pay more for one ad out of a magazine than a magazine collector will pay for the whole magazine. There are many different markets available and each has its own idiosyncrasies.

Pink luncheon plates and sugar lids or iced tea tumblers in all colors are the toughest pieces to uncover. Many Floral and Diamond butter bottoms have been robbed to be used on other U.S. Glass patterns such as Strawberry and Cherryberry. This occurred because all U.S. Glass butter bottoms are plain. They are all interchangeable with the pattern on the top only. Floral and Diamond butter dishes used to be very cheaply priced in comparison to Strawberry; so, collectors bought these bottoms for other tops. This has now created a shortage of butter bottoms in pink Floral and Diamond.

A collecting problem with all U.S. Glass patterns is the various shades of green. Some of the green is blue tinted. It is up to you as how serious you are about color matching. Another thing that new collectors need to be aware of is mould roughness along the seams of the tumblers and plates. This is "normal" for Floral and Diamond and not considered a detriment by long time collectors who have come to accept some roughness.

As you can see by the 1928 ads below, sometimes this pattern was described as "Floral and Diamond" and sometimes as "Diamond and Floral."

Only the small creamer and sugar have been found in black. These sugars and creamers are often found with a cut flower over the top of the normally found moulded flower.

The crystal pitcher and butter dishes are rare! In fact, crystal is not commonly found except for creamers and sugars.

	Pink	Green			Pink	Green
Bowl, 4½" berry	6.50	7.50	* Pitcher, 8", 42 oz..		75.00	85.00
Bowl, 5¾" handled nappy	9.00	9.00	Plate, 8" luncheon		27.50	25.00
Bowl, 8" large berry	11.00	12.00	Sherbet		6.00	7.00
* Butter dish and cover	120.00	100.00	Sugar, small		800	9.00
Butter dish bottom	80.00	77.50	Sugar, 5¼"		12.00	12.00
Butter dish top	40.00	22.50	Sugar lid		45.00	55.00
Compote, 5½" tall	13.00	14.00	Tumbler, 4" water		17.50	20.00
Creamer, small	8.00	9.00	Tumbler, 5" iced tea		27.50	32.50
Creamer, 4¾"	15.00	17.00				

* Iridescent - $250.00
  Crystal - $100.00

Seven-Piece Berry Set
You'll really be most satisfied with the purchase of this set. It's very attractive, and affords a fitting and stylish addition to your present pieces. In green pressed glass, with diamond 'and floral design. Large bowl, 8 inches in diameter, and six sauce dishes to match, 4½ inches in diameter.
35N6838—Weight, packed, 7 pounds. Per set...... **68c**

Seven-Piece   Water Set
Made from green pressed glass, with a floral and diamond design. You'll find that the sparkling scintillating pitcher and glasses are a set you'll be mighty proud to own when serving cold drinks. 3-pint pitcher. Six 8-ounce tumblers.
35N6837—Weight, packed, 12 pounds. Per set. **$1.18**

Five-Piece Table Set

Heavy pressed glass in light green, with pressed diamond and floral design. Creamer, covered sugar bowl and covered butter dish. Weight, packed, 9 pounds.
35N6836 .... **65c**

Please refer to Foreword for pricing information

FLORENTINE NO. 1, "OLD FLORENTINE," "POPPY NO. 1"
HAZEL ATLAS GLASS COMPANY, 1932-1935

Colors: Pink, green, crystal, yellow and cobalt.

Florentine No. 1 shakers have been reproduced in pink and cobalt blue. There may be other colors to follow. No cobalt blue Florentine No. 1 shakers have ever been found, so those are no problem. The pink is more difficult. I am comparing one to several old pairs from my shop. The old shakers have a major open flower on each side. There is a top circle on this blossom with three smaller circles down each side. The seven circles form the outside of the blossom. The new blossom looks more like a strawberry with no circles forming the outside of the blossom. This repro blossom looks like a poor drawing! Do not use the threading test mentioned under Floral for the Florentine No. 1 shakers, however. It won't work for Florentine although these are made by the same importing company out of Georgia. The threads are right on this reproduction pattern. The reproductions I have seen have been badly moulded, but that is not to say that it will not be corrected.

Many 5½" yellow ash trays have a V.F.W. (Veterans of Foreign Wars) embossed in the bottom. In fact I have seen more with this embossing than without it.

One of the most confusing things for new collectors is learning the difference between Florentine No. 1 and No. 2. It is simple. Notice the outline of the pattern shot on the right. The scalloped edges occur on all flat pieces of Florentine No. 1. All footed pieces such as tumblers, shakers or pitchers have the serrated edge. In Florentine No. 2 all pieces have a plain edge. Florentine No. 1 was once advertised as hexagonal and Florentine No. 2 was once advertised as round. This should also help you to remember the differences.

Pink is the hardest color to find. Butter dishes in all colors are most desirable! Sets can be collected in green, crystal or yellow with a lot of work. Serrated edges can show damage, so that is the first place to look when you pick up a piece to examine.

The 48 oz. flat bottomed pitcher was sold with both sets. It was listed as 54 oz. in catalogues but measures six ounces less. This pitcher is shown in all three colors on page 73.

There have been a multitude of fired-on colors emerging on luncheon sets, but there has also been little collector demand for these. You can find all sorts of colors and colored bands on crystal if that strikes your fancy.

Flat tumblers with panels are being found in sets with Florentine No. 1 pitchers. Evidently these paneled tumblers should be considered Florentine No. 1 rather than Florentine No. 2. That information is for purists. Since Hazel Atlas sold both styles together, why not collect them together?

	Crystal, Green	Yellow	Pink	Blue		Crystal, Green	Yellow	Pink	Blue
Ash tray, 5½"	20.00	25.00	25.00		Plate, 8½" salad	6.00	10.00	9.50	
Bowl, 5" berry	10.00	12.50	10.00	15.00	Plate, 10" dinner	14.00	19.00	20.00	
Bowl, 5", cream					Plate, 10" grill	9.00	12.00	12.00	
soup or ruffled nut	17.50		12.00	50.00	Platter, 11½" oval	12.00	18.00	17.00	
Bowl, 6" cereal	19.00	20.00	18.00		*Salt and pepper, footed	35.00	50.00	50.00	
Bowl, 8½" large berry	19.00	25.00	25.00		Saucer	3.00	4.00	4.00	15.00
Bowl, 9½" oval vegetable					Sherbet, 3 oz. footed	8.00	9.00	8.00	
and cover	45.00	50.00	50.00		Sugar	8.00	11.00	11.00	
Butter dish and cover	115.00	150.00	150.00		Sugar cover	14.00	17.00	17.00	
Butter dish bottom	45.00	80.00	80.00		Sugar, ruffled	27.50		27.50	45.00
Butter dish top	70.00	70.00	70.00		Tumbler, 3¼", 4 oz.				
Coaster/ash tray, 3¾"	15.00	17.00	22.00		footed	12.00			
Comport, 3½", ruffled	20.00		10.00	50.00	Tumbler, 3¾", 5 oz.				
Creamer	8.50	11.00	15.00		footed juice	12.00	18.00	18.00	
Creamer, ruffled	32.50		32.50	55.00	Tumbler, 4", 9 oz., ribbed	12.00		18.00	
Cup	8.00	9.00	8.00	70.00	Tumbler, 4¾", 10 oz.				
Pitcher, 6½", 36 oz.					footed water	19.00	18.00	18.00	
footed	35.00	42.50	42.50	800.00	Tumbler, 5¼", 12 oz.				
Pitcher, 7½", 48 oz.					footed iced tea	25.00	27.00	27.00	
flat, ice lip or none	60.00	155.00	105.00		Tumbler, 5¼", 9 oz.				
Plate, 6" sherbet	4.00	5.00	4.00		lemonade (like Floral)			90.00	

*Beware reproductions

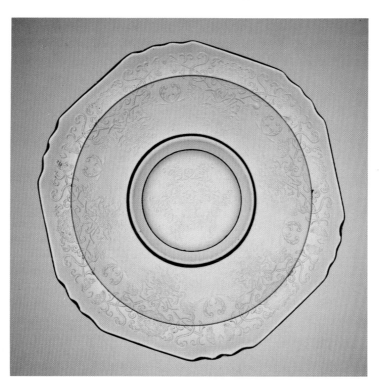

FLORENTINE NO. 2, "POPPY NO. 2" HAZEL ATLAS GLASS COMPANY 1932-1935

Colors: Pink, green, crystal, some cobalt, amber and ice blue.

Be sure to read about the differences between the Florentines in the second paragraph on page 70 (under Florentine No.1) if you are having trouble distinguishing between these patterns.

Many collectors are mixing the Florentines together. Some pieces of each pattern have been found in boxed sets over the years, so the factory must have mixed them also.

One good thing about the two Florentines is that the butter dish and oval vegetable tops are interchangeable. That ought to mean you have twice the chance of finding a lid for your butter or oval vegetable bowl. It doesn't! It means twice as many collectors are looking for tops broken over the years. I have had several letters recently asking for the measurements on the candy and butter lids since they are so similar. If you buy a candy lid thinking you are getting a butter lid, you have a problem since they are not interchangeable. The candy lid measures 4¾" but the butter dish lid measures 5" exactly. If you find a lid that measures 5", do not try to fit it on a candy bottom — it will not work!

The grill plate with the indent for the cream soup has only been found in green and crystal. Not many of these have been seen; and since they were only recently noticed, it stands to reason they are not very plentiful. Green Florentine is more in demand than crystal, but the crystal is more rarely seen.

Amber is the least found Florentine color, but there is not enough available to collect a set. It was either experimental or a small, special order. Most flat tumbler sizes have been found in amber, but still no pitcher has surfaced.

I predict that some day we will discover that the flat bottomed tumblers and flat bottomed straight sided pitchers were actually Florentine No.1. Why? The handles on the flat bottomed pitchers match the handles on the footed Florentine No. 1 pitcher. Cobalt tumblers seems to go with all the other pieces of cobalt No.1 including the rarely found pitcher. I also suspect that the ruffled comport is not a part of Florentine No. 2. Only a catalogue or a boxed set will help unravel this mystery! Somebody please find one!

Florentine fired-on blue shakers were shown in an earlier book. Now, luncheon sets of red and blue have been reported. The fired-on colors are sprayed over crystal. Once it has been fired-on, (baked, so to speak) the colors will not strip off even with paint removers as some collectors have learned. The fired-on colors are not common, but they also are not extremely collectible.

	Crystal, Green	Pink	Yellow	Blue		Crystal, Green	Pink	Yellow	Blue
Bowl, 4½" berry	10.00	12.00	16.00		Plate, 10" dinner	12.00	13.00	11.00	
Bowl, 4¾" cream soup	11.00	12.00	18.00		Plate, 10¼" grill	10.00		10.00	
Bowl, 5½"	27.50		35.00		Plate, 10¼", grill				
Bowl, 6" cereal	24.00		32.00		w/cream soup ring	28.00			
Bowl, 7½" shallow			80.00		Platter, 11" oval	13.00	13.00	15.00	
Bowl, 8" large berry	18.00	25.00	25.00		Platter, 11½" for				
Bowl, 9" oval vegetable					gravy boat			35.00	
and cover	45.00		55.00		Relish dish, 10", 3 part				
Bowl, 9" flat	22.50				or plain	16.00	22.00	25.00	
Butter dish and cover	90.00		135.00		**Salt and pepper, pr.	40.00		45.00	
Butter dish bottom	20.00		65.00		Saucer (amber 15.00)	3.00		4.00	
Butter dish top	70.00		70.00		Sherbet, footed				
Candlesticks, 2¾" pr.	40.00		55.00		(amber 40.00)	9.00		9.00	
Candy dish and cover	90.00	110.00	135.00		Sugar	7.00		9.00	
Coaster, 3¼"	11.00	14.00	19.00		Sugar cover	12.00		20.00	
Coaster/ash tray, 3¾"	16.00		20.00		Tray, condiment for				
Coaster/ash tray, 5½"	16.00		32.00		shakers, creamer and				
Comport, 3½", ruffled	20.00	10.00		50.00	sugar (round)			60.00	
Creamer	7.00		9.00		Tumbler, 3⅜", 5 oz. juice	10.00	10.00	18.00	
Cup (amber 50.00)	6.00		8.00		Tumbler, 3 9/16", 6 oz. blown	15.00			
Custard cup or jello	52.50		72.50		*** Tumbler, 4",				
Gravy boat			45.00		9 oz. water	11.00	10.00	18.00	60.00
Pitcher, 6¼", 24 oz.					Tumbler, 5", 12 oz., blown	16.00			
cone-footed			125.00		**** Tumbler, 5", 12 oz.				
* Pitcher, 7½", 28 oz.					iced tea	27.50		40.00	
cone-footed	25.00		25.00		Tumbler, 3¼", 5 oz.				
Pitcher, 7½", 48 oz.	50.00	97.50	140.00		footed	12.00	14.00		
Pitcher, 8¼", 76 oz.	80.00	197.50	325.00		Tumbler, 4", 5 oz. footed	12.00		14.00	
Plate, 6" sherbet	3.00		5.00		Tumbler, 4½", 9 oz.				
Plate, 6¼" with indent	15.00		25.00		footed	20.00		30.00	
Plate, 8½" salad	7.00	7.00	8.00		Vase or parfait, 6"	28.00		55.00	

* Blue - $450.00
** Fired-On Red, Orange or Blue, Pr. - $40.00
*** Amber - $65.00
**** Amber - $65.00

Please refer to Foreword for pricing information

FLOWER GARDEN WITH BUTTERFLIES, "BUTTERFLIES AND ROSES"
U.S. GLASS COMPANY, Late 1920's

Colors: Pink, green, blue-green, canary yellow, crystal, amber and black.

Tomorrow is my wife's birthday and she gets a surprise piece of Flower Garden with Butterflies that I bought in Oregon, a green heart shaped candy which I had never seen before! We have had blue, canary and pink heart shaped candy boxes previously. (I'm hoping this will make up for selling the canary and pink when cutting back our collection to blue and green colors only.)You will be able to see it in my later books!

Having been collectors of the blue for over 15 years, we still need a multitude of pieces for our set including the bulb of that atomizer shown. If anyone has a spare, let us know!

Flower Garden has three different powder jars; that may be why the oval and rectangular trays are so plentiful. The trays and the 8" plates are the only commonly found pieces (if there are pieces that could be considered common). Evidently more powder jars than trays were broken over the years. There are two different footed powders. The smaller, shown in green, stands 6¼" tall; the taller, shown in blue, stands 7½" high. Lids to the footed powders are interchangeable. The flat powder jar, also shown in green, has a 3½" diameter. (A blue flat powder is one of the pieces eluding our collection.)

Prices have dipped for the ash trays, as they have in almost all patterns. These are still difficult to find in Flower Garden.

In the last book, I talked about the "Shari" perfume or cologne set, but I'm still getting letters about it. It's a semi-circular, footed dresser tray which holds wedge (pie) shaped bottles. It is often confused with Flower Garden. There are two dancing girls and butterflies on it. This is not Flower Garden! Neither are the 7" and 10" trivets made by U.S. Glass with flowers all over them. They were mixing bowl covers and they do not have butterflies.

Black Flower Garden pieces are found once in a while, but these pieces are as elusive as the blue.

	Amber Crystal	Pink Green Blue-Green	Blue Canary Yellow		Amber Crystal	Pink Green Blue-Green	Blue Canary Yellow
Ash tray, match-pack holders	175.00	85.00	195.00	Mayonnaise, footed 4¾" h. x 6¼" w., w/7" plate & spoon	65.00	75.00	110.00
Candlesticks, 4" pr.	40.00	50.00	85.00	Plate, 7"	15.00	20.00	25.00
Candlesticks, 8" pr.	75.00	90.00	125.00	Plate, 8", two styles	13.50	16.50	22.50
Candy w/cover, 6", flat	125.00	150.00		Plate, 10"		32.50	42.50
Candy w/cover, 7½" cone-shaped	75.00	100.00	150.00	Plate, 10", indent for 3" comport	30.00	35.00	40.00
Candy w/cover, heart-shaped		900.00	900.00	Powder jar, 3½", flat		45.00	
* Cologne bottle w/stopper, 7½"		160.00	225.00	Powder jar, footed, 6¼"h.	65.00	82.50	150.00
Comport, 2⅞" h.		20.00	25.00	Powder jar, footed, 7½"h.	75.00	95.00	175.00
Comport, 3" h. fits 10" plate	17.50	20.00	25.00	Sandwich server, center handle	45.00	55.00	85.00
Comport, 4¼" h. x 4¾" w.			45.00	Saucer		20.00	
Comport, 4¾" h. x 10¼" w.	45.00	60.00	75.00	Sugar		60.00	
Comport, 5⅞" h. x 11" w.	50.00		85.00	Tray, 5½" x 10", oval	47.50	50.00	
Comport, 7¼" h. x 8¼" w.	55.00	75.00		Tray, 11¾" x 7¾", rectangular	47.50	57.50	77.50
Creamer		65.00		Tumbler, 7½" oz.	125.00		
Cup		55.00		Vase, 6¼"	67.50	87.50	120.00
				Vase, 10½"		100.00	175.00

*Stopper, if not broken off, ½ price of bottle

PRICE LIST FOR BLACK ITEMS ONLY

Bon Bon w/cover, 6⅝" diameter	250.00
Bowl, 7¼", w/cover, "flying saucer"	375.00
Bowl, 8½", console, w/base	150.00
Bowl, 9" rolled edge, w/base	200.00
Bowl, 11" footed orange	225.00
Bowl, 12" rolled edge console w/base	200.00
Candlestick 6" w/6½" candle, pr.	350.00
Candlestick, 8", pr.	225.00
Cheese and cracker, footed, 5⅜" h. x 10" w.	325.00
Comport and cover, 2¾" h. (fits 10"indented plate)	200.00
Cigarette box & cover, 4⅜" long	150.00
Comport, tureen, 4¼" h. x 10" w.	225.00
Comport, footed, 5⅝" h. x 10" w.	225.00
Comport, footed, 7"h.	175.00
Plate, 10", indented	100.00
Sandwich server, center-handled	125.00
Vase, 6¼", dahlia, cupped	135.00
Vase, 8", dahlia, cupped	200.00
Vase, 9", wall hanging	300.00
Vase, 10", 2-handled	225.00
Vase, 10½", dahlia, cupped	250.00

Please refer to Foreword for pricing information

FORTUNE HOCKING GLASS COMPANY, 1937-1938

Colors: Pink and crystal.

A crystal Fortune candy dish with a Royal Ruby lid was reported to me, but there was no accompanying photograph; so, if you have one, please send me a picture. The reader reported that the lid had plain beads under the knob. The candy dish *is* the best selling piece in this pattern.

There are more candy dish collectors who purchase these than do Fortune collectors. Other collectors have to compete with them for candies.

With an investment of a lot of time and little money compared to other patterns, a pink set can be collected; it will be a small set when completed. Cups, saucers and the luncheon plates are not plentiful.

Many dealers stock Fortune but do not carry it to shows. A cup and saucer in Fortune takes up the same amount of space as does a cup and saucer in any other pattern. A dealer can carry a popular pattern cup and saucer that many collectors are searching for at $25.00 or he can carry a Fortune set for $6.00 that few people are looking to buy. Which would you do? If you want to collect Fortune, leave your name with several dealers who are willing to help you find it. More and more dealers are creating "want list" files of collectors. That way the dealer has a ready made sale when he buys the glass!

Both tumblers listed below are shown on page 79. A few pitchers are surfacing that are similar to this pattern. So far, no actual Fortune pitcher has turned up; but there is always hope!

	Pink, Crystal			Pink, Crystal
Bowl, 4" berry	3.50		Cup	3.50
Bowl, 4½" dessert	4.00		Plate, 6" sherbet	2.50
Bowl, 4½" handled	4.00		Plate, 8" luncheon	8.00
Bowl, 5¼" rolled edge	5.00		Saucer	2.50
Bowl, 7¾" salad or large berry	11.00		Tumbler, 3½", 5 oz. juice	6.00
Candy dish and cover, flat	20.00		Tumbler, 4", 9 oz. water	8.00

FRUITS HAZEL ATLAS AND OTHER GLASS COMPANIES, 1931-1935

Colors: Pink, green, some crystal and iridized.

Fruits pattern water tumblers (4") in all colors are the most commonly found pieces. There are a multitude of iridized "Pears" tumblers. These were probably made by Federal Glass Company since they were making iridescent Normandie and a few pieces in Madrid during this time period. Tumblers with cherries or other fruits are commonly found in pink, but finding green tumblers is more of a problem.

Fruits collectors have all been trying to find the 5", 12 oz. tumbler. I have never seen it in pink, but a few have been reported over the years. Smaller juice tumblers are not common either, but I have not had as many folks ask for those as the iced teas. Most collectors want green tumblers because there has been no pitcher found in pink.

Crystal pitchers sell for about half the price of green. These pitchers only have cherries in the pattern. Notice that the handle is shaped like that on the flat Florentine pitchers (Hazel Atlas Company) and not like Cherry Blossom (Jeannette Glass Company) flat pitchers. This will keep you from confusing the Cherry pitchers from the Fruits. Other crystal pieces are rarely collected, but tumblers are available if you would like a cheaper beverage set.

Fruits berry bowl sets are among the hardest to collect in Depression glass. Since this is not one of the larger patterns and does not have the number of collectors that some other patterns do, the true scarcity of these berry bowls is just beginning to be recognized.

	Green	Pink		Green	Pink
Bowl, 5" berry	17.50	15.00	Sherbet	7.00	6.00
Bowl, 8" berry	45.00	35.00	Tumbler, 3½" juice	15.00	12.00
Cup	6.00	5.00	* Tumbler, 4" (1 fruit)	15.00	12.00
Pitcher, 7" flat bottom	50.00		Tumbler, 4" (combination of fruits)	20.00	12.00
Plate, 8" luncheon	5.00	5.00	Tumbler, 5", 12 oz.	60.00	55.00
Saucer	4.00	3.00			

* Iridized $7.50

GEORGIAN, "LOVEBIRDS" FEDERAL GLASS COMPANY, 1931-1936

Colors: Green and crystal.

Georgian has little "lovebirds" sitting side by side on most pieces except for some dinner plates, tumblers, and hot plates. Tumblers only have the basket design on each side. Baskets usually alternate with the birds on other pieces. Sometimes you can find a bargain priced tumbler if the seller does not see birds on it. The hot plate and some dinner plates carry only the center motif.

There are two styles of dinner plates. The harder to find style (shown on the left rear of the photo) is the least desired. This style has no "lovebirds," but only the center design. The more collectible plate (with lovebirds) is pictured in the back center. This is a case where a less plentiful piece of glass is cheaper because of lack of demand. Demand and not rarity alone affects prices. Even a rare piece can be hard to sell if no one wants it!

Georgian tumblers in both sizes are hard to find. The iced teas have almost doubled the price of the water tumblers. I have owned a dozen waters for every one of the teas over the years to give you an idea of how difficult teas are to find. In fact, just last year a collector in Illinois brought in a boxed set of 12 waters that she had found priced reasonably at a sale. No pitcher has ever been found, but it took years for someone to uncover Parrot pitchers (our other "bird" pattern that is sometimes confused with Georgian) and 37 of those were found all at once. So, there's still hope!

The next most difficult piece of Georgian to find is the sugar lid for the larger sugar. Several times I have found lids at flea markets or shows, but none of these have fit the larger sugar shown in the picture.

The 6" deep berries were heavily used; so watch out for pieces that are scratched and worn from usage. Remember that prices listed in this book are for mint condition pieces. Damaged or scratched and worn pieces should fetch less depending upon the extent of damage and wear. If you are collecting the glass to use, it may not make as much difference as collecting it to eventually resale. Mint condition glass will sell more readily and for a much better price if you ever decide to part with your collection.

Very few of the lazy susan or cold cuts servers have been found. Recently, one turned up with an original label which read "Kalter Aufschain Cold Cuts Server Schirmer Cincy." That may be why so many have been found in Kentucky and southern Ohio. These lazy susans are made of walnut and are 18½" across with seven 5" openings for holding the hot plates. Maybe someone misnamed these 5" hot plates since they are being found on a cold cuts server! One of these in the Madrid pattern can be seen in earlier editions of this book or you can see one in that pattern in my book *Very Rare Glassware of the Depression Years , Second Series*.

There are a few Georgian pieces commonly found. Berry bowls, cups, saucers sherbets, sherbet plates and luncheon plates can be seen with regularity. You may have to search a while for other pieces.

There is no true mug in Georgian. A creamer found without a spout was called a mug. There are many patterns that have creamers or pitchers without a spout; and one Federal pattern, Sharon, has at least one two spouted creamer known! Spouts were applied by hand using a wooden tool at many factories. That some escaped without the spout or that some worker had fun by adding an extra one is not surprising!

	Green
Bowl, 4½" berry	7.00
Bowl, 5¾" cereal	17.50
Bowl, 6½" deep	57.50
Bowl, 7½" large berry	50.00
Bowl, 9" oval vegetable	55.00
Butter dish and cover	65.00
Butter dish bottom	37.50
Butter dish top	27.50
Cold cuts server, 18½" wood with seven 5" openings for 5" coasters	625.00
Creamer, 3", footed	10.00
Creamer, 4", footed	13.00
Cup	8.00
* Hot Plate, 5" center design	40.00
Plate, 6" sherbet	4.00
Plate, 8" luncheon	6.50
Plate, 9¼" dinner	22.50
Plate, 9¼" center design only	18.00
Platter, 11½" closed-handled	55.00
Saucer	3.50
Sherbet	10.00
Sugar, 3", footed	8.50
Sugar, 4", footed	9.50
Sugar cover for 3"	30.00
Sugar cover for 4"	80.00
Tumbler, 4", 9 oz. flat	45.00
Tumbler, 5¼", 12 oz. flat	95.00

*Crystal-$20.00

Please refer to Foreword for pricing information

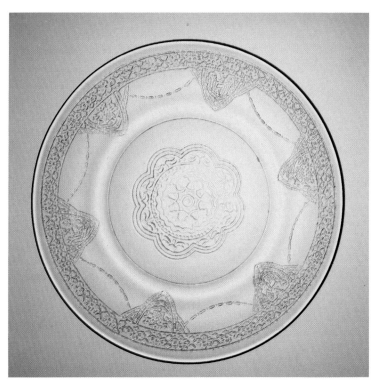

HEX OPTIC, "HONEYCOMB" JEANNETTE GLASS COMPANY, 1928-1932

Colors: Pink, green, ultramarine and iridescent in 1950's.

Hex Optic is still collected by Kitchenware buyers more than by any other collecting group. The sugar shaker, bucket reamer and butter dish are eagerly bought in both colors. Refrigerator dishes, stacking sets and mixing bowls are also available, but are not as much in demand as are the other kitchen pieces. In fact, were it not for Kitchenware collectors getting hooked on this pattern, Hex Optic might be ignored.

I recently bought a pink pitcher and will show it next time. This pitcher has the same mould shape as the hard to find lemonade pitcher in Floral.

Green is less available, but also more desirable than pink. This color preference affects Depression glass collectors more than Kitchenware collectors who seek out both colors. For now, prices for both colors are listed the same. However, if more collectors continue to spurn the pink and collect only green, prices will begin to reflect that.

Iridized tumblers, oil lamps and pitchers were all made during Jeannette's iridized craze of the 1950's. I have never been able to verify when the company made the ultramarine tumblers. A guess would be in the late 1930's when the company was making Doric and Pansy, but that is only a guess. Both of these unusual colors are shown in the photograph.

	Pink, Green		Pink, Green
Bowl, 4¼" ruffled berry	5.00	Platter, 11" round	11.00
Bowl, 7½" large berry	6.50	Refrigerator dish, 4" x 4"	9.00
Bowl, 7¼" mixing	11.00	Refrigerator stack set, 3 pc.	45.00
Bowl, 8¼" mixing	15.00	Salt and pepper, pr.	25.00
Bowl, 9" mixing	16.00	Saucer	2.00
Bowl, 10" mixing	20.00	Sugar, 2 styles of handles	5.00
Bucket reamer	50.00	Sugar shaker	130.00
Butter dish and cover, rectangular 1 lb. size	67.50	Sherbet, 5 oz. footed	4.00
Creamer, 2 style handles	5.00	Tumbler, 3¾", 9 oz.	4.00
Cup, 2 style handles	4.00	Tumbler, 5", 12 oz.	6.00
Ice bucket, metal handle	17.50	Tumbler, 4¾", 7 oz. footed	7.00
Pitcher, 5", 32 oz. sunflower motif in bottom	20.00	Tumbler, 5¾" footed	8.00
Pitcher, 9", 48 oz. footed	35.00	Tumbler, 7" footed	10.00
Plate, 6" sherbet	2.00	Whiskey, 2", 1 oz.	7.00
Plate, 8" luncheon	5.00		

HOBNAIL HOCKING GLASS COMPANY, 1934-1936

Colors: Crystal, crystal w/red trim and pink.

Hocking's Hobnail is more readily recognized by collectors because of the shapes of many pieces. Hobnail shapes are similar to those found in Miss America and those used in the 1940's to make Moonstone. This Hobnail is only one of many hobnail patterns made by dozens of other glass companies.

Hobnail serving pieces are difficult to find, but there is no lack of beverage sets! Red trimmed crystal (see photo) has caught the fancy of a few collectors; but this is found mostly on the West coast. This footed juice tumbler was sold along with the decanter as a wine set; so, it was also a wine glass.

(Terminology in glassware catalogues drives authors batty. Sometimes I have to decide whether to list what the factory said in catalogues or to list items in today's lingo. I have tried to incorporate both where feasible without creating a problem for new collectors. There is a glossary of terms listed in the back of my *Pocket Guide to Depression Glass* for those who have need to refer to it. There is not enough spare space in this book to cover all the glass terms needed; so I try to cover what I can throughout this book. That means you have to read it all to find them! It took months and some fourteen to sixteen hour days of writing to put this book together. We won't even discuss the rest of the twenty years of gathering, photographing, proofing and worrying to put it all on paper.)

For collectors who wish to purchase an economically priced set, this is just the ticket. The major problem in collecting this set is finding dealers who stock it. There are many ways collectors can overcome this handicap. I suggest you make out a want list and give it to dealers to call you collect when they find your pattern.

There are only four different pink pieces made by Hocking, five, if you count the sherbet plate and saucer as two pieces. You can pick another pink Hobnail pattern such as one made by MacBeth-Evans to go along with Hocking's; that way you add a pitcher and tumbler set, something unavailable in this Hocking ware.

	Pink	Crystal		Pink	Crystal
Bowl, 5½" cereal		3.50	Plate, 8½" luncheon	3.00	3.00
Bowl, 7" salad		4.00	Saucer/sherbet plate	2.00	1.50
Cup	4.00	4.00	Sherbet	3.00	2.50
Creamer, footed		3.00	Sugar, footed		3.00
Decanter and stopper, 32 oz.		25.00	Tumbler, 5 oz. juice		3.50
Goblet, 10 oz. water		6.00	Tumbler, 9 oz., 10 oz. water		5.00
Goblet, 13 oz. iced tea		7.00	Tumbler, 15 oz. iced tea		6.50
Pitcher, 18 oz. milk		17.00	Tumbler, 3 oz. footed wine/juice		5.50
Pitcher, 67 oz.		23.00	Tumbler, 5 oz. footed cordial		5.00
Plate, 6" sherbet	2.00	1.50	Whiskey, 1½ oz.		5.00

HOMESPUN, "FINE RIB" JEANNETTE GLASS COMPANY, 1939-1949

Colors: Pink and crystal.

Homespun tumblers are a nemesis to collectors of this pattern. Only the commonly found 5 oz. juice is readily available. Other tumblers range from hard to nearly impossible to find. Another problem is that all tumblers are found in two different styles. On some tumblers the ribs go all the way to the top; other tumblers have a plain band at the top causing the ribs to run to within a quarter or half inch of the top depending upon the size of the tumbler. There are also two styles of 15 oz. footed tumblers. One tumbler (6¼") is fatter at the bottom and has practically no stem at all; the other (6⅜") has a pronounced stem. Both of these have been listed at 6¼", but there is ⅛" difference!

This is a challenging set to complete and if you only buy one style of tumbler, then it is even more frustrating. Buy every water and tea tumbler you find! You will not go broke; there are not that many.

There is no sugar lid! The lid sometimes found on the Homespun sugar is actually a fine rib pattern powder jar top. It does fit, so many have been added to the sugars over the years. Yet, fitting the sugar does not make it Homespun.

The children's sets are still in demand. Not only do Depression glass collectors buy these sets, but doll collectors and miniature collectors buy them, also. This makes the already short supply even more so. There is no children's tea pot in crystal and there are no sugar and creamers in this tea set. The tea pot looks like a creamer with a sugar lid; so don't be fooled as I once was years ago when I first saw this set.

	Pink, Crystal		Pink, Crystal
Bowl, 4½", closed handles	6.00	Saucer	3.00
Bowl, 5" cereal	16.00	Sherbet, low flat	15.00
Bowl, 8¼" large berry	15.00	Sugar, footed	8.00
Butter dish and cover	45.00	Tumbler, 3⅞", 9 oz. straight	15.00
Coaster/ash tray	6.00	Tumbler, 4", 9 oz. water, flared top	15.00
Creamer, footed	8.00	Tumbler, 5¼", 13 oz. iced tea	25.00
Cup	6.00	Tumbler, 4", 5 oz. footed	6.00
Plate, 6" sherbet	4.00	Tumbler, 6¼", 15 oz. footed	22.50
Plate, 9¼" dinner	14.00	Tumbler, 6⅜", 15 oz. footed	22.50
Platter, 13", closed handles	12.00		

HOMESPUN CHILD'S TEA SET

	Pink	Crystal		Pink	Crystal
Cup	25.00	15.00	Tea pot cover	45.00	
Saucer	7.50	4.50	Set: 14-pieces	250.00	
Plate	10.00	6.50	Set: 12-pieces		105.00
Tea pot	35.00				

INDIANA CUSTARD, "FLOWER AND LEAF BAND" INDIANA GLASS COMPANY 1930's; 1950's

Colors: Ivory or custard, early 1930's; white, 1950's.

Indiana Custard continues to attract a few collectors, and it is great that there are only a few. There is not enough of this pattern to support a large numbers of buyers.

I have straightened up the sizes on the bowls which have been incorrect for several editions. I purchased a large set in Ohio sight unseen and paid for cereal bowls that were actually berry bowls because of mistaken size listings. (That gets corrections in an author's book real fast!)

Indiana Custard is the only pattern I know where both cups and sherbets are the hard pieces to find. Many collectors think the sherbet is overpriced; but collectors who have searched for several years without success in finding even one, would not agree! Cups are the other Achilles heel to this pattern. I have had a couple more sherbets than cups in the last two years. Both sell quickly; so there is a demand for these. More Indiana Custard collectors are in the central Indiana area than any place. Of course, it is more plentiful there, making it easier to get hooked on it!

The white (illustrated by the decorated scenic pieces) is difficult to market. I still have not met a collector of white Indiana Custard.

I wonder if there is a full set of yellow floral decorated pieces. There is a set of Indiana Custard decorated like the saucer in the front. A major problem to this set is that the decorations come off easily. If you can find a set with nicely colored pieces, you will fall in love with it. Finding it a piece or two at a time would be quite a chore! But, then, some people like a challenge! I had one collector tell me that he purposely chose a hard to get pattern because it doubled his pleasure when he found a piece!

	French Ivory		French Ivory
Bowl, 5½" berry	7.50	Plate, 7½" salad	9.50
Bowl, 6½" cereal	18.00	Plate, 8⅞" luncheon	11.00
Bowl, 7½" flat soup	28.00	Plate, 9¾" dinner	18.00
Bowl, 9", 1¾" deep, large berry	25.00	Platter, 11½" oval	28.00
Bowl, 9½" oval vegetable	24.00	Saucer	7.00
Butter dish and cover	57.50	Sherbet	82.50
Cup	35.00	Sugar	10.00
Creamer	14.00	Sugar cover	17.00
Plate, 5¾" bread and butter	6.00		

Please refer to Foreword for pricing information

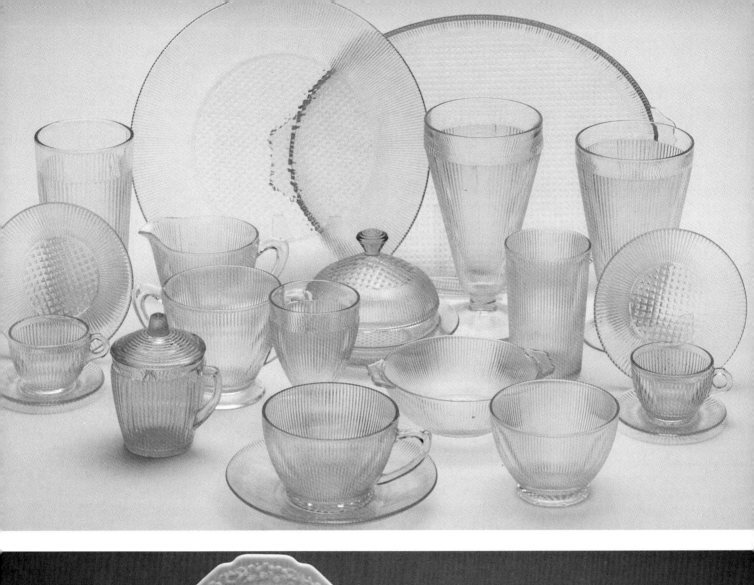

IRIS, "IRIS AND HERRINGBONE" JEANNETTE GLASS COMPANY, 1928-1932; 1950's; 1970's

Colors: Crystal, iridescent; some pink and green; recently bi-colored red/yellow and blue/green combinations and white.

Iris was one of the more difficult patterns to place in the division of this book since it fit both time periods. Actually, crystal production goes back to 1928 for its start. However, some crystal was made in the late 1940's, 1950's and some pieces such as candy bottoms and vases as late as the early 1970's. Iridescent belongs entirely within the time frame of my new book *Collectible Glassware from the 40's, 50's, 60's...*; and although I have also listed iridescent prices here now, next time they will only be in the other book.

I recently saw a green creamer on the West coast, but it had been purchased in the Carolinas. There have been sporadic reports of sugars and vases also, but this was the first green piece I had ever seen!

I said in my last book that Iris was the hottest selling crystal pattern, but little did I realize what an understatement that was! About the time the book came out with Iris on the cover, everyone seemed to want it! There was already a short supply of many pieces because of the heavy demand from the South, Tennessee in particular, where Iris is the state flower. No dealer could have enough stock of this pattern; and the demand far out stripped the supply. Dealers began to raise prices and suddenly the race was on! Many collectors got caught up in the frenzy, and some prices almost doubled. Things have settled down now that collectors have decided that prices were higher than they were willing to pay. (Collectors have always been able to control price in the market by refusing to buy. Look at the prices for art recently. Auction pieces are not bringing minimum bids!)

Demitasse cups have always been available; it is the saucers that are impossible to find. Many of these cups were originally sold on copper saucers instead of glass.

One contributing factor to the rise in price of iridescent pieces is the person in Pennsylvania who discovered a way to remove the iridescence from Iris and thus change iridescent soup bowls ($35.00 to $45.00) back to crystal (selling in the $100.00 range). However, most changed items I have seen have a very cloudy look to the Iris flowers on the pieces. It was quite an enterprising project because years ago I had been told by former glass factory workers that it could not be done!

I heard of a group of 12 iridized water goblets at a show in Springfield, Illinois, last summer; but by the time I contacted the dealer, all were sold. I still have never owned one although I have seen them in collections. This goblet and the demitasse cup and saucer are the most difficult pieces to find in the iridescent color.

Realize that candy bottoms in iridescent are a product of the 1970's when Jeannette made crystal bottoms and flashed them with two-tone colors such as red/yellow or blue/green. Many of these were sold as vases and over time the colors have washed or peeled off making them, once again, crystal candy bottoms. These can be distinguished by the lack of rays on the foot of the dish. The later made ones all are plain footed. By the same token, white vases were made and sprayed on the outside in green, red and blue. White vases of this vintage sell in the $8.00–10.00 range.

The decorated red and gold Iris that keeps turning up was called "Corsage" and "styled by Century" in 1946. This information was on a card attached to a 1946 wedding gift. Does anyone know more?

The bowls advertising "Babcock Furniture will treat you right" seem to be coming from the southern part of the country. Does anyone knows where this store was or still is?

	Crystal	Iridescent	Pink/ Green		Crystal	Iridescent	Pink/ Green
Bowl, 4½", berry, beaded edge	35.00	7.50		Goblet, 4¼", 4 oz., cocktail	20.00		
Bowl, 5", ruffled, sauce	8.00	20.00		Goblet, 4¼", 3 oz., wine	15.00		
Bowl, 5", cereal	70.00			Goblet, 5¾", 4 oz.	20.00		
Bowl, 7½", soup	100.00	45.00		Goblet, 5¾", 8 oz.	20.00	95.00	
Bowl, 8", berry, beaded edge	62.50	15.00		Lamp shade, 11½"	40.00		
* Bowl, 9½", ruffled, salad	10.00	10.00		Pitcher, 9½", footed	32.50	35.00	
Bowl, 11½", ruffled, fruit	10.00	10.00		Plate, 5½", sherbet	10.00	10.00	
Bowl, 11", fruit, straight edge	45.00			Plate, 8", luncheon	50.00		
Butter dish and cover	40.00	37.50		Plate, 9", dinner	45.00	35.00	
Butter dish bottom	12.50	10.00		Plate, 11¾", sandwich	20.00	20.00	
Butter dish top	27.50	27.50		Saucer	9.00	8.00	
Candlesticks, pr.	35.00	40.00		Sherbet, 2½", footed	20.00	11.00	
Candy jar and cover	95.00			Sherbet, 4", footed	16.00		
Coaster	65.00			Sugar	9.00	8.00	75.00
Creamer, footed	9.00	10.00	75.00	Sugar cover	10.00	10.00	
Cup	12.00	11.00		Tumbler, 4", flat	82.50		
** Demitasse cup	27.50	100.00		Tumbler, 6", footed	15.00	14.00	
** Demitasse saucer	107.50	125.00		Tumbler, 6½", footed	25.00		
Fruit or nut set	40.00	45.00		Vase, 9"	22.50	20.00	95.00
Goblet, 4", wine		27.50					

* Pink - $50.00
** Ruby, blue, amethyst priced as iridescent

Please refer to Foreword for pricing information

JUBILEE LANCASTER GLASS COMPANY, Early 1930's

Colors: Yellow and pink.

Newly discovered Jubilee pieces are turning up and many "look-alike" items are continuing to muddy the water for Jubilee collectors. New pieces include an 11½" bowl and a sherbet holding 7 oz. and standing 5½" tall. The 11" three footed bowl varies to 11½" at times depending upon the curved edges. I also photographed another style sherbet that was footed without a stem, but it only has eleven petals on the flower! Hopefully, the photo will fit next time.

Basic luncheon sets consisting of cups, saucers, luncheon plates, creamer and sugar are readily found. After finding those pieces, you have a problem getting anything else. I have found more in Florida recently than any place other than Ohio. (Of course, Florida is where I have been searching for glass; so that may account for finding more of it there.)

The mayonnaise has been fetching some wild prices! According to the catalog, the liner plate to the mayonnaise is the same piece as the 8¾" plate. There is no plate shown in the catalogues with an indent for the mayonnaise. However, you can see an indented plate as the pattern shot below. For the collector who wrote and said that my mayonnaise in the photo had sixteen petals, I show both that one and the twelve petalled flower for his magnifying glass. Both of these mayonnaise sets have indented rings that the feet of the bowl fit inside.

As I have mentioned before, TRUE Jubilee has twelve petal flowers and an open-centered flower. There are other Lancaster "look-alike" patterns that have sixteen petals or twelve petals with a smaller petal in between the larger ones. Many collectors are willing to settle for these at a lesser price; however, purist collectors will accept nothing but the twelve petal, open center pieces. As an advertiser of glass or a dealer who is offering glass for sale as Jubilee, you had better know the difference or be prepared for an onslaught of returns. Personally, I find the patterns that are similar a welcome addition to the short supply of Jubilee; and most of my customers enjoy buying "look-alike" pieces for less than prices paid for "the real thing."

The Jubilee cordial can be seen in my *Very Rare Glassware of the Depression Years, Second Series*. It is on the paneled-type blank that some tumblers have, but it was hard to cut a complete Jubilee design on this small rounded top. It does have the twelve petalled open flower! It stands 4" tall and holds 1 oz.

I finally found some pink Jubilee cup and saucer sets. I kept one and the others "flew out" of my shop for $42.50 a set! I am still looking for a creamer to go with my pink sugar.

	Pink	Yellow
Bowl, 8", 3-footed, 5⅛" high	225.00	195.00
Bowl, 9" handled fruit		95.00
Bowl, 11½", flat fruit	175.00	150.00
Bowl, 11½", 3-footed	225.00	200.00
Candlestick, pr.	175.00	145.00
Cheese & cracker set	250.00	225.00
Creamer	30.00	20.00
Cup	35.00	15.00
Goblet, 4", 1 oz., cordial		195.00
Goblet, 5", 6 oz., juice		60.00
Goblet, 6", 10 oz., water	60.00	40.00
Goblet, 6⅛", 12½ oz., tea		95.00
Mayonnaise & plate	275.00	225.00
w/original ladle	295.00	245.00
Plate, 7" salad	20.00	12.00
Plate, 8¾" luncheon	25.00	15.00
Plate, 13½" sandwich	75.00	45.00
Saucer, two styles	10.00	7.50
Sherbet/champagne, 5½", 7 oz.		45.00
Sherbet, 4¾"		40.00
Sugar	30.00	19.00
Tray, 11", 2-handled cake	60.00	40.00
Tray, 11", center-handled sandwich	175.00	125.00

"LACE EDGE," "OPEN LACE" OLD COLONY HOCKING GLASS COMPANY, 1935-1938

Colors: Pink and some crystal.

OLD COLONY is the real name of this pattern which we have called "Lace Edge" all these years! In December of 1990 I spent a day at Anchor Hocking going through files and catalogues. I got excited when I spotted these old store display photographs. After studying them for a few seconds I really could not believe what I was seeing. Both displays named the glass Old Colony. There it was in black and white! Finally, the real name of this pattern! Originally, this trip was for my book *Collectible Glassware from the 40's, 50's, 60's*...but this one discovery made the whole trip worthwhile! However, the information attained for the other book was just as invaluable.

Don't you wish you could go stock your ancestors cupboards with sherbets and plates for a dime each? Notice that the saucers were also sold as sherbet plates. At least, I am assuming those are saucers since no sherbet plate is listed in catalogues and none have ever been reported by collectors.

The true 9" comport in Old Colony has a rayed base. There is a similar comport that measures 9" also. This "pretender" has a plain foot.

The major problem to collecting Old Colony (besides finding it) concerns the damaged lace on the outside of the pieces. It chipped and cracked very easily and still does. Plates and bowls have to be stacked cautiously because of that. Candlesticks, console bowls and vases are other hard to find mint pieces in this pattern.

Ribs on the footed tumbler extend only about half way up the side as they do on the cup. This tumbler is often confused with the Coronation tumbler which has a similar shape and design. You can see the Coronation tumbler under that pattern. Notice the fine ribbed effect from the middle up on the Coronation tumbler. This is missing on the Old Colony tumbler.

The butter bottom also serves as a 7¾" salad bowl according to old catalogues, but many collectors like to think the true salad bowl is ribbed. Ribbing makes a big difference in price on this bowl! The 9½" bowl is also found ribbed or plain, but the price remains the same for both types.

Satinized or frosted pieces such as the vase shown here sell for only a fraction of their unfrosted counter parts. Lack of demand is the main reason. Although some collectors think frosted Old Colony is beautiful, most do not! My Mom handles frosted glass rarely. It adversely affects her like a squeaky chalkboard does other people.

This pattern still confuses new collectors because there were other companies that made an "open lace" type pattern. Both Lancaster and Standard had very similar designs, but their glass is better quality and "rings" when flipped on the edge with your finger. Hocking's Old Colony makes a "clunk" sound. The pink color of other companies' glass is usually a prettier shade of pink. If the piece is not shown in my listing or is in any color other than pink or crystal, the likelihood of your having a Old Colony piece is slim at best.

	*Pink		***Pink**
** Bowl, 6⅜" cereal	15.00	Plate, 8¼" salad	18.00
Bowl, 7¾" ribbed salad	40.00	Plate, 8¾" luncheon	14.00
Bowl, 8¼" (crystal)	10.00	Plate, 10½" dinner	22.50
Bowl, 9½" plain or ribbed	16.00	Plate, 10½" grill	15.00
*** Bowl, 10½", 3 legs, (frosted, $30.00)	155.00	Plate, 10½", 3-part relish	20.00
Butter dish or bon bon with cover	55.00	Plate, 13", solid lace	25.00
Butter dish bottom, 7¾"	20.00	Plate, 13", 4-part solid lace	25.00
Butter dish top	35.00	Platter, 12¾"	24.00
*** Candlesticks, pr. (frosted $40.00)	155.00	Platter, 12¾", 5-part	24.00
Candy jar and cover, ribbed	40.00	Relish dish, 7½", 3-part deep	50.00
Comport, 7"	20.00	Saucer	9.00
Comport, 7" and cover, footed	40.00	*** Sherbet, footed	70.00
Comport, 9"	650.00	Sugar	19.00
Cookie jar and cover	50.00	Tumbler, 3½", 5 oz. flat	20.00
Creamer	19.00	Tumbler, 4½", 9 oz. flat	13.00
Cup	20.00	Tumbler, 5", 10½ oz. footed	55.00
Fish bowl, 1 gal. 8 oz. (crystal only)	25.00	Vase, 7", (frosted $50.00)	285.00
Flower bowl, crystal frog	20.00		

* Satin or frosted items 50% lower in price or less

** Officially listed as cereal or cream soup

*** Price is for absolute mint condition

"OLD COLONY"
The Glass Beautiful
FOR YOUR TABLE

DISPLAYED ON
COUNTER 14

Schreick's Studio
Columbus, Ohio

LACED EDGE, "KATY BLUE" IMPERIAL GLASS COMPANY, Early 1930's

Colors: Blue w/opalescent edge and green w/opalescent edge.

Laced Edge, as this pattern was named by Imperial, is often called "Katy" by older collectors. There is a little confusion over what pieces actually fit the pattern. The bowl shown in the center of the picture and the 12" luncheon plate from which this bowl was made (by turning up the plate edges) are actually another pattern of Imperials' but were included by them as Laced Edge on the same catalogue page with all other Laced Edge pieces made. Thus, collectors accept these as being Laced Edge, albeit with variant edging, as they do the double candlesticks that were originally sold with the bowl. The white edging technique was called "Sea Foam" by Imperial and was put on many other Imperial colors and also on other patterns besides Laced Edge.

Prices for the blue have skyrocketed again. You will notice that from the prices listed below! The green follows along since it is much rarer than the blue. Notice the lack of green in my picture. I have not been able to find green in my travels. Presently, there are few collectors looking for green which helps hold the price in line or it might surpass the blue!

Platters, oval bowls (divided or not) and other serving pieces are in shorter supply than originally thought. Collectors are grabbing all the serving bowls they see. You may not find these available for much longer!

You will find pieces in this design without the white edging technique. Blue and green pieces without the white sell for about half of the prices listed if you can find a buyer. Crystal pieces do not seem to be selling at any price. I have never seen crystal pieces with white edging in this pattern; if you have a piece, I'd appreciate knowing what you have.

	Opalescent		Opalescent
Bowl, 4½" fruit	25.00	Plate, 6½" bread & butter	15.00
Bowl, 5"	30.00	Plate, 8" salad	27.50
Bowl, 5½"	30.00	Plate, 10" dinner	50.00
Bowl, 6"	32.50	Plate, 12" luncheon (per catalogue description)	60.00
Bowl, 7" soup	35.00	Platter, 13"	110.00
Bowl, 9" vegetable	85.00	Saucer	10.00
Bowl, 11" divided oval	90.00	Sugar	35.00
Bowl, 11" oval	95.00	Tidbit, 2-tiered, 8" & 10" plates	75.00
Cup	30.00	Tumbler, 9 oz.	45.00
Creamer	35.00	Vase 5½"	50.00
Mayonnaise, 3-piece	115.00		

LAKE COMO HOCKING GLASS COMPANY, 1934-1937

Color: White with blue scene.

Very rarely do you see Lake Como at shows; and if you do, it is usually the salt and pepper shakers which seem to be the most commonly found items. When displayed, Lake Como sells very quickly.

Collectors do not buy this pattern a piece at a time unless they only find one piece. They buy all that is available if the pattern is not worn. It sounds great for the dealer; but it is also discouraging to have several weeks (or months) of buying disappear in one swoop. It may take the dealer months to replace what he has just sold.

Notice the flat soup standing up on the left. The floral decoration on the edge is embossed instead of painted in blue. I have only seen a few of these in my travels. Platters are also difficult to find. One of the disappointments in finding Lake Como is that the design wears so easily. The prices below are for mint condition glass with little wear on the design. Evidently, this pattern was used heavily. Part of all the collections I have purchased have been worn. The collectors told me that they had "settled" on buying less than mint glass in order to be able to have some of the pieces. Cups are hard to find that are not worn.

You should be able to buy worn Lake Como at 50 % to 80% of the prices listed depending upon the amount of wear.

	White		White
Bowl, 6" cereal	18.00	Plate, 9¼" dinner	20.00
Bowl, 9¾" vegetable	30.00	Platter, 11"	50.00
Bowl, flat soup	80.00	Salt & pepper, pr.	35.00
Creamer, footed	20.00	Saucer	8.00
Cup, regular	25.00	Saucer, St. Denis	9.00
Cup, St. Denis	20.00	Sugar, footed	19.00
Plate, 7¼" salad	14.00		

Please refer to Foreword for pricing information

LAUREL McKEE GLASS COMPANY, 1930's

Colors: French Ivory, Jade Green, White Opal and Poudre Blue.

I have mentioned skyrocketing prices twice before in this book; but that also fits the description of what is happening to children's Laurel tea sets with the Scotty Dog decoration! Evidently, the Scotty dog collectors have discovered these sets. The same thing happened to Akro Agate Scotty dog powder jars a few years ago. (Those collectors would even buy the bottoms to the powder jars that we had not been able to give away.) In any case, the Jade Green Scotty set has doubled in price and the French Ivory has more than doubled.

Other children's sets continue to be the hot ticket in Laurel. Red, green or orange trimmed children's sets are found in a limited supply with orange the most difficult color to find.

"Poudre Blue" Laurel is still the hardest to find color; but more collectors are turning to the "Jade Green" for variety. Many blue items were never made; that is also a deterring factor in starting to collect that color. The "French Ivory" attracts few new collectors; so prices have remained rather steady. Serving bowls in all colors have always been in short supply.

Several people are beginning to buy the trimmed ivory. The red trimmed is the most plentiful, but a set can also be gathered with green trim. Both of these color trims are shown in the bottom photograph.

The shakers are hard to find with strong patterns. Many of the designs are weak or obscure. Naturally, it's better to own a patterned pair than a pair that has only the right shape!

	White Opal, Jade Green	French Ivory	Poudre Blue
Bowl, 5" berry	6.00	7.00	12.00
Bowl, 6" cereal	7.00	8.00	18.00
Bowl, 6", three legs	12.00	13.00	
Bowl, 8" soup		27.50	
Bowl, 9" large berry	16.00	18.00	35.00
Bowl, 9¾" oval vegetable	16.00	16.00	35.00
Bowl, 10½", three legs	27.00	30.00	50.00
Bowl, 11"	25.00	35.00	50.00
Candlestick, 4" pr.	27.50	27.50	
Cheese dish and cover	50.00	55.00	
Creamer, short	8.00	10.00	
Creamer, tall	11.00	12.00	25.00
Cup	7.00	7.00	18.00
Plate, 6" sherbet	4.00	5.00	8.00
Plate, 7½" salad	9.00	9.00	12.00
Plate, 9⅛" dinner	11.00	11.00	18.00
Plate, 9⅛" grill	10.00	11.00	
Platter, 10¾" oval	18.00	25.00	30.00
Salt and pepper	50.00	40.00	
Saucer	3.00	3.00	6.00
Sherbet	9.00	11.00	
Sherbet/champagne, 5"		30.00	
Sugar, short	7.50	9.00	
Sugar, tall	10.00	11.00	25.00
Tumbler, 4½", 9 oz. flat	37.50	27.50	
Tumbler, 5", 12 oz. flat		40.00	

CHILDREN'S LAUREL TEA SET

	Plain	Green or Decorated Rims	Scotty Dog Green	Scotty Dog Ivory
Creamer	20.00	35.00	100.00	75.00
Cup	15.00	25.00	55.00	35.00
Plate	7.50	12.50	50.00	30.00
Saucer	5.50	7.50	50.00	20.00
Sugar	20.00	35.00	100.00	75.00
14-piece set	150.00	250.00	800.00	500.00

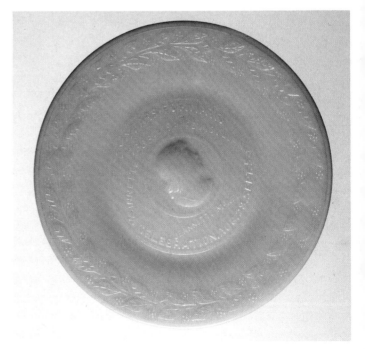

Please refer to Foreword for pricing information

LINCOLN INN   FENTON GLASS COMPANY, Late 1920's

Colors: Red, cobalt, light blue, amethyst, black, green, green opalescent, pink, crystal, amber and jade (opaque).

Lincoln Inn is the only pattern in this book that half the pieces you see are the high sherbet/champagnes. You can find a high sherbet in any color made in this pattern. I have often wondered why there are so many available. Were these the "in" cocktail glasses around Prohibition? You can find tumblers and other stems, but finding serving pieces in any color is not easily done.

The only older pitchers known are made in the colors shown in the picture. Fenton remade an iridized dark carnival colored pitcher several years ago. All of the light blue pitchers have been found in Florida; so watch for them there!

The opalescent green sugar is a rare color. It would be great to have a creamer to match. Let me know if you see one!

Shakers are difficult to find in all colors. There are collectors who only search for shakers. Although these are not the highest priced shakers in Depression glass, they are one of the toughest to find.The red and black are the most desired colors; but don't pass by any color in your travels. I found a red pair sitting with Royal Ruby in a corner of a shop a few years ago! Sometimes you have to look in some not so obvious places as you check out the shops. Many dealers who specialize in other fields do not take time to learn some of the lesser known patterns; and you can find a bargain once in a while.

Lincoln Inn plates can also be found with a fruit design in the center according to a 1930's catalogue; however, I have never seen one. Have you? I was told these were only made in crystal, so that should narrow the search.

Most red pieces are more amberina in color. Amberina is a red which has a yellowish cast to it. Red glass is made by reheating glass that comes out of the furnace yellow. Uneven reheating causes some of this to remain yellow. Some dealers have told collectors this is a rare color in order to sell it. Actually, it was a mistake and the amounts of yellow on each piece make it difficult to match pieces.

Red and cobalt blue are the easiest colors to find in Lincoln Inn. This helps, since those are the colors most desired by collectors!

	Cobalt Blue, Red	All Other Colors		Cobalt Blue, Red	All Other Colors
Ash tray	16.00	11.00	Sugar	19.00	13.00
Bon bon, handled square	14.00	11.00	Tumbler, 4 oz. flat juice	25.00	9.00
Bon bon, handled oval	15.00	11.00	Tumbler, 9 oz. flat water		19.00
Bowl, 5" fruit	11.00	8.00	Tumbler, 5 oz. footed	24.00	10.00
Bowl, 6" cereal	12.00	7.00	Tumbler, 9 oz. footed	25.00	13.00
Bowl, 6" crimped	12.00	8.00	Tumbler, 12 oz. footed	38.00	18.00
Bowl, handled olive	14.00	9.00	Vase, 12" footed	130.00	85.00
Bowl, finger	17.00	12.00			
Bowl, 9", shallow		20.00			
Bowl, 9¼" footed	30.00	18.00			
Bowl, 10½" footed	40.00	28.00			
Candy dish, footed oval	20.00	12.00			
Comport	23.00	14.00			
Creamer	20.00	14.00			
Cup	15.00	8.00			
Goblet, water	23.00	15.00			
Goblet, wine	26.00	16.00			
Nut dish, footed	16.00	11.00			
Pitcher, 7¼", 46 oz.	775.00	675.00			
Plate, 6"	7.00	4.00			
Plate, 8"	12.00	7.00			
Plate, 9¼"	25.00	11.00			
Plate, 12"	30.00	15.00			
* Salt/pepper, pr.	195.00	130.00			
Saucer	4.00	3.00			
Sherbet, 4½", cone shape	16.00	11.00			
Sherbet, 4¾"	18.00	12.00			

*Black $225.00

Please refer to Foreword for pricing information

LORAIN, "BASKET," No. 615 INDIANA GLASS COMPANY, 1929-1932

Colors: Green, yellow and some crystal.

Lorain collectors have written about the snack trays to ask what I am talking about when I said snack tray. One is shown below as a pattern shot. They are found in crystal (with colored borders of red, yellow, green and blue) and have an off center indent for the cup. The cups that go with these trays are sometimes decorated in the same colored borders, but many times they are plain crystal.

All known pieces of green and yellow Lorain are shown except for one size plate in yellow. From purchasing several collections of Lorain, and from collectors who have searched for Lorain for years, I have learned that cereal bowls are the hardest to find item and the inner rims are usually rough. The 8" deep berry in yellow is the next hardest piece to find. Green dinner plates are almost as hard to find as green cereals. Mould roughness is the biggest concern of these very particular collectors. Lorain suffers from that chronic problem!

Oval vegetable bowls have become more scarce in both colors. Saucers are harder to locate than cups because of mould roughness and wear and tear on them over the years.

New collectors please note that the white and green avocado colored sherbets (which have an open edge border) are a 1950's and later issue and should be treated as such. They were used heavily by florists and many are found with a substance used to holds flowers. They have always been assumed to be an Indiana product; but several have been found with Anchor Hocking stickers. I have not been able to corroborate this, but Hocking did attach sticker labels in the late 1950's and early 1960's. If any one out there has more information on these, please help.

Prices continue to rise in both colors. However, there have been more new collectors starting to collect green Lorain than yellow. Price and availability have something to do with that. Green is less expensive and more easily found. There are so few pieces found in crystal, I would not suggest you try to complete a set. It would be nearly impossible.

	Crystal, Green	Yellow		Crystal, Green	Yellow
Bowl, 6" cereal	30.00	50.00	Plate, 10¼" dinner	32.00	47.00
Bowl, 7¼" salad	35.00	53.00	Platter, 11½"	22.00	35.00
Bowl, 8" deep berry	75.00	125.00	Relish, 8", 4-part	16.00	30.00
Bowl, 9¾" oval vegetable	35.00	45.00	Saucer	4.00	5.00
Creamer, footed	14.00	19.00	Sherbet, footed	17.00	27.00
Cup	9.00	12.00	Snack tray, crystal/trim	20.00	
Plate, 5½" sherbet	6.00	9.00	Sugar, footed	13.00	19.00
Plate, 7¾" salad	9.00	14.00	Tumbler, 4¾", 9 oz. footed	17.00	25.00
Plate, 8⅜" luncheon	15.00	24.00			

Please refer to Foreword for pricing information

100

MADRID FEDERAL GLASS COMPANY, 1932-1939; INDIANA GLASS COMPANY, 1980's

Colors: Green, pink, amber, crystal and "Madonna" blue. (See *Reproduction Section*)

Madrid has been a genuine headache for collectors since 1976 when Federal reissued this pattern for the Bicentennial under the name "Recollection" glassware. Fine, it was dated 1976; but it WAS issued in the older color of amber instead of another color. Everyone was informed and many collectors assumed it would be collectible later. However, Indiana bought the moulds when Federal went bankrupt and there have been problems for collectors ever since. First Indiana removed the 1976 and made crystal. The old crystal butter was selling for several hundred dollars and the new one sold for $2.99. Prices plummeted!

Next, Indiana made pink and although it was lighter in color than the original, prices went down on the old. Now, Indiana has made blue; and although it is a brighter, harsher blue than the original, it has not helped the prices of the older blue. You can see the new pink in the Reproduction Section in the back. All the pieces made in pink have now been made in blue.

Blue Madrid collectors will have to be careful with their purchases for now. Only the items listed below were made in blue originally. Some of the old items have been remade, so know from whom you are buying your glass if you do not know the glass well. If a piece is found in blue that is not priced below, rest assured it is new! I was sent an ad recently advertising a teal color. I'm unsure at this writing whether it refers to this known blue or Indiana has made it in teal. Watch for it in your discount stores.

The wooden lazy susans are still being found in Eastern Kentucky and southern Ohio. A label found on one of these says "Kalter Aufschain Cold Cuts Server Schirmer Cincy." You can see one of these pictured in my *Very Rare Glassware of the Depression Years, Second Series.*

Madrid gravy boats and platters have always been found in Iowa. One is shown in the foreground of the top photograph. Mint condition sugar lids in any color are finds! Footed tumblers are harder to find than the flat ones. Collectors of green Madrid have turned out to be almost as scarce as the pattern!

A group of fourteen amber ash trays were recently purchased at an auction in Illinois. Until that time, only three or four were known!

	Amber	Pink	Green	Blue		Amber	Pink	Green	Blue
Ash tray, 6" square	180.00		130.00		Pitcher, 8", 60 oz.				
Bowl, 4¾" cream					square	40.00	35.00	135.00	150.00
soup	13.00				Pitcher, 8½", 80 oz.	55.00		200.00	
Bowl, 5" sauce	5.50	6.00	6.00		Pitcher, 8½",				
Bowl, 7" soup	14.00		15.00	28.00	80 oz. ice lip	55.00		225.00	
Bowl, 8" salad	12.00		16.00		Plate, 6" sherbet	3.00	3.50	4.00	8.00
Bowl, 9⅜" large					Plate, 7½" salad	9.00	9.00	9.00	20.00
berry	16.00	18.00			Plate, 8⅞" luncheon	7.00	7.00	9.00	18.00
Bowl, 9½" deep					Plate, 10½" dinner	30.00		30.00	65.00
salad	25.00				Plate, 10½" grill	9.00		15.00	
Bowl, 10" oval					Plate, 10¼" relish	9.00	9.00	14.00	
vegetable	14.00	14.00	15.00	35.00	Plate, 11¼" round				
* Bowl, 11" low					cake	12.00	10.00		
console	12.00	9.00			Platter, 11½" oval	12.00	11.00	14.00	20.00
Butter dish and					Salt/pepper, 3½"				
cover	62.00		75.00		footed, pr.	60.00		77.50	125.00
Butter dish bottom	25.00		35.00		Salt/pepper, 3½"				
Butter dish top	35.00		40.00		flat, pr.	40.00		50.00	
* Candlesticks,					Saucer	3.00	4.00	4.00	8.00
2¼" pr.	20.00	18.00			Sherbet, two styles	7.00		10.00	12.00
Cookie jar and					Sugar	7.00		8.00	14.00
cover	40.00	28.00			Sugar cover	30.00		35.00	150.00
Creamer, footed	8.00		10.00	17.50	Tumbler, 3⅞",				
Cup	6.00	7.00	8.00	15.00	5 oz.	11.00		30.00	35.00
Gravy boat and					Tumbler, 4¼", 9 oz.	13.00	13.00	18.00	22.00
platter	1,050.00				Tumbler, 5½",				
Hot dish coaster	35.00		35.00		12 oz. 2 styles	18.00		28.00	35.00
Hot dish coaster					Tumbler, 4", 5 oz.				
w/Indent	35.00		35.00		footed	22.00		37.00	
Jam dish, 7"	19.00		17.50	30.00	Tumbler, 5½",				
Jello mold, 2⅛"					10 oz. footed	22.00		37.00	
high	11.00				Wooden lazy				
** Pitcher, 5½"					susan, 7 hot				
36 oz. juice	35.00				dish coasters	650.00			

* Iridescent priced slightly higher
** Crystal - $150.00

Please refer to Foreword for pricing information

MANHATTAN, "HORIZONTAL RIBBED" ANCHOR HOCKING GLASS COMPANY, 1938-1943

Colors: Crystal, pink; some green, ruby and iridized.

I have received a few letters about discoveries of new pieces in Manhattan; however these have all turned out to be Anchor Hocking's newer line PARK AVENUE, so I will repeat what I said for those who do not update your books regularly.

PARK AVENUE was a new pattern line introduced by Anchor Hocking in 1987 to "re-create the Glamour Era of 1938 when Anchor Hocking first introduced a classic" according to the Inspiration '87 catalogue issued by the company. Anchor Hocking went to the trouble to preserve the integrity of their older glassware, however! None of the pieces in this line are exactly like the old Manhattan! They are only similar and Manhattan was never made in blue as this line has been. Many collectors of Manhattan have bought this new pattern to use as everyday dishes. Thus, everyone remains happy, company and collector alike. Manhattan's collectability has not been affected by the making of PARK AVENUE!

Pink Manhattan cups, saucers and dinner plates are rarely seen. You can see a cup in the top photograph, but I have never seen a saucer to go with it. The saucer/sherbet plates of Manhattan are like many of Hocking's saucers; they have no cup ring. There was a dinner plate displayed at the Houston show for at least two years. The price was high, but I guess someone must have finally purchased it, since I have not seen it there the last few years. There is also a Manhattan Royal Ruby juice pitcher in the Texas area, found in Ohio a long time ago.

The cereal bowl measures 5½" and has no handles. The handled berry measures 5⅜". These closed handled bowls are not the cereal! I mention the measurements because there is a vast price difference. In fact, the reason the 5⅜" handled berry has increased in price so much has come from dealers selling these as cereals!

Manhattan is one pattern that collectors do not seem to mind adding pieces that look similar. In fact, many collectors use Hazel Atlas shakers with Manhattan since they are round and look better to them than the original squared ones that Hocking made.

In the top photograph are several Manhattan "look-alikes." The five crystal pieces were placed here to help differentiate them from the true Manhattan. The little wine on the left (3½" tall and 2½" wide) has a similar friend which stands 3¾" tall and is 3" wide. These sell in the same price range.The two water bottles are both Hocking and were sold about the same time as Manhattan, but there are no indications in the catalogue that they were considered to be a part of that line. The bottle with the flat top sells for $10.00 to $12.50 while the one with the "Cameo" type stopper sells for $15.00 to $20.00 . The double branched candle and the candy are both products of L.E. Smith.The candy is listed below since so many people consider it to be Manhattan and the candle pairs sell in the $25.00 to $30.00 range.

The sherbet in Manhattan has a beaded bottom as can be seen left of the cup in the top picture. The center insert to the relish tray does not have these beads. The relish tray inserts can be found in crystal, pink and Royal Ruby. The center insert is always crystal on the relish trays.

	Crystal	Pink			Crystal	Pink
* Ashtray, 4" round	10.00			Relish tray, 14", 4-part	16.00	
Ashtray, 4½" square	15.00			Relish tray, 14" with inserts	45.00	45.00
Bowl, 4½" sauce, handles	8.00		***	Relish tray insert	3.50	4.00
Bowl, 5⅜" berry w/handles	15.00	15.00		Pitcher, 24 oz.	27.50	
Bowl, 5½" cereal, no handles	25.00			Pitcher, 80 oz. tilted	35.00	50.00
Bowl, 7½" large berry	10.00	10.00		Plate, 6" sherbet or saucer	6.00	45.00
Bowl, 8", closed handles	18.00	20.00		Plate, 8½ salad	12.00	
Bowl, 9" salad	17.00	18.00		Plate, 10¼" dinner	16.00	85.00
Bowl, 9½" fruit open handle	30.00	28.00		Plate, 14" sandwich	16.00	
Candlesticks, 4½" (square) pr.	12.00			Salt & pepper, 2" pr. (square)	25.00	40.00
Candy dish, 3 legs		9.00		Saucer/sherbet plate	6.00	45.00
** Candy dish and cover	32.00			Sherbet	7.00	10.00
Coaster, 3½"	12.00			Sugar, oval	9.00	9.00
Comport, 5¾"	25.00	25.00	****	Tumbler, 10 oz. footed	15.00	15.00
Creamer, oval	9.00	9.00		Vase, 8"	15.00	
Cup	16.00	130.00	**	Wine, 3½"	5.00	

* Ad for Hocking $15.00; ad for others $12.50

** "Look-Alike"

*** Ruby-$3.50

**** Green or iridized-$10.00

Please refer to Foreword for pricing information

MAYFAIR FEDERAL GLASS COMPANY, 1934

Colors: Crystal, amber and green.

After several years of observation of Federal's Mayfair, I am willing to draw some conclusions about colors and pieces that can be found. It was a very limited production because of pattern name difficulties. Amber and crystal are the colors that can be collected (in the true pattern form), but not all pieces can found in amber. Green is found only in the transitional pieces of this pattern. Let me explain.

Hocking patented the name "Mayfair" first which caused Federal to redesign their glass moulds into what became the "Rosemary" pattern. The green pieces pictured in the bottom photograph represent a "transitional period" of glassware made between the old Federal "Mayfair" pattern and what was to become "Rosemary." Notice these transitional pieces have arching in the bottom of each piece rather than the waffle design, and there is no waffling between the top arches. If you turn to the Rosemary (158-159) for reference, you will see that the glass under the arches is perfectly plain. Most collectors consider the transitional pieces a part of Mayfair rather than Rosemary, the final design after working on Mayfair at least twice. I suspect that after examining the reworking of the moulds, someone decided that the changes made were not different enough and they were again redesigned.

Crystal Mayfair can be collected as a set. Green can only be purchased in transitional form and amber is found in both; however I have found no cream soup in amber or crystal Mayfair. That may mean that cream soups were only designed for the transitional pattern and never for Mayfair. Now that I am out on this limb, feel free to prove me wrong!

I still prefer the style lines of the Mayfair to that of Rosemary, but that is only my viewpoint. This is a challenging set to collect. Once you accumulate it, you will not be sorry. Mix the transitional with the regular pattern in amber. They go well together and only an experienced collector will notice the difference. Did you notice the tumblers in the top photograph? Both styles are shown there.

There are no sherbets. The Mayfair sugar, like Rosemary, looks like a large sherbet since it does not have handles. Both the Mayfair and the transitional pattern differences can be seen in the amber creamer and sugar.

You might try carrying a four leaf clover or a rabbit's foot when searching for this. You'll need all the extra help you can get. However, when you do get lucky enough to find the pattern, you often find several pieces together, rather than a piece here and there.

	Amber	Crystal	Green		Amber	Crystal	Green
Bowl, 5" sauce	7.50	6.00	10.00	Plate, 9½" dinner	12.00	8.00	12.00
Bowl, 5" cream soup	16.00	10.00	16.00	Plate, 9½" grill	12.00	8.00	12.00
Bowl, 6" cereal	17.00	9.00	19.00	Platter, 12" oval	22.00	16.00	25.00
Bowl, 10" oval vegetable	25.00	15.00	25.00	Saucer	3.00	2.00	3.00
Creamer, footed	12.00	10.00	15.00	Sugar, footed	12.00	10.00	15.00
Cup	7.50	4.50	7.50	Tumbler, 4½", 9 oz.	20.00	12.00	25.00
Plate, 6¾" salad	6.00	4.00	8.00				

Please refer to Foreword for pricing information

MAYFAIR, "OPEN ROSE" HOCKING GLASS COMPANY, 1931-1937

Colors: Ice blue, pink; some green, yellow and crystal. *(See Reproduction Section)*

"Mayfair can not be collected in green or yellow because those colors are too rare!" I have heard that expressed since I became interested in Depression glass in the 1970's. Here's proof it can be done. Yellow and green can be collected, but it takes both time and money to do so! Of course, that holds true for pink or blue also! Even a setting for four in these easily found colors with all the pieces is expensive! However, if you try not to buy everything made, you can put a small set together for about the same money as most other patterns.

Mayfair may be the most collected pattern of Depression glass. I spend more time answering questions and calls about pieces in Mayfair than for any other pattern. Reproductions and rare pieces are the major concerns. I have updated the *Reproduction Section* in the back to take care of the odd colors of cookie jars and shakers now being found.

Few rarities in Mayfair have surfaced for a while. There was a report of a blue sugar lid, but no photograph was ever made and few ever saw it. Supposedly, it was sold with a set of blue Mayfair priced by my book. Since the blue sugar lid was not priced, the seller just "threw it in" when the set was sold. Since all the other lids are priced so highly in my book that sounds unbelievable to me!

Pink Mayfair collectors have a dilemma when picking out the tumbler size and stems to collect. Most collectors buy flat waters, footed teas and water goblets to start. After they finish these, additional stems are added. Of course, if you run into a group of other reasonably priced stems while searching for something else, don't pass them by.

There are some minor details to point out. Some Mayfair stems have a plain foot while others are rayed. All stems and tumblers shown in yellow and green are rayed. Footed iced teas vary in height. Some teas have a short stem above the foot and others have practically none. This stem causes the heights to vary somewhat. It is just a mould variation, but may account for capacity differences. Note under measurements on page 4 the listings of tumblers that I have taken from old Hocking catalogues. In two catalogues from 1935 these were listed as 13 oz., but in 1936 both catalogues listed the tumbler as 15 oz. All I have ever measured have held 15 oz.

I used to have time to get out and find rare glass. After ten weeks of self imposed prison at my computer, believe me, I would prefer to be out this weekend among all the flea markets and shows! I wish you luck in finding rare and unusual glassware! It is generally found by those who really work at it!

Several pink sugar lids and another yellow one have been found. Finally, another yellow sugar turned up; but to my amazement, it was a different style of sugar and my sugar lid would not fit it! This sugar is shaped like the odd sized, footed Princess one that was found years ago. It is 3½" tall and measures 3⅝" by 3½" across the top. The normally found sugar bowl is 2⅝" tall and 4" x 4" across the top.

Crystal Mayfair occurs in only a few pieces. Most commonly found are the pitcher, shakers and the divided platter. A reader writes that the divided platter was given as a premium with the purchase of coffee or spices in late 1930's.

To see all the rare sized stemware in pink Mayfair, you will have to find a copy of the ninth edition of this book. The 10" celery measures 11¼" handle to handle and the 9" one measures 10¼" handle to handle.

	*Pink	Blue	Green	Yellow		*Pink	Blue	Green	Yellow
Bowl, 5" cream soup	38.00				Butter dish and cover or 7" covered vegetable	50.00	250.00	1,200.00	1,200.00
Bowl, 5½" cereal	19.00	40.00	65.00	65.00	Butter bottom with indent				265.00
Bowl, 7" vegetable	20.00	40.00	110.00	110.00	Butter dish top	30.00	185.00	1,000.00	1,000.00
Bowl, 9", 3⅛ high, 3 leg console	3,750.00		3,750.00		Cake plate, 10" footed	24.00	50.00	90.00	
Bowl, 9½" oval vegetable	22.00	50.00	100.00	105.00	Candy dish and cover	45.00	225.00	500.00	400.00
Bowl, 10" vegetable	20.00	50.00		105.00	Celery dish, 9" divided			125.00	125.00
Bowl, 10" same covered	85.00	95.00		450.00	Celery dish, 10"	30.00	40.00	95.00	95.00
Bowl, 11¾" low flat	45.00	55.00	30.00	175.00	Celery dish, 10" divided	165.00	45.00		
Bowl, 12" deep scalloped fruit	45.00	65.00	30.00	195.00					

*Frosted or satin finish items slightly lower

Please refer to Foreword for pricing information

MAYFAIR, "OPEN ROSE" (Cont.)

	*Pink	Blue	Green	Yellow
Cookie jar and lid	40.00	225.00	525.00	775.00
Creamer, footed	20.00	55.00	185.00	175.00
Cup	16.00	40.00	140.00	140.00
Cup, round	225.00			
Decanter and stopper, 32 oz.	125.00			
Goblet, 3¾", 1 oz. cordial	425.00		425.00	
Goblet, 4⅛", 2½ oz.	775.00		425.00	
Goblet, 4", 3 oz. cocktail	65.00		335.00	
Goblet, 4½", 3 oz. wine	65.00		375.00	
Goblet, 5¼", 4½ oz. claret	625.00		525.00	
Goblet, 5¾, 9 oz. water	50.00		375.00	
Goblet, 7¼:, 9 oz. thin	130.00	135.00		
** Pitcher, 6", 37 oz.	45.00	115.00	475.00	425.00
Pitcher, 8", 60 oz.	45.00	130.00	425.00	375.00
Pitcher, 8½", 80 oz.	85.00	150.00	475.00	475.00
Plate, 5¾" (often substituted as saucer)	11.00	18.00	75.00	75.00
Plate, 6½" round sherbet	11.00			
Plate, 6½" round, off-center indent	20.00	20.00	100.00	
Plate, 8½" luncheon	20.00	35.00	65.00	65.00
Plate, 9½" dinner	40.00	55.00	115.00	115.00
Plate, 9½" grill	35.00	35.00	65.00	65.00
Plate, 11½" handled grill				80.00
Plate, 12" cake w/handles	32.00	46.00	30.00	
*** Platter, 12" oval, open handles	20.00	45.00	125.00	125.00
Platter, 12½" oval, 8" wide, closed handles			195.00	195.00
Relish, 8⅜", 4-part	24.00	45.00	125.00	125.00
Relish, 8⅜" non-partitioned	130.00		225.00	225.00
**** Salt and pepper, flat pr.	50.00	225.00	1,000.00	750.00
Salt and pepper, footed	5,000.00			
Sandwich server, center handle	35.00	50.00	30.00	105.00
Saucer (cup ring)	25.00			130.00
Saucer (see 5¾"plate)				
Sherbet, 2¼" flat	140.00	75.00		
Sherbet, 3" footed	14.00			
Sherbet, 4¾" footed	65.00	60.00	140.00	140.00
Sugar, footed	22.00	65.00	175.00	175.00
Sugar lid	1,350.00		1,000.00	1,000.00
Tumbler, 3½", 5 oz. juice	35.00	95.00		
Tumbler, 4¼", 9 oz. water	24.00	75.00		
Tumbler, 4¾", 11 oz. water	120.00	95.00	165.00	165.00
Tumbler, 5¼", 13½ oz. iced tea	40.00	130.00		
Tumbler, 3¼", 3 oz. footed juice	65.00			
Tumbler, 5¼", 10 oz. footed	30.00	100.00		170.00
Tumbler, 6½", 15 oz. ftd. iced tea	30.00	120.00	200.00	
Vase (sweet pea)	120.00	85.00	200.00	
Whiskey, 2¼", 1½ oz.	60.00			

* Frosted or satin finish items slightly lower
** Crystal-$15.00
*** Divided Crystal-$12.50
**** Crystal-$17.50 pr. – Beware reproductions.

Please refer to Foreword for pricing information

MISS AMERICA (DIAMOND PATTERN) HOCKING GLASS COMPANY, 1935-1938

Colors: Crystal, pink; some green, ice blue, Jad-ite and Royal Ruby. *(See Reproduction Section)*

Miss America has awakened from its doldrums! Collectors have pushed the price for pink butter dishes way past pre-reproduction prices. Crystal butter sales are even beginning to rise as are the prices of all other crystal pieces. Pink is still the desired color to collect, however.

One of the toughest reproduction problems has been the shakers. Read about these in the Reproduction Section in the back. Suffice to say, there are few green shakers available that are old. In fact, I haven't seen an older pair since the early 1970's. Pink shakers are giving me a HEADACHE! Rarely, have I had as many questions about Miss America shakers as in the last few years because there have been reproductions of the reproductions and even those have now been copied by another importer. There are at least four generations of reproduction shakers; so it depends upon which one you find as to what to look for on them. Interesting enough, there originally were two different moulds used for old shakers. The shakers that stay fat toward the base are the best ones to buy, since they have not been reproduced. The shakers which get thin (as shown in the photographs) are the style that has been reproduced. Both styles were made originally, but only the thin style has been copied. Buy shakers from a reputable dealer.

Any time a pattern was made for several years, it will be possible to find pieces that vary in design. There was more than one mould made for each piece; so items can vary as often as each mould was changed.

The footed juice goblet remains hard to find; but the footed wine is also disappearing from dealer's inventories. Supplies of pink water goblets have always been more than adequate for the demand. A pink divided relish was sold at the Peach State Depression Show last year! Few of these have surfaced in recent years.

The blue shown in the top picture is quite rare. Notice that the blue sherbet is shaped somewhat differently than that which is normally found. There is a pink sherbet that flairs out slightly at the top rim. Some collectors have confused this with English Hobnail, but it is Miss America from a different mould. Be sure to read the section under English Hobnail about the differences in these two patterns.

Royal Ruby pieces of Miss America are found occasionally. These had to be made near the end of Miss America's production and at the beginning of Royal Ruby in 1938. All known pieces are priced below. A red butter has never been found, but some reproduction red butters were made.

There are a few odd-colored or flashed pieces of Miss America that are occasionally found. Flashed-on red, green or amethyst make interesting conversation pieces, but are not plentiful enough to collect a set. A Jad-ite 8" bowl has now been found to go with the plate shown in an earlier book!

	Crystal	Pink	Green	Royal Ruby			Crystal	Pink	Green	Royal Ruby
Bowl, 4½" berry			10.00			Goblet, 5½", 10 oz.				
* Bowl, 6¼" cereal	8.00	16.00	15.00			water	20.00	38.00		175.00
Bowl, 8" curved in at						Pitcher, 8", 65 oz.	45.00	100.00		
top	35.00	60.00		375.00		Pitcher, 8½", 65 oz.				
Bowl, 8¾" straight						w/ice lip	62.00	115.00		
deep fruit	30.00	50.00			***	Plate, 5¾" sherbet	4.00	7.00	6.00	20.00
Bowl, 10" oval						Plate, 6¾"		7.00		
vegetable	12.00	22.00				Plate, 8½" salad	6.00	19.00	9.00	75.00
Bowl, 11", shallow				650.00	****	Plate, 10¼" dinner	12.00	20.00		
** Butter dish and						Plate, 10¼" grill	9.00	19.00		
cover	200.00	500.00				Platter, 12¼" oval	13.00	21.00		
Butter dish bottom	8.00	16.00				Relish, 8¾", 4 part	9.00	19.00		
Butter dish top	192.00	484.00				Relish, 11¾" round				
Cake plate, 12"						divided	20.00	500.00		
footed	22.50	35.00				Salt and pepper, pr.	28.00	50.00	285.00	
Candy jar and						Saucer	3.00	5.00		
cover, 11½"	50.00	110.00			***	Sherbet	7.00	13.00		50.00
Celery dish, 10½"						Sugar	7.00	15.00		150.00
oblong	10.00	20.00			****	Tumbler, 4", 5 oz.				
Coaster, 5¾"	13.00	24.00				juice	15.00	40.00		
Comport, 5"	12.00	20.00				Tumbler, 4½",				
Creamer, footed	7.50	15.00		155.00		10 oz. water	13.00	25.00	16.00	
Cup	8.50	19.00	10.00			Tumbler, 5¾", 14 oz.				
Goblet, 3¾", 3 oz.						iced tea	24.00	65.00		
wine	18.00	60.00		195.00						
Goblet, 4¾", 5 oz.										
juice	23.00	75.00		195.00						

*Also has appeared in Cobalt Blue $125.00   **Absolute mint price   ***Also in Ice Blue $35.00   ****Also in Ice Blue $80.00

Please refer to Foreword for pricing information

MODERNTONE HAZEL ATLAS GLASS COMPANY, 1934-1942; Late 1940's-Early 1950's

Colors: Amethyst, cobalt blue; some crystal, pink and platonite fired-on colors.

Because it fits a later time period, Platonite Moderntone has been moved into my book *Collectible Glassware from the 40's, 50's, 60's...*; but rest assured the cobalt and amethyst Moderntone will remain in this book.

Cobalt blue is a popular color. Anything cobalt sells; so this makes Moderntone doubly desirable. Many folks put cobalt colored glassware in their windows. In Florida, the sun really makes it show up!

I was asked by several collectors about the crystal "shot glasses" in the metal holder. These came in a boxed set with a Colonial Block creamer. The box was marked "Little Deb" Lemonade Server Set. I paid $20.00 for it. You can see the set in the bottom photograph. It's a shame the shot glasses and pitcher were not cobalt! That pitcher has turned up in cobalt and several have turned up with Shirley Temple's picture! There is one of these in a collection in Florida and one was displayed at the Chicago Show this Spring. I sold one years ago to a lady who wrote a book on Shirley Temple for $75.00. Now, my Mom collects Shirley Temple items and is searching for one. If you have one, let me know.

Iced tea and juice tumblers are still the tumblers to find in both cobalt and amethyst. Where have all the ruffled cream soups and sandwich plates gone? The sandwich plates can be found, but many are heavily scratched causing collectors to avoid them. The cheese dish lid has been moved to the side to show the wooden cheese plate which fits inside the metal lid. There have been some big prices paid for these recently. This cheese dish is a salad plate with a metal cover and cutting board.

Both green and pink ash trays are found occasionally, but there is little demand for them now. Blue ash trays still command a hefty price for an ash tray. Most ash trays and smoking accessories have stopped selling. Do you suppose in the year 2030, people will be searching for "rare" smoking items?

Bowls without inner rim roughness are a problem for collectors. Prices below are for mint condition pieces. That is why bowls are so highly priced. Mint condition bowls are rare; but used, nicked, battered bowls are not!

There is no true sugar or butter lid. At least there are no records of such. Evidently the butter bottom and sugar were sold to someone else who made the tops. Who knows for sure whether the lids are supposed to have black, red or blue knobs? I certainly do not! I have had reports of all those colored knobs. Red seems to be the predominate color found.

	Cobalt	Amethyst
* Ash tray, 7¾", match holder in center	115.00	
Bowl, 4¾" cream soup	17.00	15.00
Bowl, 5" berry	18.00	18.00
Bowl, 5" cream soup, ruffled	30.00	18.00
Bowl, 6½" cereal	60.00	65.00
Bowl, 7½" soup	80.00	80.00
Bowl, 8¾" large berry	40.00	30.00
Butter dish with metal cover	85.00	
Cheese dish, 7" with metal lid	400.00	
Creamer	9.00	8.00
Cup	9.00	9.00
Cup (handle-less) or custard	13.00	12.00
Plate, 5⅞" sherbet	6.00	4.00
Plate, 6¾" salad	9.00	8.00
Plate, 7¾" luncheon	9.50	8.00
Plate, 8⅞" dinner	14.00	10.00
Plate, 10½" sandwich	40.00	30.00
Platter, 11" oval	30.00	25.00
Platter, 12" oval	50.00	35.00
Salt and pepper, pr.	35.00	32.00
Saucer	4.00	3.00
Sherbet	11.00	11.00
Sugar	9.00	8.00
Sugar lid in metal	30.00	
Tumbler, 5 oz.	30.00	22.00
Tumbler, 9 oz.	25.00	22.00
Tumbler, 12 oz.	80.00	70.00
** Whiskey, 1½ oz.	22.00	

* Pink $50.00; green $75.00
** Pink or green $12.50

Please refer to Foreword for pricing information

MOONDROPS NEW MARTINSVILLE GLASS COMPANY, 1932-1940

Colors: Amber, pink, green, cobalt, ice blue, red, amethyst, crystal, dark green, light green, jadite, smoke and black.

Red and cobalt blue Moondrops continue to be the only colors rapaciously collected in this pattern! There are collectors of the other colors; but those colors sit on the shelf for long periods of time. In this pattern there are a wide range of unusual pieces from which to choose, i.e. perfume bottles, powder boxes, gravy boats and even a bud vase! The butter has to have a glass top to fetch the price listed below. The metal top with a bird finial found on butter bottoms is better than none; that top only sells for about $25.00 on a good day. However, the metal top with the fan finial brings about $55.00!

	Blue, Red	Other Colors		Blue, Red	Other Colors
Ash tray	30.00	16.00	Goblet, 5⅛", 3 oz. metal stem wine	15.00	10.00
Bowl, 5¼" berry	11.00	6.00	Goblet, 5½", 4 oz. metal stem wine	18.00	10.00
Bowl, 6¾" soup	70.00		Goblet, 6¼", 9 oz. metal stem water	22.00	15.00
Bowl, 7½" pickle	20.00	12.00	Gravy boat	115.00	85.00
Bowl, 8⅜" footed, concave top	30.00	20.00	Mayonnaise, 5¼"	50.00	30.00
Bowl, 8½" 3-footed divided relish	26.00	17.00	Mug, 5⅛", 12 oz.	35.00	22.00
Bowl, 9½" 3-legged ruffled	40.00		Perfume bottle, "rocket"	195.00	145.00
Bowl, 9¾" oval vegetable	30.00	22.00	Pitcher, 6⅞", 22 oz. small	150.00	85.00
Bowl, 9¾" covered casserole	135.00	95.00	Pitcher, 8⅛", 32 oz. medium	175.00	110.00
Bowl, 9¾" handled oval	50.00	35.00	Pitcher, 8", 50 oz. large, with lip	185.00	110.00
Bowl, 11" boat-shaped celery	30.00	22.00	Pitcher, 8⅛", 53 oz. large, no lip	180.00	120.00
Bowl, 12" round 3-footed console	80.00	30.00	Plate, 5⅞"	9.00	7.00
Bowl, 13" console with "wings"	110.00	40.00	Plate, 6⅛" sherbet	6.00	4.00
Butter dish and cover	425.00	250.00	Plate, 6" round, off-center sherbet indent	11.00	8.00
Butter dish bottom	60.00	45.00	Plate, 7⅛" salad	12.00	9.00
Butter dish top	365.00	205.00	Plate, 8½" luncheon	14.00	11.00
Candles, 2" ruffled pr.	35.00	19.00	Plate, 9½" dinner	22.00	15.00
Candles, 4½" sherbet style pr.	25.00	18.00	Plate, 14" round sandwich	35.00	16.00
Candlesticks, 5" ruffled, pr.	32.50	19.00	Plate, 14" 2-handled sandwich	40.00	22.00
Candlesticks, 5" "wings" pr.	85.00	45.00	Platter, 12" oval	30.00	20.00
Candlesticks, 5¼" triple light pr.	90.00	48.00	Powder jar, 3 footed	135.00	95.00
Candlesticks 8½" metal stem pr.	37.50	27.50	Saucer	5.00	4.50
Candy Dish, 8" ruffled	35.00	18.00	Sherbet, 2⅝"	15.00	10.00
Cocktail shaker with or without hdl.,			Sherbet, 4½"	25.00	15.00
metal top	55.00	30.00	Sugar, 2¾"	14.00	9.00
Comport, 4"	20.00	15.00	Sugar, 4"	15.00	10.00
Comport, 11½"	55.00	30.00	Tumbler, 2¾", 2 oz. shot	15.00	9.00
Creamer, 2¾" miniature	17.50	10.00	Tumbler, 2¾", 2 oz. handled shot	15.00	10.00
Creamer, 3¾" regular	15.00	9.00	Tumbler, 3¼", 3 oz. footed juice	15.00	10.00
Cup	15.00	9.00	Tumbler, 3⅝", 5 oz.	14.00	9.00
Decanter, 7¾" small	60.00	35.00	Tumbler, 4⅜", 7 oz.	15.00	9.00
Decanter, 8½" medium	65.00	35.00	Tumbler, 4⅜", 8 oz.	15.00	10.00
Decanter, 11¼" large	85.00	45.00	Tumbler, 4⅞", 9 oz. handled	27.50	15.00
Decanter, 10¼" "rocket"	350.00	200.00	Tumbler, 4⅞", 9 oz.	18.00	14.00
Goblet, 2⅞, ¾ oz. cordial	35.00	25.00	Tumbler, 5⅛", 12 oz.	25.00	13.00
Goblet, 4", 4 oz. wine	20.00	12.00	Tray, 7½", for mini sugar/creamer	35.00	18.00
Goblet, 4¾", "rocket" wine	50.00	28.00	Vase, 7¾" flat, ruffled top	55.00	55.00
Goblet, 4¾", 5 oz.	22.50	14.00	Vase, 8½" "rocket" bud	225.00	150.00
Goblet, 5¾" 8 oz.	30.00	18.00	Vase, 9¼" "rocket" style	200.00	115.00

MT. PLEASANT, "DOUBLE SHIELD" L.E. SMITH GLASS COMPANY, 1920's-1934

Colors: Black amethyst, amethyst, cobalt blue, crystal, pink, green.

The new additions to the book are a 10½" footed cake plate that stands 1¼" high and an 11¼" leaf plate. Several readers sent information on the larger leaf and I appreciate your help with the measurements!

Mt. Pleasant seems to have caught the fancy of a new collecting fraternity. Many budding collectors are drawn to this because of the cobalt blue or black color. The demand for cobalt blue is strongly evidenced at shows as dealers have trouble keeping enough Mt. Pleasant. Black is more often found, but there are more collectors for the blue. Some pieces are found in pink or green, but I have had no reports of sets being found in those colors.

More is being found in Kansas, Nebraska and western New York than any place. Mt. Pleasant was promoted heavily at hardware stores in those areas. Blue is the color mentioned in letters from those areas. Many pieces are found with a platinum (silver) band around them. This band wore off with use; thus pieces are found with only partial evidence of this decoration. (I just purchased some blue sherbets with only two having the platinum decorations intact.) The trim doesn't enhance the price.

	Pink, Green	Black Amethyst, Cobalt		Pink, Green	Black Amethyst, Cobalt
Bonbon, rolled-up handled, 7"	15.00	22.00	Leaf, 11¼"		25.00
Bowl, 4" opening, rose	17.50	25.00	Mayonnaise, 5½", 3-footed	15.00	25.00
Bowl, 4", square footed fruit	12.00	17.50	Mint, 6", center handle	15.00	20.00
Bowl, 6", 2-handled, square	12.00	15.00	Plate, 7", 2-handled, scalloped	8.50	14.00
Bowl, 7", 3 footed, rolled out edge	15.00	20.00	Plate, 8", scalloped or square	9.50	14.00
Bowl, 8", scalloped, 2-handled	17.50	25.00	Plate, 8", 2-handled	10.00	16.00
Bowl, 8", square, 2-handled	17.50	27.50	Plate 8¼, square w/Indent for cup		15.00
Bowl, 9", scalloped, 1¾" deep, footed		25.00	Plate, 9" grill		10.00
Bowl, 9¼", square footed fruit	17.50	27.50	Plate, 10½", cake, 2-handled	15.00	25.00
Bowl, 10", scalloped fruit		35.00	Plate, 10½", 1¼" high, cake		35.00
Bowl, 10", 2-handled, turned-up edge		27.00	Plate, 12", 2-handled	18.00	30.00
Cake plate, 10½", footed, 1¼" high		35.00	Salt and pepper, 2 styles	22.00	37.50
Candlestick, single, pr.	17.50	25.00	Sandwich server, center-handled		35.00
Candlestick, double, pr.	25.00	40.00	Saucer	2.00	4.00
Creamer	17.50	17.00	Sherbet	9.00	15.00
Cup (waffle-like crystal)	4.00		Sugar	17.00	17.00
Cup	8.50	10.00	Tumbler, ftd.		18.00
Leaf, 8"		15.00	Vase, 7¼"		27.50

NEW CENTURY, and incorrectly, "LYDIA RAY" HAZEL ATLAS GLASS COMPANY, 1930-1935

Colors: Green; some crystal, pink, amethyst and cobalt.

New Century collectors seek green more than any other color; in fact, sets can only be gathered in crystal and green. So far, pink, cobalt blue and amethyst have only been found in water sets and an occasional cup or saucer.

Years ago, I ran into several crystal powder jars. They were made with a sugar lid on the top of a sherbet. The knob of the sherbet had glass marbles or beads attached by a wire. I had not seen these again until recently when I saw two separate ones in Florida. There are seven different tumblers if you count the whiskey, but only two are found regularly, 9 and 10 ounce. The casserole bottom is harder to find than the top.

It has been a while since I have seen cream soups, wines or a decanter.

New Century is the *official* name for this pattern made by Hazel Atlas. "Lydia Ray" was the name used by collectors until an *official* name was found. I mention this for new collectors since the name "New Century" was also used (incorrectly) by another author to identify the *Ovide*. This has caused confusion in the past; so I want you to be aware of this minor problem.

	Green, Crystal	Pink Cobalt Amethyst		Green, Crystal	Pink Cobalt Amethyst
Ash tray/coaster, 5⅜"	27.50		Plate, 8½" salad	8.00	
Bowl, 4½" berry	11.00		Plate, 10" dinner	14.00	
Bowl, 4¾" cream soup	15.00		Plate, 10" grill	9.00	
Bowl, 8" large berry	15.00		Platter, 11" oval	13.00	
Bowl, 9" covered casserole	50.00		Salt and pepper, pr.	32.50	
Butter dish and cover	52.50		Saucer	2.50	6.00
Cup	6.00	18.00	Sherbet, 3"	8.00	
Creamer	7.00		Sugar	6.00	
Decanter and stopper	45.00		Sugar cover	12.00	
Goblet, 2½ oz. wine	22.00		Tumbler, 3½", 5 oz.	10.00	11.00
Goblet, 3¼ oz. cocktail	20.00		Tumbler, 4¼", 9 oz.	13.00	12.00
Pitcher, 7¾", 60 oz. with or			Tumbler, 5", 10 oz.	13.00	14.00
without ice lip	32.50	30.00	Tumbler, 5¼", 12 oz.	20.00	20.00
Pitcher, 8", 80 oz. with or			Tumbler, 4", 5 oz. footed	15.00	
without ice lip	35.00	38.00	Tumbler, 4⅞", 9 oz. footed	18.00	
Plate, 6" sherbet	3.00		Whiskey, 2½", 1½ oz.	13.00	
Plate, 7⅛" breakfast	7.00				

NEWPORT, "HAIRPIN" HAZEL ATLAS GLASS COMPANY, 1936-1940

Colors: Cobalt blue, amethyst; some pink, "Platonite" white and fired-on colors.

Platonite Newport can now be found in my book *Collectible Glassware from the 40's, 50's, 60's....*

There are a few size corrections below. The berry bowl measures 4¾" instead of 4¼". The plates listed at 6" and 8½" are actually 5⅞" and 8⅞". One of the problems with catalogue measurements is that they are not always accurate. Maybe workers used a ruler like I did recently. I grabbed one of my Dad's rulers to measure for a glass shelf to fit a cabinet. When time came to put the shelf in it would not fit. I was told (in very impolite terms) that ex-mathematics teachers should be able to read a ruler! I got the ruler I had used and measured again and got the same measurements as before. That is when my Dad pointed out that the ruler started at the one, not zero, since one inch had broken off the end of that ruler. It is difficult to get exact measurements with an inch missing!

Pink Newport sets were given away as premiums for buying seeds from a catalogue in the 1930's. A few of these sets are entering the market but are not selling very well. It is the cobalt blue and amethyst that draw collectors' attention. Cereal bowls and tumblers can not be found in any quantity. Many collectors are searching for both items without success. Amethyst is rarer than cobalt blue, but there are fewer collectors for amethyst.

My large berry bowls in both colors got "crunched" before our photography session. It is bad enough to lose pieces of glass, but losing them before they are pictured upsets me even more. Worse, they were so "crunched" (hundreds and hundreds of pieces) that they could not be salvaged with glue for future use.

	Cobalt	Amethyst		Cobalt	Amethyst
Bowl, 4¾" berry	13.00	11.00	Plate, 11½" sandwich	30.00	28.00
Bowl, 4¾" cream soup	15.00	14.00	Platter, 11¾" oval	35.00	28.00
Bowl, 5¼" cereal	28.00	22.00	Salt and pepper	42.50	37.50
Bowl, 8¼" large berry	35.00	28.00	Saucer	4.00	4.00
Cup	9.00	8.50	Sherbet	12.00	11.00
Creamer	13.00	11.00	Sugar	13.00	12.00
Plate, 5⅞" sherbet	5.00	4.00	Tumbler, 4½", 9 oz.	30.00	28.00
Plate, 8⅞" luncheon	10.00	10.00			

"NORA BIRD," PADEN CITY GLASS COMPANY, LINE 300, 1929-1930's

Colors: Pink, green, crystal.

"Nora Bird" is a name given to this Paden City pattern by collectors. It was a numbered etching on the popular #300 line blank. This blank is found in several additional colors; yet pink, green and crystal are the only colors on which this "Nora Bird" etching has been found.

A footed candy dish is the latest "Nora Bird" piece to be found! I am assuming that it measures 5¼" as does my Cupid candy. The reader did not send measurements with the picture. That makes two candies for you to search out in your travels. Some of these candy dishes may be in the hands of candy dish collectors and not "Nora Bird" collectors.

Note the two different styles of sugars in the picture. I have not been able to find a green creamer or the taller pink creamer. At least I did find a green cup and saucer since last time!

There may be more pieces in this pattern than I have listed; so let me know if you find something else. The bird on each piece can be found in flight or getting ready to fly. Some collectors have suggested this is a pheasant which is probably true since several pheasant patterns were present during this time frame.

	Pink, Green		Pink, Green
Candlestick, pr.	65.00	Plate, 8"	20.00
Candy dish w/cover, 6½", 3 part	85.00	Saucer	12.50
Candy with lid, footed, 5¼" high	65.00	Sugar, 4½", round handle	37.50
Creamer, 4½", round handle	40.00	Sugar, 5", pointed handle	37.50
Creamer, 5", pointed handle	40.00	Tumbler, 3"	35.00
Cup	47.00	Tumbler, 4"	45.00
Ice tub, 6"	95.00	Tumbler, 4¾", footed	50.00
Mayonnaise and liner	75.00		

Please refer to Foreword for pricing information

NORMANDIE, "BOUQUET AND LATTICE" FEDERAL GLASS COMPANY 1933-1940

Colors: Iridescent, amber, pink, crystal.

Iridescent Normandie is actually beginning to sell! For years this has been a color that no one wanted at any price. I even put some in my booth at an Antique Mall for half my book price and no one bought it. Recently, however, a rumor circulated that it was getting hard to find and suddenly there were numerous collectors buying this iridescent color of Normandie. There are enough buyers to raise all the prices a little; and the prices of the larger serving pieces have raised even more. Iridescent is still reasonably priced in comparison to the pink and amber. There has never been enough crystal found to be collectible. Any time a pattern was made in iridescent, crystal pieces are found. Crystal was made to be sprayed with the iridized color that was then heated to keep the color. Some crystal pieces ended up never being sprayed!

Dinner plates, tumblers, shakers and the sugar lid in pink are all rarely found at any price. All the same pieces are also hard to find in amber, but not quite as difficult as the pink. There are fewer collectors buying amber, but amber is available with searching; and the amber will not break your bank account when you do find it.

Amber colored Depression glassware seems to be the least desirable color in all patterns – not just Normandie. If some Women's magazine, such as *Country Living*, would feature it on the cover as a fashion statement, then we would have a run on amber like has never been seen before. Have you noticed the price of cobalt blue "Ships" glasses recently? They were shown on the cover a couple of years ago and prices almost doubled overnight.

One lady told me that pink had been easy on her purse. Of course, she had only found cups, saucers and sherbets in two years of looking! Yes, someone who enjoys buying only a few pieces is still a collector!

The console bowl and candlesticks sometimes found with the iridized Normandie are Madrid. These were sold about the same time. Several collectors have reported finding this console set with Normandie sets. That does not make it Normandie; it is still Madrid!

	Amber	Pink	Iridescent
Bowl, 5" berry	5.00	6.00	4.50
* Bowl, 6½" cereal	12.00	17.00	8.00
Bowl, 8½" large berry	14.00	19.00	11.00
Bowl, 10" oval veg.	14.00	28.00	14.00
Creamer, footed	7.00	9.50	7.00
Cup	6.50	7.50	5.50
Pitcher, 8", 80 oz.	65.00	100.00	
Plate, 6" sherbet	3.00	3.00	2.50
Plate, 7¾" salad	8.00	10.00	50.00
Plate, 9¼ luncheon	7.00	12.00	8.00
Plate, 11" dinner	25.00	90.00	14.00
Plate, 11" grill	13.00	16.00	8.50
Platter, 11¾"	15.00	20.00	11.00
Salt and pepper, pr.	42.50	65.00	
Saucer	2.50	3.00	2.00
Sherbet	6.00	8.00	6.50
Sugar	7.00	8.50	5.50
Sugar lid	80.00	125.00	
Tumbler, 4", 5 oz. juice	18.00	40.00	
Tumbler, 4¼", 9 oz. water	14.00	35.00	
Tumbler, 5", 12 oz. iced tea	22.00	60.00	

*Mistaken by many as butter bottom.

No. 610, "PYRAMID" INDIANA GLASS COMPANY, 1926-1932

Colors: Green, pink, yellow, white, crystal, blue or black in 1974-1975 by Tiara.

"Pyramid" is a collectors' name for this pattern. The official name of the pattern is No. 610. Indiana gave most patterns a number and not a name. Collectors do not seem to be fond of calling patterns by numbers however; so most of Indiana's patterns are known to collectors by an unofficial name.

This art deco style pattern has gotten very popular and prices have risen dramatically the last few years.

Crystal pitchers and tumblers are harder to find than the other colors, although there are fewer collectors searching for them. Prices on crystal pitchers are higher than all but the yellow. The yellow pitchers are found frequently; but there are so many collectors of yellow No. 610 that the price continues an upward trend! Ice buckets are readily found, even in yellow. It is the yellow lid that is nearly impossible to find! When you have both pieces, you have a rare find!

Oval bowls and pickle dishes are both 9½". The oval bowl has pointed edges as can be seen in bowls of white, green and yellow. The pickle dish is shown only in pink. The edges of that pickle dish are rounded instead of pointed.

Be careful in buying "Pyramid" because the points on the outsides of the pieces have a tendency to chip.

Blue or black pieces of "Pyramid" were made by Indiana during the 1970's for Tiara. Normally, you see two sizes of black tumblers or the 4-part center handled relish in either color. Berry bowls were also made. These colors are recent and not Depression glass! That handled 4-part relish is sometimes mistaken for Tea Room.

	Crystal	Pink	Green	Yellow
Bowl, 4¾" berry	10.00	16.00	18.00	30.00
Bowl, 8½" master berry	14.00	24.00	25.00	50.00
Bowl, 9½" oval	26.00	27.00	25.00	48.00
Bowl, 9½" pickle, 5¾" wide	18.00	28.00	25.00	50.00
Creamer	15.00	22.00	22.00	30.00
Ice tub	50.00	70.00	80.00	125.00
Ice tub lid				500.00
Pitcher	305.00	210.00	195.00	425.00
Relish tray, 4-part handled	20.00	35.00	40.00	55.00
Sugar	15.00	22.00	22.00	30.00
Tray for creamer and sugar	13.00	20.00	23.00	45.00
Tumbler, 8 oz. footed	32.00	27.00	30.00	47.50
Tumbler, 11 oz. footed	55.00	40.00	50.00	65.00

Please refer to Foreword for pricing information

No. 612, "HORSESHOE" INDIANA GLASS COMPANY, 1930-1933

Colors: Green, yellow, pink, crystal.

The official name for this Indiana pattern is No. 612, but collectors dubbed it "Horseshoe." Butter dishes have started an upward price trend again. This butter dish has always been highly priced. If you can find a first edition of my book, the butter dish was $90.00 back in 1972. As an example of how other prices stacked up against the butter dish, look at the grill plate that was only $2.25. Would you rather have one butter dish today bought for $90.00 or forty grill plates bought for $90.00. I doubt if you could have found forty grill plates back then. In fact, I doubt that you could buy forty grill plates this year!

That first edition was $9.95 and it sells in the $200 range today! I should have stocked away my old books!

Actually, new collectors have shied away from "Horseshoe" for years since it has so many highly priced pieces. Prices are finally beginning to rise for the first time in several years.

Be aware that many plates and platters are plain in the center, while others have a pattern.

Candy dishes only have the pattern on the top. The bottom is plain. No yellow butter dish, grill plate, candy dish or flat tumblers have ever been found! If you find the first of these, let me know.

Only creamers and sugars have been found in crystal. These sell in the $15.00 range, but they are quite rare!

Catalogues list a 10⅜" dinner plate, but there are doubts about its existence. Does anyone own one? The only 10⅜" plate I have seen is the grill.

	Green	Yellow		Green	Yellow
Bowl, 4½" berry	19.00	18.00	Plate, 6" sherbet	4.00	5.00
Bowl, 6½" cereal	19.00	19.00	Plate, 8⅜" salad	8.00	9.00
Bowl, 7½" salad	17.50	19.00	Plate, 9⅜" luncheon	11.00	12.00
Bowl, 8½" vegetable	19.00	25.00	Plate, 10⅜" grill	52.50	
Bowl, 9½" large berry	27.50	30.00	Plate, 11½" sandwich	13.00	15.00
Bowl, 10½" oval vegetable	18.00	22.00	Platter, 10¾" oval	18.00	19.00
Butter dish and cover	575.00		Relish, 3 part footed	18.00	35.00
Butter dish bottom	150.00		Saucer	4.00	4.50
Butter dish top	425.00		Sherbet	13.00	14.00
Candy in metal holder motif			Sugar, open	12.50	13.00
on lid	97.50		Tumbler, 4¼", 9 oz.	100.00	
also, pink	145.00		Tumbler, 4¾", 12 oz.	135.00	
Creamer, footed	13.00	14.00	Tumbler, 9 oz. footed	18.00	17.00
Cup	9.00	10.00	Tumbler, 12 oz. footed	100.00	115.00
Pitcher, 8½", 64 oz.	220.00	250.00			

No. 616, "VERNON" INDIANA GLASS COMPANY, 1930-1932

Colors: Green, crystal, yellow.

Another of Indiana's numbered lines, No. 616 is not easily found. We used this in crystal as "every day" dishes for a while when I first started buying Depression glass. After a few months, Cathy decided that she had had enough of the sharp protruding mould lines on the tumblers. Those rough lines are hard on the lips when you try to drink from them! Many of the crystal pieces are found trimmed in platinum (silver). Sandwich plates make great dinner plates. By the way, those are 11½" and not 11" as has previously been listed.

Showing the pattern is the biggest problem in photographing No. 616. The pattern is very delicate and light passes through without picking up the design well.

I still have never found my box of glass that had every piece and color of No. 616. All these years, I thought it would turn up; but it must have been a casualty of that fire in the Paducah photography studio several years ago. The studio had a fire and most of our glass got soaked during the procedure of putting it out. Apparently some of the glass got more than soaked! The glass was in wax coated (chicken) boxes but the pads that the glass was packed in mildewed before we returned to finish the session. Talk about a mess! I keep saying you wouldn't *believe* what we go through to get you these books!

Yellow and green colors are both difficult to accumulate in sets, but there is even less green than yellow available. Green tumblers are especially hard to locate. Note its conspicuous absence in the photograph!

	Green	Crystal	Yellow		Green	Crystal	Yellow
Creamer, footed	22.00	11.00	20.00	Saucer	5.00	3.00	5.00
Cup	14.00	7.00	14.00	Sugar, footed	21.50	10.00	21.00
Plate, 8" luncheon	8.00	5.00	8.00	Tumbler, 5" footed	30.00	13.00	30.00
Plate, 11½" sandwich	24.00	11.00	24.00				

Please refer to Foreword for pricing information

No. 618, "PINEAPPLE & FLORAL" INDIANA GLASS COMPANY, 1932-1937

Colors: Crystal, amber; some fired-on red, green; late 1960's, avocado; 1980's pink, cobalt blue, etc.

The same fired-on red pitcher that has been found with sets of "Pineapple and Floral" has also been found with a set of fired-on Daisy. The pitcher is of poor quality as is most of the red in this color. There is a cross hatching design on the base similar to that of No.618, but (besides the poor quality and color) there is where the similarity to Pineapple and Floral ends.

Indiana has re-made the diamond shaped comport and 7" salad bowl in all kinds of colors. Many of these have sprayed-on colors although the light pink is a nice transparent glass. The price of these older crystal pieces has dropped because of these remakes. Amber and fired-on red are safe colors to collect to avoid reproductions.

The crystal makes a nice set to collect. It is not easily put together, but it is not impossible either. You will find tumblers, cream soups and sherbets the most challenging to find.

Amber No.618 is not collected as much as the crystal, but there is much less of it available. If collectors started buying the amber all at once, it would be a sight to see the prices jump!

Remember that the mould seams on all of this pattern are rough which is a typical trademark of Indiana's glassware in that time. This is true on all size tumblers! I recently found sixteen water tumblers for $56.00 less a dealer discount! Bargains do exist!

	Amber, Crystal	Red		Amber, Crystal	Red
Ash tray, 4½"	16.00	18.00	Plate, 11½" w/indentation	22.50	
Bowl, 4¾" berry	22.00	15.00	Plate, 11½" sandwich	14.00	15.00
Bowl, 6" cereal	22.00	18.00	Platter, 11" closed handles	14.00	17.00
* Bowl, 7" salad	1.00	9.00	Platter, relish, 11½" divided	18.00	
Bowl, 10" oval vegetable	22.00	18.00	Saucer	4.00	4.00
* Comport, diamond-shaped	1.00	7.00	Sherbet, footed	17.50	17.50
Creamer, diamond-shaped	7.00	9.00	Sugar, diamond-shaped	7.00	9.00
Cream soup	18.50	18.00	Tumbler, 4¼", 8 oz.	32.50	20.00
Cup	9.00	8.00	Tumbler, 5", 12 oz.	37.50	
Plate, 6" sherbet	4.00	5.00	Vase, cone-shaped	35.00	
Plate, 8⅜ salad	7.00	7.00	Vase holder (17.50)		
** Plate, 9⅜" dinner	15.00	13.00			

* Reproduced in several colors

Please refer to Foreword for pricing information

OLD CAFE HOCKING GLASS COMPANY, 1936-1940

Colors: Pink, crystal and Royal Ruby.

Old Cafe pitchers have proven to be a problem as evidenced by the numerous letters I received! The pitcher shown is *not* Old Cafe! It was photographed for this book so I could point out that the real *Old Cafe pitcher has alternating large and small panels* as do the other Old Cafe pieces; this pitcher does not! Notice that the panels are evenly spaced. This pitcher (with evenly spaced panels) can even be found in green, a color never found in Old Cafe – yet. The pitcher is a nice "go-with" piece and it was made by Hocking. I'm sorry not to show the real pitcher. I've been looking, but I can't turn one up! If I couldn't show what it is, I opted to show what it is not!

There is also a juice pitcher that seems to be Old Cafe even though it is not shown in Hocking's catalogues, (but neither was the larger one). I have not seen a juice pitcher in my travels, but several dealers have said that they have. How about a picture?

Dinner plates continue to be the hardest pieces of Old Cafe to find besides the pitcher. All other items are available with searching. This is another pattern that you will have to ask dealers to bring to shows. Many will have this pattern back at the store, but rarely carry many pieces to shows.

There is a Hocking cookie jar with only a numbered line to its pedigree which is also a nice "go-with" piece. It is ribbed up the sides similar to Old Cafe but has a cross-hatched lid which is not even close to this pattern.

Royal Ruby "Old Cafe" cups are found on crystal saucers just as in Coronation. No Royal Ruby saucers have been found. Few lamps have been seen. Lamps were made by drilling a vase, turning it upside down and wiring it.

The low candy is 8⅜" including the handles. It was not considered to be a plate. You can see the one in the center.

	Crystal, Pink	Royal Ruby		Crystal, Pink	Royal Ruby
Bowl, 3¾" berry	2.50	4.50	Pitcher, 80 oz.	80.00	
Bowl, 5", 1 or 2 handles	4.00		Plate, 6" sherbet	2.00	
Bowl, 5½" cereal	5.00	9.00	Plate, 10" dinner	25.00	
Bowl, 9", closed handles	8.50	12.50	Saucer	2.00	
Candy dish, 8" low	10.00	10.00	Sherbet, low footed	5.00	9.00
Cup	4.00	7.00	Tumbler, 3" juice	9.00	7.50
Lamp	15.00	22.00	Tumbler, 4" water	10.00	15.00
Olive dish, 6" oblong	4.50		Vase, 7¼"	12.00	15.00
Pitcher, 6", 36 oz.	60.00				

OLD ENGLISH, "THREADING" INDIANA GLASS COMPANY

Colors: Green, amber, pink, crystal and forest green.

Old English has two newly discovered pieces, a vase measuring 8" and a 3½" two handled open compote which are both shown in the photograph. The vase has a platinum (silver) band around the top, the first piece of Old English I have seen with that treatment.

Flat pieces continue to be harder to find than other pieces (not the normal circumstance). Berry bowls in both sizes are difficult to find.

A set can be collected in green with all pieces being found in that color. A complete amber set may not be attainable since some pieces have never been seen in amber. That doesn't mean that they were never made, but it is looking bleak at best. Pink is the most elusive color. Only the center handled server, cheese and cracker and sherbets have been seen.

Decorated crystal pitcher and tumbler sets have been found with several different designs. The only one that I have seen more than once has orange and black painted flowers on each piece in the set including the pitcher lid. The pitcher lid, has the same cloverleaf type knob as the sugar and candy jars. The flat candy lid is similar in size, but the pitcher lid is notched on the bottom rim.

	Pink, Green, Amber		Pink, Green, Amber
Bowl, 4" flat	15.00	Pitcher	60.00
Bowl, 9" footed fruit	25.00	Pitcher and cover	100.00
Bowl, 9½" flat	28.00	Plate, indent for compote	18.00
Candlesticks, 4" pr.	27.50	Sandwich server, center handle	47.50
Candy dish & cover, flat	47.50	Sherbet, 2 styles	18.00
Candy jar with lid	47.50	Sugar	16.00
Compote, 3½" tall, 6⅜" across, 2 handled	20.00	Sugar cover	30.00
Compote, 3½" tall, 7" across	16.00	Tumbler, 4½" footed	20.00
Compote, 3 ½" cheese for plate	15.00	Tumbler, 5½" footed	30.00
Creamer	16.00	Vase, 5⅜", fan type, 7" wide	45.00
Egg cup (crystal only)	7.50	Vase, 8" footed, 4½" wide	40.00
Fruit stand, 11" footed	33.00	Vase, 8¼" footed, 4¼" wide	40.00
Goblet, 5¾", 8 oz.	27.50	Vase, 12" footed	50.00

Please refer to Foreword for pricing information

"ORCHID" PADEN CITY GLASS COMPANY, EARLY 1930's

Colors: Yellow, cobalt blue, green, amber, pink, red and black.

A couple of new Orchid pieces have been located. A square, flat, three part candy dish in red has been found and a cobalt blue compote, 6⅝" tall and 7" wide. Both pieces had been previously seen with other Paden City etchings, but not Orchid. There are two and maybe even three different orchid varieties being found on Paden City blanks. This pattern is so sparsely found that collectors do not mind mixing these different Orchid designs together.

Demand far exceeds all supplies of Paden City patterns. This causes prices to continue to rise, but the small amount of glass made in comparison to other companies will always keep collectors driving up prices with each purchase. Orchid prices have not gone through the roof like those of Cupid. There are fewer pieces of Orchid being found; so not as many people can own a piece or two!

Console bowls and candlesticks are the only pieces that crop up frequently. You have to realize that "frequently" for this pattern is like "hardly ever" for some major collectible patterns. I have owned more Mayfair sugar lids than I've seen Orchid consoles, for example (and I said the bowls were the most commonly found pieces)!

Although the number of collectors of Heisey's Orchid pattern is staggering, there are a relatively small number for Paden City's Orchid. Orchid growers throughout the country collect Heisey's Orchid. Availability and the heavy national distribution for Heisey Orchid are key factors.

	All Other Colors	Red Black Cobalt Blue		All Other Colors	Red Black Cobalt Blue
Bowl, 4⅞" square	15.00	30.00	Comport, 3¼" tall, 6¼" wide	17.50	35.00
Bowl, 8½", 2-handled	35.00	75.00	Comport, 6⅝" tall, 7" wide	25.00	50.00
Bowl, 8¾" square	30.00	60.00	Ice bucket, 6"	55.00	100.00
Bowl, 10", footed	45.00	90.00	Mayonnaise, 3 piece	50.00	95.00
Bowl, 11", square	35.00	67.50	Plate, 8½", square		45.00
Candlesticks, 5¾" pr.	50.00	100.00	Sandwich server, center handled	35.00	65.00
Candy with lid, 6½", square, three part	45.00	95.00	Sugar	25.00	45.00
Creamer	25.00	45.00	Vase, 10"	45.00	95.00

OVIDE, incorrectly dubbed "NEW CENTURY" HAZEL ATLAS GLASS COMPANY, 1930-1935

Colors: Green, black, white platonite trimmed with fired-on colors in 1950's.

Ovide is another of Hazel Atlas' Platonite patterns that fit into both this and my *Collectible Glassware from the 40's, 50's, 60's....* Due to photography schedules being done months ahead of writing, I ran into a problem with my photographs of this pattern. I received a letter saying a set of the "flying ducks" (geese) was a wedding gift to a lady in 1942; so that fact placed them in the *Collectible Glassware from the 40's, 50's, 60's...* book. However, the photograph showing those birds was taken with the Art Deco designed pieces. I had to decide a way to break up the pictures taken to end up with that picture in the other book. Since the Art Deco design photos have been in this book previously, I will only price it in this book.

The "flying ducks" (geese) belongs to the same collector who owns the Art Deco set. Evidently, there was a strong distribution of decorated sets in the north central Ohio region. I have a letter telling of an egg cup being discovered in the "flying ducks" pattern!

The black floral decorated set crosses over into Kitchenware with those stacking sets and mixing bowls. A stacking refrigerator set is shown in the photo. These sell in the $30.00-35.00 range when complete.

Very little black, green or yellow is being found. A luncheon set in black can be assembled if wanted, but it would be even easier to put together the same set in black Cloverleaf. Depression glass dealers would be inclined to bring the black Cloverleaf patterns to shows, but few stock black Ovide.

One collector surmised that most of the Ovide pieces he saw probably were intended to be Cloverleaf but had lousy or weak patterns. I would not go that far, but it is a point well taken. Many Cloverleaf pieces are found with very weak patterns. Weak enough that Cloverleaf collectors pass them.

	Black	Green	Decorated White	Art Deco		Black	Green	Decorated White	Art Deco
Bowl, 4¾" berry			6.00		Plate, 8" luncheon		2.00	12.50	40.00
Bowl, 5½" cereal			12.00		Plate, 9" dinner			18.00	
Bowl, 8" large berry			20.00		Platter, 11"			20.00	
Candy dish and cover	40.00	20.00	30.00		Salt and pepper, pr.	25.00	25.00	22.50	
Cocktail, footed fruit	4.00	3.00			Saucer	2.50	2.00	4.00	15.00
Creamer	6.00	3.00	15.00	75.00	Sherbet	5.50	2.00	12.50	40.00
Cup	6.00	3.00	12.00	45.00	Sugar, open	6.00	3.50	15.00	75.00
Plate, 6" sherbet		1.50	5.50		Tumbler			16.00	75.00

Please refer to Foreword for pricing information

OYSTER AND PEARL ANCHOR HOCKING GLASS CORPORATION, 1938-1940

Colors: Pink, crystal, Ruby Red, white with fired-on pink or green.

Royal Ruby Oyster and Pearl can be seen under the Royal Ruby pattern shown later in this book, but prices will still be included below. Collectors buy Oyster and Pearl as accessory pieces. The relish dish and candlesticks are hard to keep in my shop because they are reasonably priced and are usually purchased as gifts for non-collectors. Several times this has created a "new" collector who knew nothing about Depression glass until they received it as a gift. That relish dish is 11½" including the handles.

I have made a point to talk about measurements with handles in my commentary since I have been getting so many letters about measurements on pieces that I have already listed. Normally bowls and plates are measured without the handles. That is the how all glass factories listed the pieces and I can not change that now. There is no divided bowl in Oyster and Pearl; it was listed as a relish!

It has become expected by members of my wife's family to receive a pretty Depression glass bowl or plate on special occasions. Wedding gifts of antique glass seem to be received better than one of three blenders.

Red decorated crystal pieces are rarely found, but they sell faster than getting plain crystal. The 10½" fruit bowl is a great salad bowl with the 13½" plate as a liner, but several collectors have told me that it also makes an ideal small punch bowl. It wouldn't hold enough for our family gatherings!

The pink color fired-on over white was called "Dusty Rose"; the fired-on green was christened "Springtime Green" by Hocking. Collectors do not seem to have a middle ground on these fired-on colors. They either love them or hate them. There seem to be more of the fired-on colors available than the plain white.

The spouted 5¼" bowl is often referred to as heart shaped. The same bowl is also found without the spout. Although pictured in "Dusty Rose" and "Springtime Green" last time, this bowl was omitted in the price listings in those colors. Sorry!

	Crystal, Pink	Royal Ruby	White and Fired-On Green Or Pink
Bowl, 5¼" heart-shaped, 1-handled	6.50	8.50	7.50
Bowl, 5½", 1-handled	6.50	11.00	
Bowl, 6½" deep-handled	9.50	17.50	
Bowl, 10½" deep fruit	20.00	40.00	12.00
Candle holder, 3½" pr.	20.00	40.00	13.00
Plate, 13½" sandwich	15.00	35.00	
Relish dish, 10¼" oblong	8.50		

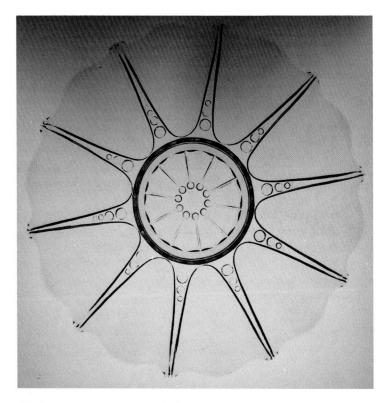

"PARROT," SYLVAN FEDERAL GLASS COMPANY, 1931-1932

Colors: Green, amber; some crystal and blue.

I expected some comments on our photographer's folly of placing that plastic bird on the glass, but not one letter or remark was made at a show. Green Parrot prices are sailing full speed ahead, but prices of amber Parrot have not increased as fast, even though it is more rare. The amber butter dish, creamer and sugar lid are all harder to find than green.

The 8½" round yellow plate (shown on the right front of the photograph of amber) was made by Indiana. These are also found in green. If you see one, you may notice that the birds more closely resemble parakeets than parrots. In any case, they are not a part of Federal's Parrot pattern. However, including this plate in the photo saves me answering about 20 letters a year!

People recognize the Madrid shapes on which we find Parrot. You will notice that most Parrot tumblers are found on these Madrid blanks except for the heavy footed tumbler. Evidently, the thin, moulded, footed tumbler did not accept the Parrot design very well and a new style tumbler was made. This thin, 10 oz. footed tumbler has only been found in amber. The supply of heavy, footed tumblers and thin, flat iced teas in amber have more than met the demand of collectors. Price for these two tumblers has remained steady. Other prices in amber have more than compensated for the few steady ones.

The hot plate has now been found in two styles! One is shaped like the Madrid hot plate with the pointed edges. This can be seen in the photo of green Parrot. The other is round, and more like Federal's other bird pattern, Georgian. (It can be seen below.) It seems the round hot plate may be the harder to find; but right now, *any* hot plate is hard to find!

There has been only one *mint* condition butter dish top found in amber. The butter bottom has an indented ledge for the top. The jam dish is the same as the butter bottom without the ledge, but has never been found in green.

There are quantities of sugar and butter lids found. The major concern is finding MINT condition lids. The pointed edges and ridges on Parrot chipped then and now. You should carefully check these points when purchasing this pattern. Damaged or *repaired* glassware should not bring *mint* prices. I emphasize that here because many sugar and butter lids have been repaired. If it has been reworked, it should be sold as "repaired."

My main concern is that there are many so-called "glass grinders" who are just that. They grind glass, but they do not repair it. You would not let a doctor cut off your arm if it were broken. By the same token, you should not expect to have a chipped glass cut off below the chip and left so sharp you would fear a cut lip if you tried to drink out of it. The glass would have been better left alone.

Ask to see an example of a glass grinder's work before you hand over your treasures. If the edges are rounded and smoothed to the touch and not flattened or sharp, look no further. Can you feel the repair? Are chips and flakes ground away leaving no noticeable dips in the surface or can you see scratches and cracks in the work? You should find an edge that is worked to uniformity. Unless it was a badly damaged piece, you should not notice the repair until close examination. If you can find where the piece was repaired without much difficulty, this grinder is not for you.

	Green	Amber
Bowl, 5" berry	18.00	15.00
Bowl, 7" soup	35.00	27.50
Bowl, 8" large berry	65.00	70.00
Bowl, 10" oval vegetable	45.00	55.00
Butter dish and cover	265.00	1,100.00
Butter dish bottom	30.00	200.00
Butter dish top	235.00	900.00
Creamer, footed	27.50	45.00
Cup	30.00	30.00
Hot plate, 5", 2 styles	625.00	
Jam dish, 7"		27.50
Pitcher, 8½", 80 oz.	1,300.00	
Plate, 5¾" sherbet	25.00	15.00
Plate, 7½" salad	28.00	
Plate, 9" dinner	38.00	30.00
Plate, 10½" round grill	25.00	
Plate, 10½" square grill		22.00
Plate, 10¼" square (crystal only)	25.00	
Platter, 11¼" oblong	35.00	55.00
Salt and pepper, pr.	200.00	
Saucer	11.00	11.00
* Sherbet, footed cone	19.00	18.00
Sherbet, 4¼" high	250.00	
Sugar	25.00	30.00
Sugar cover	115.00	350.00

	Green	Amber
Tumbler, 4¼", 10 oz.	100.00	95.00
Tumbler, 5½", 12 oz.	120.00	100.00
Tumbler, 5¾" footed heavy	105.00	95.00
Tumbler, 5½", 10 oz. footed (Madrid mould)		120.00

* Blue-$100.00

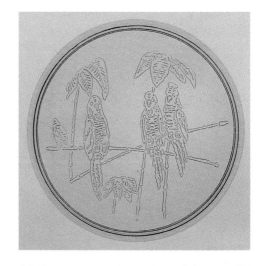

PATRICIAN, "SPOKE" FEDERAL GLASS COMPANY, 1933-1937

Colors: Pink, green, crystal and amber ("Golden Glo").

Patrician is one of the few amber patterns of Depression glass that is collected by large numbers of people. Amber is found easily and the large 10½" dinner plates will hold enough for the heartiest of appetites. That may be one of the reasons that several collectors I have met expound on the virtues of Patrician for everyday use! I discovered that these plates were given away in flour sacks as "cake" plates. They saturated my area!

There is nothing in amber that can truly be considered rare; but mint condition sugar lids, cookie or butter bottoms and footed tumblers are harder to find than other pieces. Check sugar lids for signs of repair. The cookie bottom is rare in green. There are several lids found for each bottom. Most people think that all tops are harder to find than bottoms. This does not hold true for butter dishes and cookie jars in Patrician. Saucers are also harder to find than cups. This phenomenon occurs in few patterns, but Patrician is one of them.

The hexagonal shape of Patrician cookie jars, pitchers and tumblers has always infatuated new collectors. I received a letter calling me to task on hexagonal. Plates, bowls and other pieces are somewhat pentagonal.

There are two styles of pitchers found. The one pictured has a moulded handle and is easier to find in amber than the one with an applied handle. In crystal, the applied handle pitcher is the easiest to find!

Green Patrician is more easily found and collected than pink or crystal. To complete a set in pink is difficult, but not yet impossible. It is in crystal. Not all pieces have been found in crystal; so you would have to settle for a smaller set – if you could find enough!

	Amber, Crystal	Pink	Green		Amber, Crystal	Pink	Green
Bowl, 4¾" cream soup	14.00	16.00	17.00	Plate, 6" sherbet	8.50	6.50	7.00
Bowl, 5" berry	10.00	11.00	10.00	Plate, 7½" salad	13.00	14.00	13.00
Bowl, 6" cereal	20.00	20.00	23.00	Plate, 9" luncheon	10.00	8.00	9.00
Bowl, 8½" large berry	40.00	22.00	30.00	Plate, 10½" dinner	6.00	25.00	30.00
Bowl, 10" oval vegetable	27.50	11.00	23.00	Plate, 10½" grill	12.50	11.00	12.00
Butter dish and cover	80.00	195.00	95.00	Platter, 11½" oval	27.50	20.00	20.00
Butter dish bottom	55.00	150.00	50.00	Salt and pepper, pr.	50.00	75.00	55.00
Butter dish top	25.00	45.00	45.00	Saucer	7.50	7.50	7.50
Cookie jar and cover	80.00		400.00	Sherbet	11.00	11.00	12.00
Creamer, footed	8.50	9.50	10.00	Sugar	7.50	8.00	8.00
Cup	7.50	8.00	9.00	Sugar cover	45.00	42.00	48.00
Jam dish	25.00	25.00	30.00	Tumbler, 4", 5 oz.	26.00	23.00	28.00
Pitcher, 8", 75 oz. moulded				Tumbler, 4¼", 9 oz.	23.00	19.00	23.00
handle	95.00	90.00	100.00	Tumbler, 5½", 14 oz.	35.00	25.00	35.00
Pitcher, 8¼", 75 oz., applied				Tumbler, 5¼", 8 oz. ftd	40.00		45.00
handle	125.00	100.00	125.00				

"PATRICK," LANCASTER GLASS COMPANY, EARLY 1930's

Colors: Yellow and pink.

I received a letter from a lady who thinks she has a Patrick three footed candy! I have never seen one except in a catalogue. As more Jubilee collectors turn their attention to collecting Patrick, the smaller supply of this pattern is diminishing rapidly and prices are rising! Although Jubilee was distributed heavily in the Northwest, I have not had any reported findings of Patrick there.

Jubilee and Patrick make great complimentary sets. There is not enough Patrick for everyone who wants a set; but by mixing it with Jubilee, you can stretch your collecting reach. While I bought about sixty pieces of Jubilee in Florida last month, I did not see one piece of Patrick in my travels.

As in Jubilee, serving dishes are few and far between in Patrick. I had a lady write that cups were given away and you had to buy the saucers. Since the cups are also more plentiful in Jubilee, this might have been a marketing ploy in that pattern, too. It would appear people took the free cups and did without saucers.

There are a few pieces of pink Patrick, but this color seems to be in shorter supply than the yellow. There are several floral patterns made by Lancaster with the same shapes of Patrick and Jubilee that can be blended into these sets if you get stymied in finding serving pieces.

	Pink	Yellow		Pink	Yellow
Bowl, 9", handled fruit	65.00	40.00	Mayonnaise, 3-piece	125.00	80.00
Bowl, 11", console	75.00	45.00	Plate, 7" sherbet	10.00	6.00
Candlesticks, pr.	75.00	45.00	Plate, 7½" salad	18.00	10.00
Candy dish, 3-footed	75.00	45.00	Plate, 8" luncheon	25.00	15.00
Cheese & cracker set	85.00	35.00	Saucer	10.00	5.00
Creamer	53.00	20.00	Sherbet, 4¾"	40.00	25.00
Cup	35.00	15.00	Sugar	35.00	20.00
Goblet, 4" cocktail	45.00	25.00	Tray, 11", 2-handled	50.00	35.00
Goblet, 4¾", 6 oz. juice	45.00	27.50	Tray, 11", center-handled	50.00	35.00
Goblet, 6", 10 oz. water	65.00	35.00			

"PEACOCK REVERSE," LINE 412 PADEN CITY GLASS COMPANY, 1930's

Colors: Cobalt blue, red, amber, yellow, green, pink, black and crystal.

New pieces of Peacock Reverse continue to be found! Another style comport and several pieces in yellow have been reported. The new comport stands only 3¼" high, but is 7" wide. Ten inch bud vases have now been found in pink, amber and green!

I had a report of an eight sided plate; have you seen one?

All colors are collectible, but crystal is the least desirable. Prices here are not determined by color as much as in other patterns. Collectors accept any color they can find!

Paden City's Line #412 (commonly called "Crow's Foot" by collectors) and Line #991 (which is Penny Line) make up the blanks on which Peacock Reverse has been seen. Paden City lines were used for many different designs; so it is not unusual to spot a piece only to find that it does not have the pattern for which you are searching.

Any piece listed in Orchid, Cupid or Peacock and Wild Rose could be found with the Peacock Reverse design. Let me know what you turn up!

	All Colors		All Colors
Bowl, 4⅞" square	30.00	Plate, 8½" luncheon	35.00
Bowl, 8¾" square	75.00	Plate 10⅜", 2-handled	45.00
Bowl, 8¾" square with handles	80.00	Saucer	15.00
Bowl, 11¾" console	75.00	Sherbet, 4⅝" tall, 3⅜" diameter	40.00
Candlesticks, 5¾" square base, pr.	110.00	Sherbet, 4⅞" tall, 3⅝" diameter	40.00
Candy dish, 6½" square	125.00	Server, center-handled	60.00
Comport, 3¼" high, 6¼" wide	47.50	Sugar, 2¾" flat	75.00
Creamer, 2¾" flat	75.00	Tumbler, 4", 10 oz. flat	55.00
Cup	65.00	Vase, 10"	85.00
Plate, 5¾" sherbet	20.00	Vase, 10", bud	125.00

"PEACOCK & WILD ROSE," PADEN CITY GLASS COMPANY, LINE #1300, 1930's

Colors: Pink, green, cobalt blue, black, crystal and red.

An elliptical vase is the only new item I have found in Peacock and Rose, but I was shown a newly discovered 12" vase in pink at the Springfield, Missouri, show recently! The bulbous base showed signs of being faintly paneled. Vases are the most commonly found pieces in this pattern. There are two styles of 10" vases. The bulbous-bottomed vase is pictured in three colors, but there is a more straight-sided one that can be found in black.

No more information has been forthcoming on the 5" pitcher, so I will not list it yet. Although there are several "bird" designs in Paden City patterns, there is more recognition for the peacock patterns than for any other.

	All Colors
Bowl, 8½", flat	50.00
Bowl, 8½", fruit, oval, footed	75.00
Bowl, 8¾", footed	65.00
Bowl, 9½", center-handled	60.00
Bowl, 9½", footed	65.00
Bowl, 10½", center-handled	70.00
Bowl, 10½", footed	80.00
Bowl, 10½", fruit	80.00
Bowl, 11", console	65.00
Bowl, 14", console	75.00
Candlestick, 5", pr.	100.00
Candy dish w/cover, 7"	125.00
Cheese and cracker set	95.00
Comport, 3¼" tall, 6¼" wide	45.00
Ice bucket, 6"	110.00
Ice tub, 4¾"	100.00
Pitcher, 5" high	100.00
Plate, cake, low foot	75.00
Relish, 3-part	50.00
Vase, 8¼" elliptical	125.00
Vase, 10", two styles	85.00
Vase, 12"	100.00

PETALWARE MacBETH-EVANS GLASS COMPANY, 1930-1940

Colors: Monax, Cremax, pink, crystal, cobalt and fired-on red, blue, green and yellow.

Petalware collectors have never been the same since the red trimmed Petalware appeared on both the covers of my eighth edition book and my sixth edition *Pocket Guide to Depression Glass*. It was the first pattern ever to be on both books! What can I say except my publisher loved it! No, I have little decision in what goes on the covers of my books. I make suggestions, but…. The red trimmed Petalware also has three sizes of tumblers decorated to match it. Prices for this red trimmed pattern have "gone out of sight!"

I have tried to show as wide a variety of the Monax decorated Petalware as possible this time. Below and on the bottom of page 143 are plates from different series of fruits, birds and flowers. Most of the fruit-decorated Petalware come in sets of eight. One such set consists of plates showing cherry, apple, orange, plum, strawberry, blueberry, pear and grape. You may find other sets with different fruits. Some sets have the fruits named; others do not. Some sets have colored bands and others have 22K gold trim. My all-time favorite (besides the Florence Cherry) are the Bluebird plates. Maybe it's the Bluebird of happiness.

Monax and Cremax are terms given these colors by MacBeth-Evans. Cremax refers to the beige colored Petalware represented by a few pieces in the top photo on page 145. The wall hanging bowl in the left foreground and the plate with black windmill decoration are Cremax. The rarely found flat soup is also shown in that photograph. The pastel-banded Cremax is the most collected. I'll have several pieces of that in the next book! Florette is the name given to the red floral pattern shown in this photograph. Notice that it does not have a red trim and is not as colorful as the other red flowered pattern.

Cremax will show green under a black light, but Monax does not.

Pink Petalware sells very well in my shop. Note the big price increases in pink. I suggested in the last edition that pink was inexpensive and a good pattern for new collectors to start. That was the end of inexpensive; but pink Petalware is still less expensive than many other pink patterns.

Lamp shades do not sell very well; but if you want a cheap shade to go with this pattern, you should have little trouble finding one.

The cobalt mustard has a metal lid and it is Petalware! There are a few other pieces of cobalt blue Petalware, but they are rarely seen. The 9" berry bowl varies from 8¾" at times.

PETALWARE MacBETH-EVANS GLASS COMPANY, 1930-1940 (Cont.)

	Crystal	Pink	Monax Plain	Cremax, Monax Florette, Fired-On Decorations	Red Trim Floral
Bowl, 4½" cream soup	4.00	10.00	9.00	10.00	
Bowl, 5¾" cereal	3.50	8.00	5.00	10.00	27.50
Bowl, 7" soup			50.00		
* Bowl, 9" large berry	7.50	12.50	15.00	22.50	95.00
Cup	2.50	6.00	4.50	8.00	20.00
** Creamer, footed	2.50	6.00	5.00	10.00	25.00
Lamp shade (many sizes) $8.00 to $15.00					
Mustard with metal cover in cobalt blue only, $8.00					
Pitcher, 80 oz. (crystal decorated bands)	22.00				
Plate, 6" sherbet	1.50	2.00	2.00	5.00	
Plate, 8" salad	1.75	3.50	3.00	8.00	
Plate, 9" dinner	3.50	7.50	5.00	12.00	22.50
Plate, 11¾" salver	4.00	8.00	8.00	15.00	
Plate, 12" salver		8.00	17.50		32.50
Platter, 13" oval	7.50	12.50	14.00	17.50	
Saucer	1.00	1.50	1.50	2.50	5.00
Saucer, cream soup liner			15.00		
Sherbet, 4" low footed			25.00		
** Sherbet, 4½" low footed	3.00	6.00	6.00	10.00	27.50
** Sugar, footed	2.50	6.00	5.00	9.00	25.00
Tidbit servers or lazy susans, several styles 12.00 to 17.50					
*** Tumblers (crystal decorated bands) 2.50 to 7.50					

* Also in cobalt at $45.00
** Also in cobalt at $30.00
*** Several sizes

PRIMO, "PANELLED ASTER" U.S. GLASS COMPANY, EARLY 1930's

Colors: Green and yellow.

Primo is another obscure pattern where little catalogue information is available. I continue to add new pieces to the listing as they are found. The report of a three-footed round console bowl in Primo turned out to be another U.S. Glass pattern known as "Thorn" which is found in pink, green and black. There have been no new reports of center handled servers, but it is possible these do exist!

Berry bowls and cake plates seem to be the hardest to find pieces. I still have not found a green berry bowl to photograph. Mould seam roughness is the norm for this pattern; so if you are turned off by that; look for some other pattern to collect.

The coaster/ash tray combinations do not have the pattern on them. Evidently, they were made by U.S. Glass to go with other patterns besides Primo, since no pieces of Primo have been found in the pink or black to go with those colored coasters (shown). Notice how exactly the tumbler fits the coaster! These coasters have been found in boxed Primo sets which were advertised as "Bridge Sets."

	Yellow, Green			Yellow, Green
Bowl, 4½"	8.50	Plate, 10" dinner		14.00
Bowl, 7¾"	18.00	Plate, 10" grill		8.50
Cake plate, 10", 3-footed	18.00	Saucer		2.50
Coaster/ash tray	7.50	Sherbet		8.50
Creamer	9.00	Sugar		9.00
Cup	8.00	Tumbler, 5¾", 9 oz.		15.00
Plate, 7½"	7.00			

Please refer to Foreword for pricing information

PRINCESS HOCKING GLASS COMPANY, 1931-1935

Colors: Green, Topaz yellow, apricot yellow, pink and blue.

Yellow Princess continues to give collectors headaches due to color variations. "Topaz" is the official color listed by Hocking, and it is a pretty shade of yellow. However, some yellow is almost amber and has been called "apricot" by collectors. Most prefer the "Topaz" which makes the darker, amber shade difficult to sell. The hardest to find yellow pieces include the butter dish, juice pitcher, footed iced tea, undivided relish, coasters and ash trays.

The undivided relish is called a soup bowl by some dealers, so you need to be aware of that. It is so shallow, I wouldn't want to eat my soup out of it. It's what Cathy's grandmother called a "polite" soup bowl (you eat just enough to "be polite").

The handled sandwich plate actually measures 10¼" or 11¼" if measured with handles. These are rarely found in yellow and have been fetching high prices when they do occasionally turn up. They are common in pink and green. The grill plate and dinner plate have also been corrected to read 9½" instead of what old catalogues had listed.

An unusual, three footed bowl has been found in Texas. It is 8¾" square and stands only 1½" high. What it was designed for is anyone's guess, but it is like the undivided relish in that it doesn't hold much!

Tumblers and bowls are hard to acquire in all colors. One of the problems in finding mint condition bowls is inner rim roughness. Green Princess collectors have to search long and hard for footed iced teas, cereal and berry bowls, undivided relishes and the elusive footed pitcher and tumblers to match.

Collectors of pink Princess have problems finding the coasters, footed iced teas and the footed pitcher with matching tumblers.

Blue Princess collectors are pretty much out of luck! There have been only a few different pieces found in this pattern. They are all marked with an asterisk in the listing below. There are still reports of blue sets being seen in Texas. I can confirm the existence of one set, since I have a photograph of it! The pitcher found with this set is damaged; however, the pitcher is not Princess. It is blue Florentine like the one shown in my second book in 1975.

From 1975 to date, almost all of the blue reported has been found in the Southwest and Mexico. It must have been distributed or test marketed there!

	Green	Pink	Topaz, Apricot			Green	Pink	Topaz, Apricot
Ash tray, 4½"	65.00	82.50	85.00	**	Plate, 9½" grill	11.00	10.00	5.00
Bowl, 4½" berry	20.00	16.00	40.00		Plate, 10¼" handled sandwich	11.00	9.00	125.00
Bowl, 5" cereal or oatmeal	25.00	20.00	26.00		Plate, 10½" grill, closed			
Bowl, 9" octagonal salad	32.50	22.50	100.00		handles	9.00	8.00	5.00
Bowl, 9½" hat-shaped	35.00	22.00	100.00		Platter, 12" closed handles	18.00	18.00	50.00
Bowl, 10" oval vegetable	22.00	17.50	50.00		Relish, 7½" divided	22.00	20.00	95.00
Butter dish and cover	80.00	80.00	600.00		Relish, 7½" plain	95.00	100.00	130.00
Butter dish bottom	25.00	25.00	200.00		Salt and pepper, 4½" pr.	45.00	40.00	55.00
Butter dish top	55.00	55.00	400.00		Spice shakers, 5½" pr.	37.50		
Cake stand, 10"	19.50	20.00		***	Saucer (same as sherbet			
Candy dish and cover	45.00	45.00			plate)	6.50	5.00	3.00
Coaster	30.00	60.00	80.00		Sherbet, footed	18.00	15.00	30.00
* Cookie jar and cover	45.00	50.00			Sugar	9.00	8.00	8.00
Creamer, oval	12.00	11.00	12.00		Sugar cover	18.00	15.00	15.00
** Cup	10.00	9.00	7.50		Tumbler, 3", 5 oz. juice	24.00	19.00	24.00
Pitcher 6", 37 oz.	40.00	38.00	500.00		Tumbler, 4", 9 oz. water	22.00	18.00	20.00
Pitcher, 7⅜", 24 oz. footed	500.00	425.00			Tumbler, 5¼", 13 oz. iced tea	32.00	20.00	24.00
Pitcher, 8", 60 oz.	45.00	45.00	75.00		Tumbler, 4¾", 9 oz. sq. ftd	55.00	45.00	
*** Plate, 5½" sherbet	7.00	7.00	3.00		Tumbler, 5¼", 10 oz. footed	28.00	19.00	18.00
Plate, 8" salad	12.00	10.00	9.00		Tumbler, 6½", 12½ oz. ftd.	75.00	60.00	125.00
Plate, 9½" dinner	22.00	18.00	14.00		Vase, 8"	28.00	25.00	

*Blue $600.00
**Blue $100.00
***Blue $55.00

Please refer to Foreword for pricing information

QUEEN MARY (PRISMATIC LINE), "VERTICAL RIBBED"
HOCKING GLASS COMPANY, 1936-1949

Colors: Pink, crystal and some Royal Ruby.

Queen Mary collectors have been asking about the footed creamer and sugar shown. I still have not found any confirmation on them at Anchor Hocking, but I did see another set sell for $45.00 last month. The long time collector was ecstatic and positive that they were, indeed, Queen Mary.

Pink dinner plates and footed tumblers have always been hard to find, but I am hearing reports that those pieces in crystal are also hiding. Other tumblers and the pink candy dish are beginning to appear on more collector "want lists." This is a pattern that dealers now carry to shows!

The 6" cereal bowl has the same shape as the butter bottom. Butter dishes were also called preserve dishes. There are two sizes of cups. The smaller cup sits on the saucer with cup ring. The larger cup sits on the combination saucer/sherbet plate.

A crystal set can still be captured at reasonable prices. Pink has begun to reach higher price levels. Now could be a good time to start rounding up this pattern before more people discover it.

Several pieces of Queen Mary were made in Royal Ruby including the candlesticks and large bowl. In the 1950's, the 3½" ash tray was made in Forest Green and Royal Ruby.

The 2" x 3¾" ash tray and 2" x 3¾" oval cigarette jar have been found labeled "Ace Hi Bridge Smoking Set."

There were a pair of lamp shades found in this pattern. These had been made from candy lids using metal decorations, not the most beautiful pieces I have seen, but interesting!

	Pink	Crystal		Pink	Crystal
Ash tray, 2" x 3¾" oval	4.00	2.50	Creamer, footed	17.50	
* Ash tray, 3½" round		2.50	Creamer, oval	6.00	5.00
Bowl, 4" one handle or none	4.00	3.00	Cup (2 sizes)	6.00	5.00
Bowl, 4½", berry	5.00	3.00	Plate, 6" and 6⅝"	4.00	3.00
Bowl, 5" berry	5.00	3.00	Plate, 8¾" salad		5.00
Bowl, 5½", two handles	6.00	5.00	Plate, 9¾" dinner	35.00	12.50
Bowl, 6" cereal	20.00	6.00	Plate, 12" sandwich	12.00	8.00
Bowl, 7" small	10.00	6.50	Plate, 14" serving tray	15.00	10.00
Bowl, 8¾" large berry	13.00	9.00	Relish tray, 12", 3-part	12.00	8.00
Butter dish or preserve and cover	95.00	20.00	Relish tray, 14", 4-part	12.00	10.00
Butter dish bottom	25.00	4.00	Salt and pepper, pr.		17.50
Butter dish top	70.00	16.00	Saucer	2.00	2.00
Candy dish and cover	30.00	16.00	Sherbet, footed	4.50	3.50
** Candlesticks, 4½" double branch, pr.		13.50	Sugar, footed	17.50	
Celery or pickle dish, 5" x 10"	19.50	8.00	Sugar, oval	5.00	4.00
Cigarette jar, 2" x 3" oval	6.00	5.00	Tumbler, 3½", 5 oz. juice	8.50	3.50
Coaster, 3½"	3.00	2.00	Tumbler, 4", 9 oz. water	9.50	5.00
Coaster/ash tray, 4¼" square	5.00	4.50	Tumbler, 5", 10 oz. footed	35.00	24.00
Comport, 5¾"	9.00	6.00			

* Royal Ruby $5.00; Forest Green $3.00
** Royal Ruby $30.00

RAINDROPS, "OPTIC DESIGN" FEDERAL GLASS COMPANY 1929-1933

Colors: Green and crystal.

Raindrops has two styles of cups. One is flat bottomed and the other has a slight foot. The flat bottomed is 2⁵⁄₁₆" high and the footed is 2¹¹⁄₁₆" (as reported by a Raindrops collector). A new size tumbler has also been reported which holds 14 oz. and is 5⅜" tall. Mr. Shaker still has not found a mate! A collector in Illinois would "kill" for the one shown!

Sugar bowl lids are still hard to find, but since there are few Raindrops collectors, the supply is adequate for now. Raindrops makes a great little luncheon set. It even has a few extra pieces that many smaller sets do not. You can find three sizes of serving bowls in Raindrops.

Raindrops design has rounded bumps and not elongated ones as does Pear Optic or Thumbprint. Don't confuse the cups of these patterns as my photography help once did!

	Green		Green
Bowl, 4½" fruit	4.50	Sugar	6.00
Bowl, 6" cereal	6.50	Sugar cover	35.00
Bowl, 7½" berry	32.50	Tumbler, 3", 4 oz.	4.00
Cup	5.00	Tumbler, 2⅛", 2 oz.	4.00
Creamer	6.00	Tumbler, 3⅞", 5 oz.	6.00
Plate, 6" sherbet	2.00	Tumbler, 4⅛", 9½ oz.	8.50
Plate, 8" luncheon	5.00	Tumbler, 5", 10 oz.	8.50
Salt and pepper, pr.	200.00	Tumbler, 5⅜", 14 oz.	10.00
Saucer	1.50	Whiskey, 1⅞", 1 oz.	6.00
Sherbet	6.00		

RADIANCE NEW MARTINSVILLE GLASS COMPANY, 1936-1939

Colors: Red, cobalt and ice blue, amber, crystal, pink and emerald green.

Colored punch bowls in Radiance remain elusive. The crystal punch bowl sets being found on green and other colored plates may have been made by Viking after they bought out New Martinsville. You can see each style on the bottom of page 151. These crystal bowls are selling in the $35.00 range and cups are selling for $4.00 each. If anyone can shed some light on the crystal style punch bowls, I would appreciate hearing from you. A few collectors have suggested that Radiance is "too good" a glassware to be in this book. It is better made glassware than those mass-produced wares of the Depression era and belongs in my *Elegant Glassware of the Depression Era*.

Red and the ice blue are the most collected colors. Few pieces were made in cobalt blue but include a recently found vase.

A few pieces are also being found in pink including creamer, sugar, tray, cup, saucer and shakers. These are selling in the same range as the red since they are scarce at this time.

Rarely found pieces in this pattern include the butter dish, pitcher, handled decanter and the five-piece condiment set. The vase has been found made into a lamp. I doubt this was a factory project, but it could have been.

There are several different designs decorated in gold and platinum. The major problem with these is finding matching pieces. Many collectors have shied away from buying decorated pieces; but, if not worn, they make an interesting addition to your collection.

	Ice Blue, Red	Amber		Ice Blue, Red	Amber
Bowl, 5", nut 2-handled	14.00	8.00	Condiment set, 4-piece w/tray	225.00	130.00
Bowl, 6", bonbon	15.00	9.00	Creamer	20.00	12.00
Bowl, 6", bonbon, footed	17.50	10.00	Cruet, indiv.	50.00	35.00
Bowl, 6", bonbon w/cover	45.00	28.00	Cup	15.00	11.00
Bowl, 7", relish, 2-part	18.00	12.00	Cup, punch	12.00	6.00
Bowl, 7", pickle	17.50	11.00	* Decanter w/stopper, handled	135.00	80.00
Bowl, 8", relish, 3-part	25.00	17.50	Goblet, 1 oz., cordial	35.00	25.00
Bowl, 10", celery	20.00	12.00	Ladle for punch bowl	115.00	85.00
Bowl, 10", crimped	32.50	17.50	Lamp, 12"	95.00	55.00
Bowl, 10", flared	32.50	19.00	Mayonnaise, 3 piece, set	50.00	22.00
Bowl, 12", crimped	37.50	25.00	** Pitcher, 64 oz.	195.00	135.00
Bowl, 12", flared	35.00	22.00	Plate, 8", luncheon	15.00	9.00
Bowl, punch	165.00	85.00	*** Plate, 14", punch bowl liner	65.00	30.00
Butter dish	395.00	175.00	Salt & pepper, pr.	75.00	45.00
Candlestick 6" ruffled pr.	105.00	65.00	Saucer	7.50	5.00
Candlestick 8" pr.	55.00	35.00	Sugar	19.00	11.00
Candlestick 2-lite, pr.	85.00	55.00	Tray, oval	27.50	22.00
Cheese/cracker, (11" plate) set	45.00	25.00	**** Tumbler, 9 oz.	25.00	16.00
Comport, 5"	25.00	15.00	***** Vase, 10", flared	50.00	25.00
Comport, 6"	27.50	18.00			

* Cobalt blue $185.00
** Cobalt blue $350.00
*** Emerald green $25.00
**** Cobalt blue $28.00
***** Cobalt blue $75.00

"RIBBON" HAZEL ATLAS GLASS COMPANY, Early 1930's

Colors: Green; some black, crystal and pink.

Ribbon bowls are elusive! The 5" cereal is pictured on the left in a plate holder. The black bowl was turned over to show the pattern which is on the outside. I see very little Ribbon for sale in my travels about the country. I made three trips to the West coast last year and one so far this year. Some patterns are not seen out there and Ribbon was one of them! I talked to one collector who had about twenty pieces, but all her pieces had come from the East by mail order.

You may notice that the Ribbon shapes are the same as Cloverleaf and Ovide which are two other Hazel Atlas patterns. Either some glass designer really liked those shapes or the company reworked moulds to make the new patterns.

Tumblers, sugars and creamers are not as difficult to find as bowls, but even they are getting to be in shorter supply.

The candy dish is the most commonly seen piece of Ribbon. That fact and the economical price make it a perfect gift for non-collectors. It is also practical!

Collecting lesser known, and smaller patterns such as Ribbon is a fairly common practice among young collectors. They do not have to pawn the family's jewels because the price is still reasonable; and it is unlikely they will find more than five or six pieces at any one time. Plus, they get the invaluable experience and the fun of participating in collecting Depression glass!

Shakers are the only pieces of pink that have been reported to me. If you have any other pieces, I would like to hear from you.

	Green	Black		Green	Black
Bowl, 4" berry	9.00		Plate, 8" luncheon	4.00	12.00
Bowl, 5" cereal	13.50		Salt and pepper, pr.	25.00	37.50
Bowl, 8" large berry	22.50	27.50	Saucer	2.00	
Candy dish and cover	32.50		Sherbet, footed	4.50	
Creamer, footed	12.00		Sugar, footed	10.00	
Cup	4.00		Tumbler, 6", 10 oz.	22.50	
Plate, 6¼" sherbet	2.00				

RING, "BANDED RINGS" HOCKING GLASS COMPANY, 1927-1933

Colors: Crystal, crystal w/pink, red, blue, orange, yellow, black, silver, etc. rings; green, some pink, "Mayfair" blue and red.

Ring collectors usually start by collecting one particular color "scheme." Colored rings in a particular order on crystal is what I am calling a "scheme." Some collectors have been known to call it other things. Printable words include headache and "pain in the butt." There is a predominant "scheme" involving black, yellow, red and orange colored rings in that order. There are many others, also. It is those others which drive perfectionists crazy!

Crystal with platinum bands is another widely collected form of this pattern. Worn borders bedevil collectors in this decoration.

Green Ring can be collected, but not as easily as the crystal or decorated crystal. A reader tells me that for subscribing to *Country Gentleman* in the 1930's, you received a green berry bowl set consisting of an 8" berry and six 5" berry bowls.

Pink seems to be found only in pitcher and tumbler sets. A Wisconsin collector reports that the pink pitchers are very common in his part of the country. Tumblers were not mentioned in that letter; so, perhaps, only the pitchers were premium items.

	Crystal	Decor., Green		Crystal	Decor., Green
Bowl, 5" berry	3.00	4.50	** Plate, 8" luncheon	2.00	4.00
Bowl, 7" soup	8.00	12.00	Plate, 11¾", sandwich	6.00	10.00
Bowl, 5¼", divided	9.00		***Salt and pepper, pr., 3"	16.00	32.00
Bowl, 8" large berry	6.50	9.00	Sandwich server, center handle	15.00	23.00
Butter tub or ice tub	15.00	27.50	Saucer	1.25	1.50
Cocktail shaker	17.50	22.50	Sherbet, low (for 6½" plate)	4.50	11.00
** Cup	4.00	4.50	Sherbet, 4¾" footed	4.50	8.50
Creamer, footed	4.00	5.00	Sugar, footed	4.00	5.00
Decanter and stopper	20.00	32.00	Tumbler, 3½", 5 oz.	3.00	6.00
Goblet, 7¼", 9 oz.	7.00	13.50	Tumbler, 4¼", 9 oz.	4.00	6.50
Goblet, 3¾", 3½ oz. cocktail	10.00	15.00	* Tumbler, 4¾", 10 oz	7.00	
Goblet, 4½", 3½ oz., wine	12.50	17.50	Tumbler, 5⅛", 12 oz.	5.00	8.00
Ice bucket	13.00	20.00	Tumbler, 3½" footed juice	5.00	7.00
Pitcher, 8", 60 oz.	14.00	13.50	Tumbler, 5½" footed water	5.00	8.00
* Pitcher, 8½", 80 oz.	17.00	27.50	Tumbler, 6½", footed iced tea	6.50	12.00
Plate, 6¼" sherbet	1.50	2.00	Vase, 8"	15.00	30.00
Plate, 6½", off-center ring	1.50	5.00	Whiskey, 2", 1½ oz.	4.00	7.50

* Also found in pink. Priced as green.
** Red $17.50. Blue $27.50
*** Green $55.00

Please refer to Foreword for pricing information

ROCK CRYSTAL, "EARLY AMERICAN ROCK CRYSTAL" McKEE GLASS COMPANY,
1920's and 1930's in colors

Colors: Four shades of green, aquamarine, vaseline, yellow, amber, pink and frosted pink, red slag, dark red, red, amberina red, crystal, frosted crystal, crystal with goofus decoration, crystal with gold decoration, amethyst, milk glass, blue frosted or "Jap" blue and cobalt blue.

Collecting Rock Crystal (as we have for seventeen years) continues to be a challenge.One of the most unusual pieces found recently is the silver decorated red bowl in the bottom photograph. It actually is crystal, sprayed red with silver decoration. There is a partial original label showing an orchestra conductor and reading "MAESTRO Reg. U. S. Pat. Off." It photographs a lot better than it really looks!

Remember that there are two different size punch bowls. The base opening for our bowl is 5" across and stands 6¹⁄₁₆" tall. This base fits a punch bowl that is 4³⁄₁₆" across the bottom. The other style base has only a 4⅛" opening but also stands 6¹⁄₁₆" tall. The bowl to fit this base must be around 3½" across the bottom; but I am only guessing since we do not have a punch bowl to fit it. There should be ¾" difference to make the base fit. No one has sent in measurements for that punch bowl as yet.

Photographing the red again, we included pieces that were not shown in the last edition. We have found a center handled bowl which is 8½" across. That bowl must be a candy or nut dish since the handle would be in the way if using it for a serving bowl.

Red, crystal and amber sets can be assembled with patience. There are so many different pieces available that you need to determine how much you are willing to spend on a set by choosing what items to purchase. Instead of buying every available tumbler and stem, you can pick up a couple of each. That way even collectors with limited budgets can start crystal or amber. Red takes a deeper pocket!

Rock Crystal can be collected as a simple luncheon set, a dinner set or a complete service with many unusual serving and accessory pieces. In fact, many Rock Crystal pieces are purchased by collectors of other patterns to use as accessory items with their own patterns. Vases, cruets, candlesticks and a multitude of serving pieces are some of the items usually garnered for use.

	Crystal	All Other Colors	Red
* Bon bon, 7½" s.e.	17.50	27.50	47.50
Bowl, 4" s.e.	10.00	14.00	22.50
Bowl, 4½" s.e.	11.00	14.00	25.00
Bowl, 5" s.e.	13.50	18.00	37.50
** Bowl, 5" finger bowl with 7" plate, p.e.	18.00	27.50	55.00
Bowl, 7" pickle or spoon tray	17.50	27.50	52.50
Bowl, 7" salad s.e.	18.00	25.00	50.00
Bowl, 8" salad s.e.	22.00	25.00	65.00
Bowl, 8½" center handle			125.00
Bowl, 9" salad s.e.	21.00	25.00	65.00
Bowl, 10½" salad s.e.	22.00	28.00	70.00
Bowl, 11½" 2-part relish	28.00	35.00	60.00
Bowl, 12" oblong celery	22.50	32.50	55.00
*** Bowl, 12½" footed center bowl	47.50	80.00	225.00
Bowl, 12½", 5 part relish	40.00		
Bowl, 13" roll tray	28.00	45.00	95.00
Bowl, 14" 6-part relish	32.50	47.50	
Butter dish and cover	300.00		
Butter dish bottom	175.00		
Butter dish top	125.00		
**** Candelabra, 2-lite pr.	37.50	75.00	185.00
Candelabra, 3-lite pr.	45.00	85.00	225.00
Candlestick, flat, stemmed pr.	35.00	45.00	75.00
Candlestick, 5½" low pr.	30.00	47.50	125.00
Candlestick, 8" tall pr.	65.00	85.00	275.00
Candy and cover, round	37.50	65.00	145.00
Cake stand, 11", 2¾" high, footed	30.00	45.00	95.00

* s.e. McKee designation for scalloped edge
** p.e. McKee designation for plain edge
*** Red Slag-$350.00 Cobalt-$165.00
**** Cobalt-$185.00

Please refer to Foreword for pricing information

	Crystal	All Other Colors	Red
Comport, 7"	30.00	40.00	57.50
Creamer, flat s.e.	32.50		
Creamer, 9 oz. footed	17.50	28.00	57.50
Cruet and stopper, 6 oz. oil	75.00		
Cup, 7 oz.	15.00	25.00	60.00
Goblet, 7½ oz., 8 oz. low footed	14.00	24.00	50.00
Goblet, 11 oz. low footed iced tea	17.50	26.00	60.00
Jelly, 5" footed s.e.	15.00	25.00	42.50
Lamp, electric	150.00	250.00	500.00
Parfait, 3½ oz. low footed	15.00	35.00	65.00
Pitcher, qt. s.e.	150.00	200.00	
Pitcher, ½ gal., 7½" high	95.00	175.00	
Pitcher, 9" large covered	150.00	275.00	600.00
Pitcher, fancy tankard	150.00	450.00	750.00
Plate, 6" bread and butter s.e.	5.00	8.50	15.00
Plate, 7½" p.e. & s.e.	7.50	11.00	19.00
Plate, 8½" p.e. & s.e.	8.50	11.50	27.50
Plate, 9" s.e.	15.00	20.00	50.00
Plate, 10½" s.e.	15.00	20.00	45.00
Plate, 10½" dinner s.e. (large center design)	45.00	65.00	150.00
Plate, 11½" s.e.	16.00	22.00	50.00
Punch bowl and stand, 14" (2 styles)	375.00		
Punch bowl stand only (2 styles)	125.00		
Salt and pepper (2 styles) pr.	67.50	110.00	
Salt dip	32.50		
Sandwich server, center-handled	24.00	37.50	90.00
Saucer	6.50	7.50	17.50
Sherbet or egg, 3½ oz. footed	15.00	22.00	55.00
Spooner	35.00		
Stemware, 1 oz. footed cordial	17.50	37.50	55.00
Stemware, 2 oz. wine	17.00	25.00	47.50
Stemware, 3 oz. wine	17.00	27.50	47.50
Stemware, 3½ oz. footed cocktail	14.00	19.00	32.50
Stemware, 6 oz. footed champagne	15.00	20.00	30.00
Stemware, 8 oz. large footed goblet	15.00	25.00	50.00
Sundae, 6 oz. low footed	10.00	17.50	30.00
Sugar, 10 oz. open	14.00	20.00	35.00
Sugar, lid	27.50	40.00	75.00
Syrup with lid	125.00		
Tray, 5⅜" x 7⅜", ⅞" high	55.00		
Tumbler, 2½ oz. whiskey	15.00	20.00	50.00
Tumbler, 5 oz. juice	15.00	23.00	50.00
Tumbler, 5 oz. old fashioned	15.00	23.00	50.00
Tumbler, 9 oz. concave or straight	17.50	25.00	45.00
Tumbler, 12 oz. concave or straight	22.00	33.00	60.00
Vase, cornucopia	57.50	78.00	
Vase, 11" footed	45.00	85.00	135.00

ROSE CAMEO BELMONT TUMBLER COMPANY, 1931

Color: Green.

There is no confirmation as to what company made this pattern. Belmont Tumbler Company had a 1931 patent on Rose Cameo, but glass shards of Rose Cameo have been found at the factory site of Hazel Atlas. Maybe time will unravel this mystery. Of course, a yellow Cloverleaf shaker was dug up at the site of Akro Agate's factory in Clarksburg, West Virginia; and we know that Akro had nothing to do with making Cloverleaf. (Did you know some glass collectors dabble in archaeology in pursuit of glass?)

The straight sided bowl has been set upright to show the different shape from the cereal. It was set on a plate stand last time and confused some readers who thought it was small plate.

Rose Cameo is not confusing new collectors as it once did. Cameo, with its dancing girl, and this cameo encircled rose were often mixed up in earlier times.

Remember that there are two styles of tumblers. The difference in these is noted by the flaring of the rims. One does not flare.

	Green
Bowl, 4½" berry	7.50
Bowl, 5" cereal	10.00
Bowl, 6" straight sides	15.00
Plate, 7" salad	7.50
Sherbet	9.50
Tumbler, 5" footed (2 styles)	15.00

ROSEMARY, "DUTCH ROSE" FEDERAL GLASS COMPANY 1935-1937

Colors: Amber, green, pink; some iridized.

You can read the story of Rosemary's transformation from Federal's Mayfair pattern on page 106. Needless to say, Rosemary's existence came about inadvertently because of another glass company's action.

Rosemary cereal bowls, cream soups, grill plates and tumblers are the pieces seldom seen in all colors. I might add for new collectors that grill plates are the divided plates usually associated with diners at the time. Food was kept from running together by those divisions. These are especially tough to find in pink. Pink is the most difficult set to put together with amber being the easiest. However, a full complement of amber cereals, cream soups, tumblers and grill plates will take you some time to find.

No new reports of iridescent or hand decorated Rosemary has been made in the last few years. From reports in the past there are a few of these to be found.

Note that the sugar has no handles and is often mislabelled as a sherbet. There is no sherbet known in Rosemary!

You will find Rosemary an intriguing pattern whether you are a beginning collector or a collector looking for a new set to challenge your collecting abilities.

	Amber	Green	Pink
Bowl, 5" berry	5.00	7.00	9.00
Bowl, 5" cream soup	12.50	17.50	20.00
Bowl, 6" cereal	22.50	25.00	30.00
Bowl, 10" oval vegetable	12.50	24.00	25.00
Creamer, footed	7.50	11.00	14.00
Cup	5.00	8.00	8.50
Plate, 6¾" salad	5.00	7.50	7.50
Plate, dinner	8.50	12.00	14.00
Plate, grill	7.00	12.00	17.50
Platter, 12" oval	13.00	18.00	25.00
Saucer	3.00	3.50	4.00
Sugar, footed	7.50	11.00	15.00
Tumbler, 4¼", 9 oz.	25.00	27.50	40.00

Please refer to Foreword for pricing information

ROULETTE, "MANY WINDOWS" HOCKING GLASS COMPANY, 1935-1939

Colors: Green, pink and crystal.

Roulette has plenty of green basic pieces: cups, saucers, sherbets and luncheon plates. The sandwich plate, pitcher and fruit bowl are available. After that, you will spend a lot of time looking for the six different tumblers! Juice tumblers and the old fashioned are the most elusive of all.

Pink is found only as a pitcher and tumblers. All five sizes of pink flat tumblers are pictured but I still am missing a green juice. Pink tumblers are easier to find than green, but I have never seen a pink footed tumbler.

Crystal tumbler and pitcher sets are found infrequently, and some are decorated with colored stripes. In fact, this colored stripe effect makes an "Art Deco" look which is now catching on with collectors.

The name, "Many Windows" was given this pattern before Roulette was found to be the real pattern name. I assume that was from the windowed effect the design makes as it encircles each piece.

	Crystal	Pink, Green
Bowl, 9" fruit	9.00	12.50
Cup	35.00	5.00
Pitcher, 8", 65 oz.	22.50	30.00
Plate, 6" sherbet	3.00	3.50
Plate, 8½" luncheon	4.50	5.00
Plate, 12" sandwich	10.00	10.00
Saucer	1.25	2.50
Sherbet	3.00	5.00
Tumbler, 3¼", 5 oz. juice	6.50	18.00
Tumbler, 3¼", 7½ oz. old fashioned	22.50	35.00
Tumbler, 4⅛", 9 oz. water	12.00	17.00
Tumbler, 5⅛", 12 oz. iced tea	15.00	20.00
Tumbler, 5½", 10 oz. footed	13.00	22.00
Whiskey, 2½", 1½ oz.	6.50	12.50

"ROUND ROBIN" MANUFACTURER UNKNOWN, Probably early 1930's

Colors: Green, iridescent and crystal.

Round Robin is another small pattern whose manufacturer has remained anonymous. The domino tray is the unusual piece in this small pattern. Hocking's Cameo is the only other pattern to offer a sugar cube tray. It has only been found in green. For new readers, the domino tray held the creamer in the center ring with sugar cubes surrounding it. Sugar cubes were made by a famous sugar company, and the tray became synonymous with this name.

Sherbets are the hardest pieces to find outside the domino tray. These are particularly hard to find in green.

Crystal has to be made to have iridescent pieces. Crystal is sprayed with the iridescent color and put back into the furnace and baked. Obviously, not all the crystal was sprayed; and thus, some crystal Round Robin is found today.

Round Robin cups are footed. Not many mass produced Depression glass patterns had a footed cup.

	Green	Iridescent
Bowl, 4" berry	4.50	4.25
Cup, footed	4.50	5.00
Creamer, footed	6.50	6.00
Domino tray	30.00	
Plate, 6" sherbet	2.00	2.00
Plate, 8" luncheon	3.00	3.00
Plate, 12" sandwich	6.50	6.50
Saucer	1.50	1.50
Sherbet	4.50	5.00
Sugar	5.50	5.50

Please refer to Foreword for pricing information

ROXANA, HAZEL ATLAS GLASS COMPANY, 1932

Colors: Yellow, crystal and some white.

For years I have listed a saucer in Roxana; and no one has ever written to say that what I was listing as a saucer is actually a 5½" plate! I purchased a six piece setting last year and that plate was my surprise from the set. All seven known pieces are shown, but I also included a gold decorated plate in hope it would "show off" the pattern a little better in the photograph. This delicate pattern is difficult to capture on film since the light shade of yellow has a tendency to disappear under bright lights.

Roxana was only listed in Hazel Atlas catalogues for one year. It is a rare pattern when compared to thousands of pieces made over the years in many other patterns. Unfortunately, there are so few pieces available that some collectors avoid it. The common denominator of many collectors of this pattern is the name. Only one Roxana I have met at shows did not collect it. At the time I autographed her book, she was just starting and had not selected a pattern. I have often wondered if I caused her to look for Roxana after talking to her about it.

Only the 4½" bowl has been found in white. The yellow 4½" bowl and tumblers are difficult to find, but that 5½" plate seems to be even harder.

	Yellow	White
Bowl, 4½" x 2⅜"	8.00	12.00
Bowl, 5" berry	6.00	
Bowl, 6" cereal	9.50	
Plate, 5½"	5.00	
Plate, 6" sherbet	4.00	
Sherbet, footed	6.00	
Tumbler, 4¼", 9 oz.	14.00	

ROYAL RUBY ANCHOR HOCKING GLASS COMPANY, 1938-1940

Colors: Ruby red.

Royal Ruby was introduced in 1938 with Anchor Hocking fashioning the ware from many of their existing patterns. I have tried to include all pieces introduced before 1940 in my list, but I am sure there will be others added as additional information appears. Pieces of Royal Ruby made after 1940 are included in my book *Collectible Glassware from the 40's, 50's, 60's...*

The two catalogue pages shown on pages 163 and 164 are from one of Anchor Hocking's first catalogues after the introduction of Royal Ruby. Remember that experimental pieces of Royal Ruby have been found in many of Hocking's lines including Colonial and Miss America. There are others, but my point is to show regular issued lines.

	Royal Ruby		Royal Ruby
Bonbon, 6½"	8.00	Creamer, ftd.	8.50
Bowl, 3¾" berry (Old Cafe)	4.50	Cup (Coronation)	5.00
Bowl, 4½", handled (Coronation)	6.00	Cup (Old Cafe)	7.00
Bowl, 4⅞", smooth (Sandwich)	12.00	Cup, round	4.50
Bowl, 5¼" heart-shaped, 1-handled (Oys & Prl)	8.50	Goblet, ball stem	9.00
Bowl, 5¼", scalloped (Sandwich)	18.00	Jewel box, 4¼", crys. w/Ruby cov.	9.50
Bowl, 5½" cereal (Old Cafe)	9.00	Lamp (Old Cafe)	22.00
Bowl, 5½", 1-handled (Oys & Prl)	11.00	Marmalade, 5⅛", crys. w/Ruby cov.	6.50
Bowl, 6½" deep-handled (Oys & Prl)	17.50	Plate, 8½", luncheon (Coronation)	7.00
Bowl, 6½", handled (Coronation)	10.00	Plate, 9⅛", dinner, round	9.00
Bowl, 6½", scalloped (Sandwich)	25.00	Plate, 13½" sandwich (Oys & Prl)	35.00
Bowl, 8", handled (Coronation)	14.00	Puff box, 4⅝", crys. w/Ruby cov.	8.00
Bowl, 8", scalloped (Sandwich)	35.00	Relish tray insert (Manhattan)	3.50
Bowl, 9", closed handles (Old Cafe)	12.50	Saucer, round	1.50
Bowl, 10½" deep fruit (Oys & Prl)	40.00	Sherbet, low footed (Old Cafe)	9.00
Candle holder, 3½" pr. (Oys & Prl)	40.00	Sugar, ftd.	6.50
Candle holder, 4½" pr. (Queen Mary)	30.00	Sugar, lid	9.00
Candy dish, 8" mint, low (Old Cafe)	10.00	Tray, 6" x 4½"	10.00
Candy jar, 5½", crys. w/Ruby cov. (Old Cafe)	12.50	Tumbler, 3" juice (Old Cafe)	7.50
Cigarette box/card holder, 6⅛" x 4" crys.		Tumbler, 4" water (Old Cafe)	15.00
w/Ruby top	50.00	Vase, 7¼" (Old Cafe)	15.00
		Vase, 9", two styles	15.00

Please refer to Foreword for pricing information

ARE .... CRYSTAL, ROSE and "ROYAL RUBY"

THE BUY OF THE YEAR

Hurricane Lamps have been on the market at prices ranging from 25c each to as high as $2.00 or $3.00. Even at those prices they have struck the public's fancy. Now we are offering a Hurricane Lamp, outstanding in design, that retails in the popular price bracket—**FOR THE FIRST TIME.**

1000A—7" Hurricane Lamp—Complete

4 doz. ctn.—35 lbs.

Packed bulk in 2 cartons—Chimneys in 1 carton, bases in another.

5" Handled Jelly
A866—Ruby
4 doz. ctn.—23 lbs.

5¼" Fancy Bowl
A1486—Ruby
4 doz. ctn.—33 lbs.

6"x4½" Tray
A577—Ruby
4 doz. ctn.—32 lbs.

6½" Bonbon
A573—Ruby
4 doz. ctn.—32 lbs.

Sugar and Creamer
A1753—Sugar—Ruby
2 doz. ctn.—13 lbs.
A1754—Creamer—Ruby
2 doz. ctn.—13 lbs.

6½" Handled Bowl
A4476—Ruby
4 doz. ctn.—33 lbs.

8" Footed Mint Tray
A977—Ruby
4 doz. ctn.—40 lbs.

E522—4⅝" Crystal Puff Box with Ruby Cover
2 doz. ctn.—23 lbs.

E599—4¼" Crystal Jewel Box with Ruby Cover
2 doz. ctn.—29 lbs.

E514—5⅛"x3⅝" Crystal Marmalade Jar with Ruby Cover
2 doz. ctn.—22 lbs.

E775—5½" Crystal Candy Jar with Ruby Cover
2 doz. ctn.—30 lbs.

FLOWER VASES

4¾" Vase
5010—Crystal
4 doz. ctn.—30 lbs.

7" Vase
1942—Crystal
2 doz. ctn.—43 lbs.

8¾" Vase
R597—Rose
1 doz. ctn.—28 lbs.

9" Vase
A53—Royal Ruby
2 doz. ctn.—36 lbs.

CONSOLE SETS
(Candle Holders and Console Bowls and Plates)

PROMOTE CONSOLE SETS
Display Sets but price and sell both sets and individual pieces.

IN "ROYAL RUBY"
A881—3½" Candle Holder
   2 doz. ctn.—14 lbs.
A889—10½" Console Bowl
   1 doz. ctn.—30 lbs.
A890—13½" Console Plate
   1 doz. ctn.—28 lbs.

IN "POLISHED CRYSTAL"
881—3½" Candle Holder
   2 doz. ctn.—14 lbs.
889—10½" Console Bowl
   1 doz. ctn.—30 lbs.
890—13½" Sandwich Plate
   1 doz. ctn.—29 lbs.

7-Pc. Dessert Set

BULK PACKED
IN "ROYAL RUBY" GLASS

A4400/8—7-Piece Set

Bulk Packed:

   1 Ctn., 1 doz. A4478—8" Bowl
      (Weight 16 lbs.)

   1 Ctn., 6 doz. A4474—4½" Dessert
      (Weight 26 lbs.)

   Minimum 12 Sets in 2 cartons—42 lbs.

ROYAL LACE HAZEL ATLAS GLASS COMPANY, 1934-1941

Colors: Cobalt blue, crystal, green, pink; some amethyst.

Royal Lace is one of the shining stars of Depression glass. I wish I could find another collection for sale! I hope you enjoy this expanded selection of six photographs of Royal Lace. It may be a long time before I find so much again.

There are five different pitchers made in Royal Lace: 1) 48 oz. straight side; 2) 64 oz., 8", no ice lip; 3) 68 oz., 8", w/ice lip; 4) 86 oz., 8", no ice lip; 5) 96 oz., 8½", w/ice lip. The ten ounce difference in the last two listed above is caused by the spout on the pitcher without lip dipping below the top edge of the pitcher. This causes the liquid to run out before you get to the top.

Crystal and pink pitchers can be found in all five styles. Green can only be found in four styles. (There is no 68 oz. with ice lip in green). There are four styles found in blue. I had to change that statement from three last time since several 68 oz. pitchers with ice lip came on the market! There have been no blue 86 oz. without ice lip found.

More water tumblers (9 oz.) without panels are found than with the panel. Most collectors prefer the plain style to match their other tumblers.

Over the years there has been some confusion over the cobalt blue straight side and rolled edge console bowls because of the vast price difference. Showing all three bowls eliminated that problem! The straight edge bowl (which is commonly found) is in the center of the top picture. In the bottom picture the ruffled edge bowl is on the left and the rolled edge is on the right behind the creamer and sugar. A candlestick to match each bowl is also shown.

The straight edge candlestick, behind and to the right of the cup in the top photograph, can be found without the candle holder in the center. This is called a nut cup by collectors, probably from Fostoria's nut cups made on purpose from candle holders. This Royal Lace nut cup may have been a manufacturing mistake by Hazel Atlas. In any case, these are in demand by collectors who have large sets and did not know about this piece until recently! You can see pink, green and blue nut cups pictured in my book *Very Rare Glassware of the Depression Years, Second Series*.

The 4⅞",10 oz. tumblers are still the most difficult tumbler to find, but iced tea and juice tumblers are also drying up. This is true for all colors. It would be even worse if all collectors bought four sizes of tumblers! Many only purchase water tumblers and the straight sided pitcher. Even though so many of this style pitcher and water tumblers were made, demand still continues to drive up the price!

Collectors prefer all glass sherbets to the ones found in metal holders, which makes for higher prices on them. Be sure to check the inside rims for mould roughness and nicks. That inner rim is why mint condition pieces cost more. Even stacking bowls and plates will cause damage to these rims if not carefully done. That is why you see so many dealers placing paper plates between their merchandise. A mint piece can rapidly deteriorate from careless handling of the "lid bangers" as they are known in the business. Sunday afternoons at many shows sometimes seem to be a contest of shoppers seeing who can lift the most lids without buying a piece of glass. Respect the glass! If your bifocals cause distance discrepancies as mine do, don't lift lids and bang them back down unless you're examining the piece with the clear thought of buying it. Dealers will probably stand up and applaud when they read that.

	Crystal	Pink	Green	Blue
Bowl, 4¾" cream soup	9.50	16.00	25.00	28.00
Bowl, 5" berry	12.00	22.00	25.00	38.00
Bowl, 10" round berry	15.00	22.00	25.00	50.00
Bowl, 10", 3-legged straight edge	15.00	25.00	35.00	50.00
Bowl, 10", 3-legged rolled edge	125.00	35.00	65.00	255.00
Bowl, 10", 3-legged ruffled edge	22.50	35.00	55.00	350.00
Bowl, 11" oval vegetable	18.00	22.00	25.00	45.00
Butter dish and cover	60.00	130.00	250.00	475.00
Butter dish bottom	40.00	85.00	165.00	320.00
Butter dish top	25.00	45.00	85.00	155.00
Candlestick, straight edge pr.	25.00	35.00	55.00	90.00
Candlestick, rolled edge pr.	40.00	45.00	60.00	140.00
Candlestick ruffled edge pr.	25.00	45.00	55.00	155.00
Cookie jar and cover	27.50	42.00	65.00	295.00
Cream, footed	10.00	15.00	20.00	40.00
Cup	6.00	11.00	18.00	26.00
Nut bowl	85.00	175.00	165.00	350.00
Pitcher, 48 oz., straight sides	35.00	46.00	85.00	95.00

	Crystal	Pink	Green	Blue
Pitcher, 64 oz., 8", w/o/l	40.00	60.00	95.00	135.00
Pitcher, 8", 68 oz., w/lip	45.00	55.00		200.00
Pitcher, 8", 86 oz., w/o/l	45.00	65.00	110.00	
Pitcher, 8½", 96 oz., w/lip	50.00	70.00	120.00	190.00
Plate, 6", sherbet	3.00	6.00	8.00	12.00
Plate, 8½" luncheon	7.00	11.00	12.00	30.00
Plate, 9⅞" dinner	11.00	16.00	20.00	32.00
Plate, 9" grill	8.50	12.00	20.00	30.00
Platter, 13" oval	15.00	22.00	30.00	47.00
Salt and pepper, pr.	37.50	50.00	110.00	225.00
Saucer	3.00	5.00	7.00	9.50
Sherbet, footed	8.50	14.00	20.00	38.00
* Sherbet in metal holder	3.50			25.00
Sugar	8.00	11.00	18.00	25.00
Sugar lid	14.00	30.00	35.00	125.00
Tumbler, 3½", 5 oz.	13.00	17.00	25.00	38.50
Tumbler, 4⅛", 9 oz.	9.50	14.00	25.00	35.00
Tumbler, 4⅞", 10 oz.	18.00	35.00	38.00	68.00
Tumbler, 5⅜", 12 oz.	18.00	35.00	38.00	60.00
** Toddy or cider set: includes cookie jar metal lid, metal tray, 8 roly-poly cups and ladle				145.00

* Amethyst $35.00   **Amethyst $125.00

"S" PATTERN, "STIPPLED ROSE BAND" MacBETH-EVANS GLASS COMPANY, 1930-1933

Colors: Crystal; crystal w/trims of silver, blue, green, amber; pink; some amber, green, fired-on red, Monax, and light yellow.

"S" Pattern collectors continue to buy more of the platinum trimmed and pastel banded crystal than they do the plain crystal. The only problem with that is there is not enough of the decorated to meet the demand! If you mix the platinum trimmed with plain crystal there is a better chance to complete a set. Collectors have never yet found a dinner plate in crystal.

Color variances in the amber make some of it more yellow than amber. As in other yellow Depression Glass patterns, matching colors consistently is a problem. The differences are almost as distinct as they are in Hocking's Princess; however amber "S" Pattern collectors do have a dinner plate to use!

A pink or green pitcher and tumbler set still turns up occasionally, but the demand for these has dwindled considerably. Years ago, there were a large group of pitcher collectors; rare pitchers sold fast. Today, there are few pitcher collectors and most of these collectors already own the hard to find pitchers. A rare piece of glass has to have someone who wishes to own it before it will sell. No matter how rare an item is, it takes demand to make it sell. It is simple economics; no demand means no sale, and rarity be hanged!

The fired-on red items and the red items that are like red American Sweetheart both fit the rare category; but like the pink and green pitchers, there are few collectors who care.

	Crystal	Yellow, Amber, Crystal With Trims		Crystal	Yellow, Amber, Crystal With Trims
* Bowl, 5½" cereal	3.50	4.50	Plate, grill	6.00	7.50
Bowl, 8½" large berry	8.50	13.50	Plate, 11¾" heavy cake	35.00	38.00
* Creamer, thick or thin	5.00	6.00	*** Plate, 13" heavy cake	52.50	62.50
* Cup, thick or thin	3.00	4.00	Saucer	1.50	2.00
Pitcher, 80 oz. (like "Dogwood")			Sherbet, low footed	4.00	6.50
(green or pink 500.00)	45.00	90.00	* Sugar, thick and thin	4.50	6.00
Pitcher, 80 oz. (like "American			Tumbler, 3½", 5 oz.	3.50	5.00
Sweetheart")	55.00		Tumbler, 4", 9 oz. (green or		
Plate, 6" sherbet (Monax 8.00)	2.00	2.50	pink 50.00)	4.00	6.00
** Plate, 8¼" luncheon	4.00	4.50	Tumbler, 4¾, 10 oz.	4.00	7.00
Plate, 9¼" dinner		6.50	Tumbler, 5", 12 oz.	8.00	12.00

* Fired-on red items will run approximately twice price of amber   **Red-$40.00; Monax-$10.00   ***Amber-$77.50

SANDWICH INDIANA GLASS COMPANY, 1920's-1980's

Colors: Crystal late 1920's-today; teal blue 1950's-1980's; milk white mid 1950's; amber late 1920's-1980's; red 1933,1969-early 1970's; Smokey Blue 1976-1977; pink, green 1920's-early 1930's.

Collecting Indiana's Sandwich pattern thrills some people. Most dealers and many collectors avoid it like the plague because of the company's total disregard of protecting old Indiana patterns by continually reissuing them. The pink and green shown here is from the Depression era, but Indiana has made a darker green in recent years.

I can vouch for six items in red Sandwich dating from 1933, i.e. cups, saucers, luncheon plates, water goblets, creamers and sugars. However, in 1969, Tiara Home Products produced red pitchers, 9 oz. goblets, cups, saucers, wines, wine decanters, 13" serving trays, creamers, sugars and salad and dinner plates. Today, there is no difference in pricing the red unless you have some red marked 1933 Chicago World's Fair. Crystal was made as early as the late 1920's but few people can tell it apart from the Tiara issues of the last 20 years. You, alone, will have to decide how seriously you want to collect Indiana's Sandwich. Those decanter stoppers are hard to find as evidenced by their being absent in the photograph.

	Amber Crystal	Teal Blue	Red	Pink/Green
Ash trays(club, spade, heart, diamond shapes, ea.)	3.00			
Basket, 10" high	30.00			
Bowl, 4¼" berry	3.00			
Bowl, 6"	3.50			
Bowl, 6", hexagonal	4.50	12.50		
Bowl, 8½"	10.00			
Bowl, 9" console	15.00			35.00
Bowl, 11½" console	18.00			45.00
Butter dish and cover, domed	20.00	*150.00		
Butter dish bottom	5.00	40.00		
Butter dish top	15.00	110.00		
Candlesticks, 3½" pr.	15.00			40.00
Candlesticks 7" pr.	22.50			
Creamer	8.50		40.00	
Celery, 10½"	15.00			
Creamer and sugar on diamond shaped tray	15.00	30.00		
Cruet, 6½ oz. and stopper	22.50	130.00		150.00
Cup	3.00	7.50	25.00	
Decanter and stopper	20.00		75.00	100.00
Goblet, 9 oz.	12.50		40.00	
Mayonnaise, ftd.	12.50			27.50
Pitcher, 68 oz.	20.00		125.00	
Plate, 6" sherbet	2.50	6.00		
Plate, 7" bread and butter	3.50			
Plate, 8" oval, indent for cup	5.00	10.00		
Plate, 8⅜" luncheon	4.50			17.50
Plate, 10½" dinner	7.50			17.50
Plate, 13" sandwich	12.50	22.50	32.50	22.50
Puff box	15.00			
Salt and pepper pr.	15.00			
Sandwich server, center	17.50		45.00	27.50
Saucer	2.00	4.50	5.00	
Sherbet, 3¼"	5.00	10.00		
Sugar, large	8.50		40.00	
Sugar lid for large size	12.50			
Tumbler, 3 oz. footed cocktail	7.00			
Tumbler, 8 oz. footed water	8.50			
Tumbler, 12 oz. footed iced tea	9.50			
Wine, 3", 4 oz.	5.50		12.50	22.50

*Beware recent vintage sell $20.00

SHARON, "CABBAGE ROSE" FEDERAL GLASS COMPANY, 1935-1939

Colors: Pink, green, amber; some crystal. *(See Reproduction Section)*

Sharon is once again being briskly collected! Sharon is another Depression pattern that has suffered loss of collectors' interest in the past because of many reproductions. Due to education of the differences between old and new, Sharon has new life! It was not that people stopped collecting as much as new collectors did not start. Without new collectors, basic pieces stop selling and dealers stop buying them. It became a vicious cycle with only the rarely found and under priced pieces selling. Now every dealer who stopped buying, is crying that he can't find enough Sharon to meet today's demand!

This rising market is a great sign, unless you are an author trying to keep up with it! It is a good problem except that I also need to be out buying glass for my shop instead of just writing about it!

I was asked recently if the pink cheese dish would be the first piece of Sharon to break the $1,000.00 mark. Since the cheese dish just reached the $700.00 plateau, it will not come close. About 15 years ago, the Sharon oil lamp base (pictured below) broke that mark by a big margin. No others have ever been found!

Besides the cheese dish, thick iced teas and jam dishes are the only other pink pieces difficult to locate. The jam dish is like the butter bottom, but it has no indentation for the top. It differs from the 2" deep soup bowl by standing only 1½" tall. I stopped at an Antique Mall in Tennessee last week as I was driving back from Florida. I was amazed to see three of the pink 2" deep soup bowls labelled "Depression dish - $15.00." I forced myself to buy them without much fanfare. People still do not recognize the most basic patterns and you can still find a bargain!

A cheese dish can be seen in the amber picture next to the butter. The butter is pictured on the outside of the cheese. Notice how the butter is much taller, although the butter base is only 1½" tall. The tops are the same; but the cheese bottom is like a salad plate with a raised band on top of it. The lid fits inside this raised band! Amber cheese dishes can be found without too much searching. There is no cheese dish in the original green.

Other hard to find green pieces include the pitchers and candy dish. Surprisingly enough, the green pitcher without ice lip is rarer than the one with an ice lip. Both the amber and green pitchers photographed have ice lips. This lip was supposed to keep the ice in the pitcher when pouring.

You can easily see the difference in the thick and thin tumblers in either picture! The heavy tumblers are easier to find in green; and the price reflects that. In amber, as in pink, the heavy iced teas are more rarely seen.

Amber footed teas are the most scarce of all Sharon tumblers. Fewer collectors of amber Sharon make the true price of these tumblers a mystery. Many collectors just do without them at today's prices; that attitude may make it hard for prices to go much higher!

	Amber	Pink	Green
Bowl, 5" berry	7.50	9.00	11.00
Bowl, 5" cream soup	22.50	35.00	40.00
Bowl, 6" cereal	15.00	18.00	20.00
Bowl, 7½" flat soup, 2" deep	40.00	35.00	
Bowl, 8½" large berry	5.00	20.00	25.00
Bowl, 9½" oval vegetable	14.00	18.00	22.00
Bowl, 10½" fruit	20.00	28.00	28.00
Butter dish and cover	45.00	45.00	75.00
Butter dish bottom	22.50	22.50	32.50
Butter dish top	22.50	22.50	42.50
* Cake plate, 11½" footed	20.00	30.00	50.00
Candy jar and cover	40.00	35.00	150.00
Cheese dish and cover	175.00	725.00	
Creamer, footed	12.00	15.00	18.00
Cup	8.50	11.50	15.00
Jam dish, 7½"	30.00	115.00	35.00
Pitcher, 80 oz. with ice lip	120.00	115.00	325.00
Pitcher, 80 oz. without ice lip	115.00	105.00	350.00
Plate, 6" bread and butter	4.00	5.00	6.00
** Plate, 7½" salad	12.00	18.00	18.00
Plate, 9½" dinner	10.00	14.00	15.00
Platter, 12½" oval	13.00	16.00	20.00
Salt and pepper, pr.	37.50	42.50	60.00
Saucer	5.00	7.50	7.50
Sherbet, footed	11.00	12.00	27.50
Sugar	8.00	10.00	11.00
Sugar lid	20.00	20.00	32.00
Tumbler, 4⅛", 9 oz. thick	23.00	27.00	55.00
Tumbler, 4⅛", 9 oz. thin	23.00	27.00	60.00
Tumbler, 5¼", 12 oz. thin	45.00	35.00	87.50
Tumbler, 5¼", 12 oz. thick	55.00	65.00	82.50
*** Tumbler, 6½", 15 oz. footed	85.00	37.50	

* Crystal $5.00
** Crystal $13.50
*** Crystal $15.00

"SHIPS" or "SAILBOAT" also known as "SPORTSMAN SERIES"

HAZEL ATLAS GLASS COMPANY, LATE 1930's

Color: Cobalt blue w/white, yellow and red decoration.

A "Ships" shot glass is shown in the top picture on page 175. It is the tiny (2¼", 2 oz.) tumbler in the front on the right. It is not the heavy bottomed tumbler shown on the left which holds 4 oz. and is 3¼" tall. I have letters from people who purchased the 4 oz. tumbler believing it to be a shot glass! You will notice there's a great difference in price between the actual 2 oz. shot and the 4 oz. tumbler!

The "Ships" decorated Moderntone is not abundant. Look for unworn white, not beige, decorations on these pieces. Prices are for mint pieces. Worn and discolored items should fetch much less if someone will even purchase them.

We have found one yellow "Ships" old fashioned tumbler that is not a discoloration. It really is "raincoat" yellow rather than white! Note the pieces with red "Ships" and even a crystal tumbler with a blue boat. You can expand this pattern to your heart's content!

Pictured below are other items in the "Sportsman Series." The "Polo" series sells well in our "horse country" of Kentucky. People who collect Dutch related paraphernalia enjoy the "Windmills." There are "Nursery Rhymes," dogs, fish and whatever sports interest you – skiing, boating, fishing, golfing, dancing, or horse riding; you can surely find a beverage set to your liking!

In the bottom photo on page 175, Cathy likes to refer to the cocktail shaker, ice tub and tumblers as "fancy ships." Also shown here are some of the accessory pieces that can go with this pattern that has its beginnings on the Moderntone blank. None of these are in the Hazel Atlas listing below; so I will put prices for these in parentheses as I mention them.

The round metal tray ($30.00) was bought years ago with a pitcher and tumbler set on it. These accessory items are fun to look for and you never know what will pop up. The square or round ash trays ($35.00) and the three sectional box ($125.00) on the left may be manufactured by the same company since the designs are very similar. I have seen that box priced as high as $225.00. The ash tray with the metal ship ($65.00) is more than likely Hazel Atlas. The smaller glass tray ($50.00), which has a tumbler with a sailor and matching anchor and rope design, and the larger glass tray ($75.00), which has a matching tumbler, are rarely seen. The crystal ash tray with light blue ship ($12.50) was a piece bought solely because it had a ship.

	Blue/White		Blue/White		Blue/White
Cup (Plain) "Moderntone"	8.50	Plate, 5⅞", bread & butter	17.50	Tumbler, 6 oz., roly poly	8.50
Cocktail mixer w/stirrer	22.50	Plate, 8", salad	19.00	Tumbler, 8 oz., 3⅜", old fashion	14.00
Cocktail shaker	27.50	Plate, 9", dinner	25.00	Tumbler, 9 oz., 3¾", straight water	12.00
Ice bowl	27.50	Saucer	14.00	Tumbler, 9 oz., 4⅝", water	9.50
Pitcher w/o lip, 82 oz.	45.00	Tumbler, 2 oz., 2¼" shot glass	105.00	Tumbler, 10½ oz., 4⅞", iced tea	12.00
Pitcher w/lip, 86 oz.	40.00	Tumbler, 5 oz., 3¾", juice	9.50	Tumbler, 12 oz., iced tea	18.00

SIERRA, "PINWHEEL" JEANNETTE GLASS COMPANY, 1931-1933

Colors: Green, pink and some ultramarine.

No saucer for the Sierra ultramarine cup has been seen! I do have a photograph of a cereal sent in by a reader. These were experimental or more would be turning up. Possibly they were made at the time that Doric and Pansy or Swirl was being made in that color.

Sierra pitchers, tumblers and oval vegetable bowls have disappeared in both pink and green. You could find these pieces in pink a few years ago with diligent looking, but finding them now is a major chore. I was able to round up all but the green tumbler for the photograph. Some avid Sierra collectors have said that finding the green oval vegetable is the most difficult task, but finding six or eight tumblers takes about the same amount of looking.

Sugar bowls are harder to find than the lids. It is the pointed edges on the sugar bowl which chip so easily that make this bowl so hard to find in mint condition. That is the one flaw in collecting any Sierra pieces. The points have to be inspected carefully. You can miss a "chigger bite" off one of these points very easily.

You need to look carefully at all pink Sierra butter dishes. You might run into the Adam/Sierra combination. Be sure to read about this under Adam.

Oft times the wrong cup is placed on Sierra saucers. You always have to be on your toes when you are buying! That cup, pitcher and tumblers all have smooth edges instead of the serrated of the other pieces. I imagine drinking or pouring out of serrated edges would make a 1930's version of the prankster's dribble glass.

	Pink	Green		Pink	Green
Bowl, 5½" cereal	9.50	11.00	Platter, 11" oval	32.50	37.50
Bowl, 8½" large berry	15.00	22.00	Salt and pepper, pr.	35.00	35.00
Bowl, 9¼" oval vegetable	35.00	80.00	Saucer	4.50	6.00
Butter dish and cover	55.00	60.00	Serving tray, 10¼", 2 handles	12.50	15.00
Creamer	15.00	18.00	Sugar	15.00	20.00
Cup	9.50	12.00	Sugar cover	12.00	12.00
Pitcher, 6½", 32 oz.	57.50	90.00	Tumbler, 4½", 9 oz. footed	37.50	60.00
Plate, 9" dinner	14.00	16.00			

SPIRAL HOCKING GLASS COMPANY, 1928-1930

Colors: Green and pink.

I have always included a Twisted Optic piece in my Spiral pictures for comparison to the Spiral. Can you spot it this time? Remember that Spiral swirls go to the left or clockwise while Twisted Optic spirals go to the right or counterclockwise.

The problem spiral designed patterns give collectors occurs with the placement of the spirals on the piece. Inside or outside affects the left or right handed spiraling. It makes a difference in the way you look at it!

The footed tumbler pictured was omitted from the last listing. It is 5⅞" tall.

Green Spiral is the color normally found, but there is some pink available. Maybe that will tell you that the blue mayonnaise is the Twisted Optic example in this picture since Spiral is not found in blue.

The Spiral center-handled server has a solid handle and the Twisted Optic center-handled server has an open handle if you have trouble identifying these.

The Spiral platter is not commonly found. Note that it has closed or tabbed handles as does Cameo, also made by Hocking. A small luncheon set can be purchased rather economically.

	Green		Green
Bowl, 4¾" berry	4.50	Preserve and cover	27.50
Bowl, 7" mixing	8.00	Salt and pepper, pr.	27.50
Bowl, 8" large berry	11.00	Sandwich server, center handle	20.00
Creamer, flat or footed	7.00	Saucer	1.50
Cup	4.50	Sherbet	3.50
Ice or butter tub	22.50	Sugar, flat or footed	7.00
Pitcher, 7⅝", 58 oz.	27.50	Tumbler, 3", 5 oz. juice	4.00
Plate, 6" sherbet	1.50	Tumbler, 5", 9 oz. water	7.00
Plate, 8" luncheon	3.00	Tumbler, 5⅞" footed	10.00
Platter 12"	20.00		

Please refer to Foreword for pricing information

STARLIGHT HAZEL ATLAS GLASS COMPANY, 1938-1940

Colors: Crystal, pink; some white, cobalt.

Crystal Starlight collectors still have problems finding sherbets, cereals and the large salad bowls. The 5½" cereal is handled and measures 6" including the handles. I ought to mention that the 13" sandwich plate is also elusive. Many collectors use the salad bowl with sandwich plate as a salad set.

There is so little pink and cobalt found that few collectors pay any attention to it. Bowls are all that are found in these colors.

Generally speaking, Starlight is another one of the smaller sets that can be collected without loans having to be obtained. The only difficulty comes in finding it. The pink and blue bowls make nice accessory pieces that can be used alongside the crystal. There is not enough white found to make a set of it practical. If you love a challenge, you would be one of the few folks looking for the white.

Sometimes the pink, closed-handled bowl can be found in a metal holder. This metal holder encircles the base and extends up and over the handles in a swirled fashion which holds a salad spoon and fork. Finding these with a sterling fork and spoon is a bonus!

I have often wondered why Starlight shakers are found with a one-holed shaker top. I have now found out! It was a specially designed top made to keep the salt "moisture proof." Shakers with these tops are often found in Florida and other southern areas where the humid air has caused shaker holes to clog. Did you realize we've only "shaken" salt since the turn of the century. Prior to that, you pinched it from salt dips.

	Crystal, White	Pink		Crystal, White	Pink
Bowl, 5½" cereal, closed handles	6.00	8.00	Plate, 9" dinner	6.00	
* Bowl, 8½", closed handles	6.00	13.00	Plate, 13" sandwich	11.00	13.00
Bowl, 11½" salad	16.00		Relish dish	12.00	
Bowl, 12", 2¾" deep	22.50		Salt and pepper, pr.	20.00	
Creamer, oval	4.50		Saucer	1.50	
Cup	3.50		Sherbet	11.00	
Plate, 6" bread and butter	2.50		Sugar, oval	4.00	
Plate, 8½" luncheon	3.00				

* Cobalt $30.00

STRAWBERRY U.S. GLASS COMPANY, Early 1930's

Colors: Pink, green, crystal; some iridized.

Strawberry and Cherryberry are now split into two separate patterns. See page 30 for the Cherryberry listing.

The iridescent Strawberry pitcher is quite rare! Carnival collectors cherish this iridescent pitcher more highly than Depression glass collectors. The one main concern is that it have full vivid color and not fade out toward the bottom. You will see few pitchers in your travels.

Crystal is priced the same as iridescent because it is so rare. There are few crystal Strawberry collectors; that is good since so little of it is found! Strawberry sugar covers are another item that is missing from most collections as is the 2" deep bowl. Some collectors have mistakenly called the sugar with missing lid a spooner. It is a sugar bowl without handles which is most times seen in older glassware.

Strawberry is another of those U.S. Glass patterns that has very rough mould seams. This occurs on the tumblers, pitchers and even the plates. If mould roughness offends your collecting sensibilities, then this pattern is not for you.

Strawberry also has a plain butter dish bottom that is interchangeable with other U.S. Glass patterns. This is the pattern for which most other U.S. Glass pattern butter dishes were robbed to take the bottom for use with Strawberry tops. Strawberry butter dishes have always been coveted by collectors. Strawberry has no cup or saucer.

	Crystal, Iridescent	Pink, Green		Crystal, Iridescent	Pink, Green
Bowl, 4" berry	6.00	8.00	Olive dish, 5" one-handled	7.50	12.00
Bowl, 6¼", 2" deep	40.00	60.00	Pickle dish, 8¼" oval	7.50	12.00
Bowl, 6½" deep salad	13.00	16.00	Pitcher, 7¾"	150.00	130.00
Bowl, 7½" deep berry	14.00	18.00	Plate, 6" sherbet	4.50	6.50
Butter dish and cover	130.00	140.00	Plate, 7½" salad	8.00	12.00
Butter dish bottom	75.00	85.00	Sherbet	6.00	7.00
Butter dish top	55.00	55.00	Sugar, small open	11.00	15.00
Comport, 5¾"	12.00	18.00	Sugar large	20.00	30.00
Creamer, small	10.00	16.00	Sugar cover	35.00	45.00
Creamer, 4⅝" large	20.00	30.00	Tumbler, 3⅝", 8 oz.	17.50	25.00

SUNFLOWER JEANNETTE GLASS COMPANY, 1930's

Colors: Pink, green, some Delphite; some opaques.

Sunflower cake plates still are found in numbers to stagger the imagination. They were packed in twenty pound bags of flour for several years. Everyone bought flour in large quantities since home baking was necessary, then. This cake plate is the only commonly found green piece in Sunflower. One problem that occurs regularly with the green cake plate is that many are found in a deep dark green that does not match any other green pieces of Sunflower. A pink cake plate is shown against the back of the picture.

A 7" pink trivet is shown in the center of the photograph. Notice that the edges are slightly upturned and it is three inches smaller than the ever present cake plate. The trivet still remains the only difficult to find piece of Sunflower. Collector demand keeps prices increasing steadily. Green is found less often than pink; therefore, prices for green are outdistancing prices in pink. Both colors make nice sets.

Several collectors have told me that this pattern has a shortage of saucers, but more so in green than in pink. I do not see enough in my travels to agree or disagree with that observation. In any case, if you run into a stack of Sunflower saucers, be forewarned that they might be a good buy!

The ultramarine ash tray is the only piece found in that color. Opaque colors show up once in a while. A set in Delphite blue would be great; but that creamer is all I have found. I have heard of a cup in Delphite! I have always called the odd creamer color "mustard" and the sugar "mayonnaise" because my editing wife always marks out my goose and cow fertilizer remarks that perfectly describe these colors!

	Pink	Green		Pink	Green
* Ash Tray, 5", center design only	8.00	11.00	Saucer	6.00	8.00
Cake Plate, 10", 3 legs	12.00	12.00	Sugar (opaque 85.00)	14.00	16.00
** Creamer (opaque 85.00)	14.00	16.00	Tumbler, 4¾", 8 oz. footed	22.00	27.50
Cup (opaque 75.00)	9.00	11.00	Trivet, 7", 3 legs, turned up edge	255.00	265.00
Plate, 9" dinner	11.00	14.00			

* Found in ultramarine $25.00   **Delphite $75.00

SWANKY SWIGS 1930's-early 1940's

Swanky Swigs originally came with a Kraft cheese product in them. I have included those Swankys that were made in the 1930's and early 1940's in this book. There is some overlap; but all of the later made Swankys are now found in my book *Collectible Glassware from the 40's, 50's, 60's....*

Top Row	Band No.1		Red & Black	3⅜"	2.00-3.00
			Red & Blue	3⅜"	3.00-4.00
			Blue	3⅜"	3.50-5.00
	Band No.2		Red & Black	4¾"	4.00-5.00
			Red & Black	3⅜"	3.00-4.00
	Band No.3		Blue & White	3⅜"	3.00-4.00
	Circle & Dot:		Blue	4¾"	6.00-8.00
			Blue	3½"	5.00-6.00
			Red, Green	3½"	4.00-5.00
			Black	3½"	5.00-6.00
			Red	4¾"	6.00-8.00
	Dot		Black	4¾"	7.00-9.00
			Blue	3½"	5.00-6.00
2nd Row	Star:		Blue	4¾"	5.00-6.00
			Blue, Red, Green, Black	3½"	3.00-4.00
			Cobalt w/White Stars	4¾"	15.00-18.00
	Centennials:		W.Va. Cobalt	4¾"	20.00-22.00
			Texas Cobalt	4¾"	25.00-30.00
			Texas Blue, Black, Green	3½"	25.00-30.00
	Checkerboard		Blue, Red	3½"	22.50-25.00
3rd Row	Checkerboard		Green	3½"	25.00-27.50
	Sailboat		Blue	4½"	12.00-15.00
			Blue	3½"	10.00-12.00
			Red,Green	4½"	12.00-15.00
			Green, Lt. Green	3½"	10.00-15.00
	Tulip No.1		Blue, Red	4½"	12.50-15.00
			Blue, Red	3½"	3.00-4.00
4th Row	Tulip No.1		Green	4½"	12.50-15.00
			Green, Black	3½"	3.00-4.00
			Green w/Label	3½"	8.00-10.00
	*Tulip No.2		Red, Green, Black	3½"	20.00-25.00
	Carnival		Blue, Red	3½"	4.00-6.00
			Green, Yellow	3½"	4.00-6.00
	Tulip No. 3		Dk. Blue, Lt. Blue	3¾"	2.50-3.50

*West Coast lower price

SWIRL, "PETAL SWIRL" JEANNETTE GLASS COMPANY, 1937-1938

Colors: Ultramarine, pink, Delphite; some amber and "ice" blue.

A correction in my listings needs to be made. The cereal bowl only measures 5¼" and not 6¼". Some where between the eighth and ninth editions of my book, that bowl grew an inch. I have never figured out how a piece is listed properly for years and then suddenly it isn't!

Almost all pieces of Swirl can be found with two different edges. Some pieces have ruffled edges and some are plain. Pink comes mostly with plain edges while ultramarine comes with both. This makes a difference if you order merchandise by mail. It is your responsibility to specify what style you want if you place an order. Either style is acceptable to most collectors, but some will not mix styles in their collection. If you only want plain edged pieces, please tell the dealer before he ships your order. This is not a problem when you are shopping and see the merchandise.

Candy and butter dish bottoms are more abundant than tops in Swirl. Remember that before you buy only the bottom. I missed an ultramarine candy at the Webster Florida flea market last month for $7.00. The person buying it made the dealer guarantee that it was old. He liked the color and only had a ten dollar bill in his wallet. It was one time I wished a dish had been a little higher priced!

As with other patterns that come in ultramarine, there are green tinted pieces as well as the regular color. This green tint is hard to match, and most collectors avoid this shade. Because of this avoidance, many times you can buy the green tint at a super bargain price if you are willing to accept that shade.

Another ultramarine Swirl pitcher has been reported, but so far there has not been a pink one seen. I say, so far, because many collectors of Swirl combine this pattern with Jeannette's "Jennyware" kitchenware line which does have a pink pitcher in it! Some people have confused the two patterns because they are similar in style and made in the same colors. If you find mixing bowls, measuring cups or reamers, then you have crossed over into the kitchenware line and out of the Swirl dinnerware set. See *Kitchen Glassware of the Depression Years* for complete "Jennyware" listings.

Swirl can be found in several experimental colors. A small set can be collected in Delphite blue. Vegetable bowls (9") seem to be the primary experimental piece. Notice the amber and "ice" blue in the photo. I have seen the ice blue priced at $60.00, but I have never seen an amber priced since I bought this one years ago in Nashville. I had a report of one in crystal, but it was never confirmed. There are two styles of this bowl found. Notice how the ultramarine and pink bowls have a rimmed inside edge. Other 9" Swirl bowls can be found without this rimmed edge.

The pink coaster shown in the foreground is often found inside a small rubber tire. These were souvenir pieces distributed by tire companies. These small tires have become collectible advertising items. Those with the company name on the glass insert are more in demand; but those with a plain Swirl glass insert (such as this coaster) are collected if the miniature tire is embossed with the name of a tire company.

	Pink	Ultra-marine	Delphite		Pink	Ultra-marine	Delphite
Bowl, 5¼" cereal	8.50	12.50	11.00	Plate, 6½" sherbet	3.50	5.00	4.00
Bowl, 9" salad	12.50	20.00	25.00	Plate, 7¼"	6.00	10.00	
Bowl, 9" salad, rimmed	15.00	22.50		Plate, 8" salad	7.00	12.50	7.00
Bowl, 10" footed, closed				Plate, 9¼" dinner	10.00	13.00	10.00
handles	20.00	25.00		Plate, 10½"		25.00	15.00
Bowl, 10½" footed console	17.50	22.00		Plate, 12½" sandwich	10.00	22.00	
Butter dish	175.00	235.00		Platter, 12" oval			30.00
Butter dish bottom	30.00	35.00		Salt and pepper, pr.		37.50	
Butter dish top	145.00	200.00		Saucer	2.50	3.50	3.00
Candle holders, double				Sherbet, low footed	9.00	15.00	
branch pr.		37.50		Soup, tab handles (lug)	18.00	22.50	
Candle holders, single				Sugar, footed	9.50	12.50	9.00
branch pr.			100.00	Tray, 10½", two-handled			22.50
Candy dish, open, 3 legs	10.00	15.00		Tumbler, 4", 9 oz.	12.00	24.00	
Candy dish with cover	75.00	110.00		Tumbler, 4⅝", 9 oz.	15.00		
Coaster, 1" x 3¼"	7.50	10.00		Tumbler, 5⅛", 13 oz.	35.50	85.00	
Creamer, footed	4.50	12.50	9.50	Tumbler, 9 oz. footed	15.00	30.00	
Cup	6.00	12.50	8.00	Vase, 6½" footed, ruffled	14.50		
Pitcher, 48 oz. footed		1,500.00		Vase, 8½" footed, two styles		22.50	

Please refer to Foreword for pricing information

TEA ROOM INDIANA GLASS COMPANY, 1926-1931

Colors: Pink, green, amber and some crystal.

Tea Room collecting has slowed somewhat since two of the "big" collectors who helped dry up the short supply have both completed or slowed down in their collecting pursuits. When a few collectors call every major dealer in the country looking for particular pieces of any pattern no matter what the price, you had better believe some one will come up with those pieces!

There is supposed to be a club formed by Tea Room and Pyramid collectors. They have their own newsletter. You may be able to ascertain information about this on your own if you are interested. So far, I still haven't gotten copies; so I can't supply more information.

There are some problems with sugar and creamer measurements. These all measure close to 4". The footed listed as 3½" are actually 4" and the larger footed listed as 4½" are actually 4". Oh well, that really makes for fun when advertising sugar and creamer sets!

Green is collected more often than pink; and a few collectors are beginning to seek the crystal. Crystal pieces are bringing half the prices of the pink except for the commonly found 9½" ruffled vase and the pitcher (priced separately below).

For those who have had trouble distinguishing the two styles of banana splits, look at the picture of pink. The flat banana split is in front and the footed banana split is behind it. Both styles of banana splits are very desirable pieces of Tea Room to own in any color!

The small, green sugar with handles and cover in the front of the top picture has created some interesting comments. (There is also a pink one and matching creamer in lower photo.) This creamer and sugar are on the same mould shape as another Indiana pattern known as "Cracked Ice." These are not "Cracked Ice" since the design shows parallel lines just as on Tea Room. In any case, this creamer and sugar are great "look-alike" pieces if not the real thing.

Amber pitchers and tumblers continue to be found in the Atlanta area as do a few creamers and sugars. Some interesting lamps are showing up which used tumblers that had been frosted. The regular lamp (shown here in pink) is not as plentiful as it once was. It has been a while since I have seen one in green.

The flat sugar and the marmalade bottom are the same. The marmalade takes a notched lid; the sugar lid is not notched. Finding either of these is not an easy task! The mustard also comes with a plain or notched lid. Examples of mustards with notched lids are shown in pink and crystal.

As the name implies, Tea Room was intended to be used in the "tea rooms" and "ice cream" parlors of the day. That is why you find so many soda fountain type items in this pattern.

	Green	Pink		Green	Pink
Bowl, finger	45.00	35.00	Salt and pepper, pr.	50.00	45.00
Bowl, 7½" banana split, flat	77.50	72.00	* Saucer	25.00	25.00
Bowl, 7½" banana split, footed	65.00	55.00	Sherbet, low footed	20.00	18.00
Bowl, 8¼" celery	27.50	22.50	Sherbet, low flared edge	27.50	24.00
Bowl, 8¾" deep salad	75.00	60.00	Sherbet, tall footed	35.00	30.00
Bowl, 9½" oval vegetable	60.00	50.00	Sugar w/lid, 3"	100.00	95.00
Candlestick, low, pr.	45.00	40.00	Sugar, 4½" footed (amber $75.00)	15.00	14.00
Creamer, 3¼"	22.50	22.50	Sugar, rectangular	18.00	16.00
Creamer, 4½" footed (amber $60.00)	15.00	14.00	Sugar, flat with cover	165.00	125.00
Creamer, rectangular	16.00	14.00	Sundae, footed, ruffled top	85.00	65.00
Creamer & sugar on tray, 4"	65.00	60.00	Tray, center-handled	175.00	140.00
* Cup	45.00	45.00	Tray, rectangular sugar & creamer	45.00	35.00
Goblet, 9 oz.	67.50	57.50	Tumbler, 8 oz., 4³⁄₁₆" flat	80.00	70.00
Ice bucket	50.00	45.00	Tumbler, 6 oz. footed	30.00	30.00
Lamp, 9" electric	42.50	37.50	Tumbler, 8 oz., 5¼" high, footed		
Marmalade, notched lid	177.50	150.00	(amber $75.00)	28.00	26.00
Mustard, covered	130.00	110.00	Tumbler, 11 oz. footed	40.00	35.00
Parfait	60.00	55.00	Tumbler, 12 oz. footed	50.00	45.00
** Pitcher, 64 oz. (amber $400.00)	125.00	110.00	Vase, 6½" ruffled edge	95.00	80.00
Plate, 6½" sherbet	27.50	25.00	*** Vase, 9½" ruffled edge	85.00	70.00
Plate, 8¼", luncheon	30.00	25.00	Vase, 9½" straight	55.00	45.00
Plate, 10½", 2-handled	45.00	40.00	Vase, 11" ruffled edge	155.00	180.00
Relish, divided	20.00	16.00	Vase, 11" straight	85.00	80.00

  * Prices for absolutely mint pieces
  ** Crystal-$275.00
  *** Crystal-$12.50

Please refer to Foreword for pricing information

THISTLE MacBETH-EVANS, 1929-1930

Colors: Pink, green; some yellow and crystal.

Thistle and Fire-King blue are "favorites" of the photographer who takes hours of his time to record our Depression glass. When we unpack these patterns he says "special words" and asks if we *really want a pattern* to show! There is almost no way to see the pattern on film. The lights make the pattern do a disappearing act. That disappearance is sort of familiar to Thistle collectors. This pattern has been known to hide very well. All seven pieces found in pink are shown here. I have had little luck in finding green.

Green is more scarce than pink except for the large fruit bowl which is almost nonexistent in pink. The one in the picture is one of two I have ever seen.

The mould shapes in this pattern are the same as Dogwood. In Thistle, however, there's only the thin style cup instead of the thicker style. No creamer and sugar has ever been found!

The thick butter dish, pitcher, tumbler and other heavy moulded pieces with Thistle designs are new! They are being made by Mosser Glass Company in Cambridge, Ohio. They are not a part of this pattern, but copies of a much older pattern glass. If your piece of Thistle is not in the photograph, then you probably do not have a piece of MacBeth-Evans' Thistle pattern.

	Pink	Green
Bowl, 5½" cereal	18.00	20.00
Bowl, 10¼" large fruit	225.00	150.00
Cup, thin	17.00	20.00
Plate, 8" luncheon	10.00	15.00
Plate, 10¼" grill	15.00	18.00
Plate, 13" heavy cake	100.00	125.00
Saucer	8.50	8.50

"THUMBPRINT," PEAR OPTIC FEDERAL GLASS COMPANY, 1929-1930

Color: Green

"Thumbprint" is the common collector's name for a pattern called Pear Optic by Federal. Most companies had a "Thumbprint" type pattern; so, there are similar pieces from other companies that are collected with this Federal pattern. Many of Federal's pieces have the **F** in a shield symbol used by the company to mark their glassware.

I had a letter from a lady who said she had a sugar with lid, but she never sent a picture for confirmation.

The photo shown here (taken by photographer Raymond Mills) is of a set owned by Imogene McKinney of Texas. I started to replace this photograph; but I have been able to find so little of this pattern in my travels, my box of Thumbprint for photography is almost empty!

"Thumbprint" is often confused with Raindrops, but notice how the "bumps" on Thumbprint are elongated whereas the "bumps" on Raindrops are round.

	Green
Bowl, 4¾" berry	3.00
Bowl, 5" cereal	4.50
Bowl, 8" large berry	9.00
Creamer, footed	11.50
Cup	3.00
Plate, 6" sherbet	2.00
Plate, 8" luncheon	3.00
Plate, 9¼" dinner	6.00
Salt and pepper, pr.	22.50
Saucer	1.50
Sherbet	5.00
Sugar, footed	11.50
Tumbler, 4", 5 oz.	4.50
Tumbler, 5", 10 oz.	5.00
Tumbler, 5½", 12 oz.	5.00

Please refer to Foreword for pricing information

TWISTED OPTIC IMPERIAL GLASS COMPANY, 1927-1930

Colors: Pink, green, amber; some blue and canary yellow.

All the pieces shown belong to Twisted Optic. You can see an additional blue piece under Spiral placed there to help in differentiating the two patterns which are often confused. If you find a Spiral piece in some color besides pink or green, then it is most likely Twisted Optic since Spiral is only found in pink or green. You should know that many different glass companies made spiraling patterns besides Hocking and Imperial! There were a lot of smaller glass factories that never issued catalogues and others that were in business for so short a duration that records were never kept or have long since disappeared.

Twisted Optic spirals to the right and Spiral's go to the left!

Many collectors collect these patterns together in order to be able to have a bigger collection! Others are purists and will not mix patterns. You, alone, have to make this decision. I will say that more and more collectors are telling me at shows about mixing patterns, as well as colors.

	*All Colors		*All Colors
Bowl, 4¾" cream soup	10.00	Plate, 7½" x 9" oval with indent	4.50
Bowl, 5" cereal	4.50	Plate, 8" luncheon	3.00
Bowl, 7" salad	8.00	Plate, 10", sandwich	8.50
Candlesticks, 3" pr.	15.00	Preserve (same as candy with slotted lid)	25.00
Candy jar and cover	25.00	Sandwich server, open center handle	18.00
Creamer	6.50	Sandwich server, two-handled	10.00
Cup	3.50	Saucer	1.50
Mayonnaise	18.00	Sherbet	5.50
Pitcher, 64 oz.	27.50	Sugar	6.00
Plate, 6" sherbet	1.75	Tumbler, 4½", 9 oz.	5.00
Plate, 7" salad	2.50	Tumbler, 5¼", 12 oz.	7.50

* Blue, Canary Yellow 50% more

U.S. SWIRL U.S. GLASS COMPANY, Late 1920's

Colors: Pink, green iridescent and crystal.

An iridescent butter dish has been discovered in U.S. Swirl as well as some crystal sherbets. I do not know if there is enough of these to collect a set or not! Time will tell, but my experience says that these colors are not plentiful since they are just now being spotted! The tumbler listing 3⅝" corresponds with the only known size of Aunt Polly and Cherryberry/Strawberry tumblers, but the 12 oz. tumbler has only been found in this U.S. Glass Company pattern.

U.S. Swirl has the plain butter bottom that is interchangeable with all the other patterns made by U.S. Glass. The butter dish in this pattern is the one that many Strawberry collectors have purchased over the years to "steal" the bottom for their Strawberry tops. Now, this robbery has stressed the search for butters in this pattern, particularly in pink.

I still need a green creamer. If you have an extra one, let me hear from you! I have been seeing more pink than green in my travels. This pattern is so rarely seen that many of you are only acquainted with it through this picture.

	Green	Pink		Green	Pink
Bowl, 4⅜", berry	5.00	6.00	Pitcher, 8", 48 oz.	40.00	40.00
Bowl, 5½", 1 handle	9.00	10.00	Plate, 6⅛", sherbet	2.00	2.00
Bowl, 7⅞, large berry	12.00	15.00	Plate, 7⅞", salad	5.00	6.00
Bowl, 8¼", oval	22.50	22.50	Salt and pepper, pr.	40.00	40.00
Butter and cover	62.50	67.50	Sherbet, 3¼"	4.00	4.50
Butter bottom	42.50	52.50	Sugar w/lid	27.50	27.50
Butter top	10.00	15.00	Tumbler, 3⅝", 8 oz.	8.00	9.00
Candy w/cover, 2-handled	25.00	27.50	Tumbler, 4¾", 12 oz.	10.00	12.00
Creamer	12.00	14.00	Vase, 6½"	15.00	18.00

Please refer to Foreword for pricing information

"VICTORY" DIAMOND GLASS-WARE COMPANY, 1929-1932

Colors: Amber, pink, green; some cobalt blue and black.

Victory collectors seek all colors; sets can be assembled in pink and green with a lot of searching. Amber, cobalt blue and black will take more searching and require some luck.

Cobalt blue Victory attracts collectors interested in the color more than the pattern. For example, when we took a six piece setting of cobalt blue Victory to a Depression glass show, several of the pieces were bought by collectors who had to be told what the pattern was. Those collectors were only interested in the color!

That same concept applies to black Victory, but not to the same extent that it does with cobalt blue. Flat black pieces have to be turned over to see the pattern.

The Victory gravy boat and platter are the most desirable pieces to own in any color. I have only seen one amber set which was purchased years ago on my way to an Extravaganza on Route 30 in Pennsylvania. A green gravy and platter can be seen on the bottom of page 191.

Finding goblets, cereal and soup bowls, as well as the oval vegetable will keep you searching long and hard, no matter which color you choose.

There are several styles of decorations besides the 22K gold trimmed pieces shown here. There are floral decorations and even a black decorated design that is very "Art Deco" looking. I have only seen this "Art Deco" design on pink and green. I have observed more floral decorated console sets (bowl and candlesticks) than anything, Complete sets of floral decorated ware may not be available. I assume that whole sets can be found with gold trim.

	Amber, Pink, Green	Black, Blue
Bon bon, 7"	10.00	18.00
Bowl, 6½" cereal	9.50	25.00
Bowl, 8½" flat soup	15.00	35.00
Bowl, 9" oval vegetable	27.50	70.00
Bowl, 11" rolled edge	25.00	40.00
Bowl, 12" console	30.00	60.00
Bowl, 12½" flat edge	27.50	60.00
Candlesticks, 3" pr.	27.50	80.00
Cheese & cracker set, 12" indented plate & compote	37.50	
Comport, 6" tall, 6¾" diameter	12.00	
Creamer	12.00	40.00
Cup	7.00	28.00
Goblet, 5", 7 oz.	18.00	
Gravy boat and platter	150.00	280.00
Mayonnaise set: 3½" tall, 5½" across, 8½" indented plate, w/ladle	37.50	90.00
Plate, 6" bread and butter	4.00	12.00
Plate, 7" salad	6.00	12.00
Plate, 8" luncheon	6.00	15.00
Plate, 9" dinner	17.50	32.00
Platter, 12"	22.00	60.00
Sandwich server, center handle	24.00	55.00
Saucer	3.00	8.00
Sherbet, footed	12.00	22.00
Sugar	12.00	40.00

Please refer to Foreword for pricing information

VITROCK, "FLOWER RIM" HOCKING GLASS COMPANY, 1934-1937

Colors: White and white w/fired-on colors, usually red or green.

Want to go shopping at Kresge's? This mid 1930's store display photograph was found in Anchor Hocking's files. Vitrock was Hocking's venture into the "milk glass" market. Note the emphasis that Vitrock "Will not craze or check" on the display sign.

To my knowledge only this "Flower Rim" pattern and Lake Como were made into dinnerware sets in this very durable line. Vitrock competed at the time with Hazel Atlas' "Platonite"; and by all indications, "Platonite" won.

Vitrock is better known for kitchenware reamers, measuring cups and mixing bowls found in this white color. Notice that the Vitrock Kitchenware items are also shown in the display. I now know why those big Vitrock mixing bowls are so hard to find. They cost a quarter when a working man's wages were in the range of a $1.00 a day!

You can see more of this in my *Kitchen Glassware of the Depression Years.* Some collectors are gathering different patterns that can "cross-over" into other fields. This is a very good example of a pattern that fits into both collecting areas.

Vitrock fired-on colors make decorative accessory pieces for special occasions. You can find fired-on blue as well as the three colors shown!

Platters and the cream soups are pieces that are impossible to find. I am only looking at a poor overexposed copy of the photo while writing, but I do not see any cream soups in this introductory display! Perhaps they were added to the line later.

	White		White
Bowl, 4" berry	4.00	Plate, 7¼" salad	2.00
Bowl, 5½" cream soup	14.00	Plate, 8¾" luncheon	4.00
Bowl, 6" fruit	5.00	Plate, 9" soup	10.00
Bowl, 7½" cereal	5.00	Plate, 10" dinner	6.00
Bowl, 9½" vegetable	10.00	Platter, 11½"	24.00
Creamer, oval	4.00	Saucer	1.50
Cup	3.00		

Schreick's Studio
Columbus, Ohio

WATERFORD, "WAFFLE" HOCKING GLASS COMPANY, 1938-1944

Colors: Crystal, pink; some yellow, white; Forest Green 1950's.

Price of hard to find pink Waterford pieces is not an issue with collectors. Most would like to see some cereal bowls, a pitcher or butter dish! I am not encountering pink Waterford at Depression glass shows either. Of these three pieces, the cereal is the most elusive. It was even hard to find the cereals when they were priced at $1.50 in my first book in 1972!

There is a "look-alike" footed cup that is sometimes sold as a Waterford punch cup. This cup and the larger lamps that are often displayed as Waterford are only similar to Waterford. Waterford has a flattened, not rounded, "diamond" shape on each section of the design. There is also a large, pink pitcher with a indented, circular design in each diamond that is not Waterford. This pitcher was made by Hocking, but has more of a "bullseye" look. These only sell for $20.00, so do not pay Waterford prices for one!

A crystal Waterford collection can still be completed, but there are pieces in crystal that are hard to find. Cereal bowls and even water goblets are disappearing. Check the inside rims for roughness on this pattern. A little roughness is normal; don't let that keep you from owning a hard to find piece. Because of the rim design, Waterford does chip.

You will find a few pieces of white and some "Dusty Rose" and "Springtime Green" which are the names for colors usually found on ash trays selling at crystal prices. Examples of these colors can be seen in Oyster and Pearl on page 135. Forest Green 13¾" plates were made in the 1950's promotion; these are usually found in the $12.00 range. Some crystal has also been found trimmed in red.

Advertising ash trays such as the "Post Cereals" shown below are now selling for $12.00 to $15.00 depending upon the desirability of the advertising on the piece!

The items listed below with Miss America style in parentheses are Waterford patterned pieces that have the same mould shapes as Miss America. You can see some of these in the seventh edition of this book or in the first *Very Rare Glassware of the Depression Years.* It seems likely that the first designs for Waterford were patterned on the shapes of Miss America which had been discontinued the year before Waterford was introduced. For some unknown reason, a newly designed shape was chosen and the experimental (?) pieces have been found in small quantities. It is unlikely that a full set could be found, but one never knows!

The yellow and amber goblets shown below are compliments of Anchor Hocking's photography from items stored in their morgue.

	Crystal	Pink		Crystal	Pink
* Ash tray, 4"	6.50		Pitcher, 80 oz. tilted ice lip	28.00	125.00
Bowl, 4¾" berry	5.00	10.00	Plate, 6" sherbet	2.00	4.00
Bowl, 5½" cereal	14.00	22.00	Plate, 7⅛" salad	4.00	6.00
Bowl, 8¼" large berry	9.00	15.00	Plate, 9⅝" dinner	8.00	15.00
Butter dish and cover	23.00	195.00	Plate, 10¼" handled cake	6.50	12.00
Butter dish bottom	5.00	25.00	Plate, 13¾" sandwich	8.50	22.00
Butter dish top	18.00	170.00	Relish, 13¾", 5-part	15.00	
Coaster, 4"	3.00		Salt and pepper, 2 types	8.00	
Creamer, oval	4.00	8.50	Saucer	2.00	4.00
Creamer (Miss America style)	30.00		Sherbet, footed	3.50	10.00
Cup	6.00	12.00	Sherbet, footed, scalloped base	3.25	
Cup (Miss America style)		30.00	Sugar	4.00	8.50
Goblets, 5¼", 5⅝"	14.00		Sugar cover, oval	4.00	20.00
Goblet, 5½" (Miss America style)	30.00	75.00	Sugar (Miss America style)	30.00	
Lamp, 4" spherical base	24.00		Tumbler, 3½", 5 oz. juice (Miss America style)		55.00
Pitcher, 42 oz. tilted juice	20.00		Tumbler, 4⅞", 10 oz. footed	10.00	16.00

* With ads $15.00

Please refer to Foreword for pricing information

WINDSOR, "WINDSOR DIAMOND" JEANNETTE GLASS COMPANY, 1936-1946

Colors: Pink, green, crystal; some Delphite, amberina red and ice blue.

Windsor has always been the last pattern written in this book; a friend always accused me of being tired when I got to Windsor and not treating it equally. Windsor is a difficult pattern to write about because of the many crystal items found in unusual shapes that are not found in color. There are many collectors of pink and green, but few collect crystal at this time. Color was discontinued about 1940, but some crystal pieces were made into 1946. A restyled butter and sugar were then transferred to Holiday when that pattern was introduced in 1947.

Notice the two different styles of butter tops in the upper photograph. One is similar to the shape of Holiday! There are also two styles of sugars and lids. In that photograph, the crystal sugar bowl has no lip for the lid to rest against (shaped like Holiday); in the lower shot, the pink sugar represents the style with lip. The pink sugar and lid without the lip are hard to find.

You can see an unusual piece of Windsor in my first *Very Rare Glassware of the Depression Years*. It is a yellow (vaseline) powder jar which has a Cube top and Windsor bottom. A pink powder jar with Windsor top and Cube bottom has also been reported!

A new style pink ash tray and a tab handled berry bowl can be seen in the *Very Rare Glassware of the Depression Years, Second Series*. While looking there, check out the blue Windsor butter dish!

Relish trays can be found with or without tab handles. The trays without handles can be seen in crystal. Pink trays without handles are much in demand!

Green Windsor tumblers are elusive. Even the water tumbler (which is commonly found in pink), is in short supply. As with many patterns there is a lot of mould roughness on seams of tumblers and Windsor tumblers have a tendency to chip on the sides. Check these out carefully before you buy!

The 13⅝" plate is often found as a beverage set with a pitcher and six water tumblers. That may have been a premium item since so many pitcher and water tumblers are available today.

The 10½" pointed edge bowl is hard to find in pink. This same bowl in crystal, along with the comport, makes up a punch bowl and stand. The comport fits up inside the base of this bowl to keep it from sliding off the base. In recent years, there have been newly made comports in crystal and sprayed-on, multi-colored ones which have a beaded edge. The recent crystal will not work as a punch stand because of the beaded edge. This beaded edge comport was made in the late 1950's in Jeannette's Shell Pink, one of the patterns in my latest book *Collectible Glassware from the 40's, 50's, 60's....*

	Crystal	Pink	Green		Crystal	Pink	Green
* Ash tray, 5¾"	12.50	32.00	42.00	Plate, 6" sherbet	2.00	4.00	6.00
Bowl, 4¾" berry	3.00	7.00	9.00	Plate, 7" salad	3.50	13.00	15.00
Bowl, 5" pointed edge	4.00	15.00		** Plate, 9" dinner	4.00	12.00	15.00
Bowl, 5" cream soup	5.00	16.50	22.00	Plate, 10¼" handled sandwich	5.00	12.00	12.00
Bowls, 5⅛, 5⅜" cereal	8.00	16.00	17.00	Plate, 13⅝" chop	8.00	40.00	40.00
Bowl, 7⅛", three legs	7.00	22.00		Platter, 11½" oval	5.00	16.00	17.00
Bowl, 8" pointed edge	8.50	35.00		****Powder jar		50.00	
Bowl, 8", 2-handled	6.00	13.00	18.00	Relish platter, 11½" divided	9.50	175.00	
Bowl, 8½" large berry	6.00	13.00	14.00	Salt and pepper, pr.	15.00	32.50	45.00
Bowl, 9½" oval vegetable	6.00	14.00	20.00	Saucer (ice blue $15.00)	2.00	3.50	4.00
Bowl, 10½" salad	7.50			Sherbet, footed	3.00	9.00	11.00
Bowl, 10½" pointed edge	22.00	100.00		Sugar & cover	6.00	20.00	25.00
Bowl, 12½" fruit console	22.00	95.00		Sugar & cover (like "Holiday")	10.00	90.00	
Bowl, 7" x 11¾" boat shape	14.00	25.00	28.00	Tray, 4", square, w/handles	4.00	8.00	9.00
Butter dish (two styles)	25.00	45.00	75.00	Tray, 4", square, wo/handles	5.00	32.00	
Cake plate, 10¾" footed	7.50	15.00	16.00	Tray, 4⅛" x 9", w/handles	3.00	7.50	14.00
Candlesticks, 3" Pr.	16.00	70.00		Tray, 4⅛" x 9", wo/handles	8.50	45.00	
Candy jar and cover	15.00			Tray, 8½" x 9¾", w/handles	6.00	20.00	28.00
Coaster, 3¼"	3.00	12.00	15.00	Tray, 8½" x 9¾", wo/handles	12.50	75.00	35.00
Comport	8.00			** Tumbler, 3¼", 5 oz.	7.50	20.00	30.00
** Creamer	4.00	9.50	10.00	** Tumbler, 4", 9 oz. (red 50.00)	5.00	16.00	25.00
Creamer (shaped as "Holiday")	6.00			Tumbler, 5", 12 oz.	7.50	22.00	40.00
** Cup	3.00	8.00	9.00	Tumbler, 4" footed	6.00		
Pitcher, 4½", 16 oz.	19.00	100.00		Tumbler, 5" footed, 11 oz.	9.00		
*** Pitcher, 6¾", 52 oz.	12.00	19.00	45.00	Tumbler, 7¼" footed	12.00		

*Delphite-$40.00   **Blue-$55.00   ***Red-$400.00   ****Yellow-$150.00

Please refer to Foreword for pricing information

Patterns Henceforth In *Collectible Glassware from the 40's, 50's and 60's...*

ANNIVERSARY JEANNETTE GLASS COMPANY, 1947-49; late 1960's - mid 1970's

Colors: Pink, crystal, and iridescent.

	Crystal	Pink	Iridescent		Crystal	Pink	Iridescent
Bowl, 4⅞" berry	2.50	6.00	4.00	Plate, 6¼" sherbet	1.25	2.00	1.50
Bowl, 7⅜" soup	6.00	12.50	6.50	Plate, 9" dinner	4.00	8.00	5.75
Bowl, 9" fruit	9.00	17.50	10.00	Plate, 12½" sandwich server	4.00	10.00	7.50
Butter dish bottom	10.00	25.00		Relish dish, 8"	4.50	8.50	6.00
Butter dish top	12.50	22.50		Saucer	1.00	1.50	1.25
Butter dish and cover	22.50	47.50		Sherbet, ftd.	2.50	6.50	
Candy jar and cover	17.50	37.50		Sugar	2.00	6.00	4.00
Cake plate, 12½"	5.50	12.50		Sugar cover	4.00	8.50	2.50
Cake plate w/metal cover	12.00			Tid-bit, berry & fruit bowls			
Candlestick, 4⅞" pr.	15.00			w/metal hndl.	12.00		
Comport, open, 3 legged	3.50	9.00	4.50	Vase, 6½"	12.00	25.00	
Creamer, footed	3.50	8.50	5.00	Vase, wall pin-up	12.00	22.50	
Cup	2.50	6.50	3.75				
Pickle dish, 9"	4.00	9.00	6.00				

"BUBBLE," "BULLSEYE," "PROVINCIAL" ANCHOR HOCKING GLASS COMPANY, 1940-1965

Colors: Pink, Sapphire blue, Forest Green, Royal Ruby, crystal and any known Hocking color.

	Crystal	Forest Green	Blue	Royal Ruby
Bowl, 4" berry	2.50		12.00	
Bowl, 4½" fruit	3.50	5.50	9.00	7.50
Bowl, 5¼" cereal	4.00	9.50	10.00	
Bowl, 7¾" flat soup	4.50		12.00	
Bowl, 8⅜" large berry (pink $6.00)	5.50	11.00	14.00	15.00
Bowl, 9" flanged			175.00	
Candlesticks, pr.	12.50	22.50		
Creamer	4.50	9.50	27.50	
* Cup	3.00	5.00	3.00	6.00
Lamp, 3 styles	37.50			
Pitcher, 64 oz. ice lip	55.00			45.00
Plate, 6¾" bread and butter	1.50	3.00	3.00	
Plate, 9⅜" grill			17.50	
Plate, 9⅜" dinner	4.00	12.50	6.00	8.00
Platter, 12" oval	7.50		14.00	
** Saucer	1.00	3.00	1.50	3.00
***Stem, 3½ oz., cocktail	3.50	7.00		8.00
***Stem, 4 oz., juice	4.00	9.00		10.00
Stem, 4½ oz., cocktail	4.00	8.00		9.00
Stem, 5½ oz., juice	5.00	10.00		11.00
***Stem, 6 oz., sherbet	3.00	7.00		8.00
Stem, 6 oz., sherbet	3.50	7.50		8.50
***Stem, 9 oz., goblet	7.00	12.00		12.50
Stem, 9½ oz., goblet	6.00	11.00		11.50
***Stem, 14 oz., iced tea	7.00	17.50		
Sugar	4.50	9.00	15.00	
Tidbit (2 tier)				30.00
Tumbler, 6 oz., juice	3.50			7.00
Tumbler, 8 oz., 3¼", old fashioned	6.00			15.00
Tumbler, 9 oz., water	5.00			8.00
Tumbler, 12 oz., 4½", iced tea	7.00			10.00
Tumbler, 16 oz., 5⅞", lemonade	9.00			16.00

*Pink - $75.00   **Pink - $25.00   ***"Boopie"

"CHRISTMAS CANDY," NO. 624 INDIANA GLASS COMPANY, 1950's

Colors: Teal and crystal.

	Crystal	Teal
Bowl, 7⅜" soup	6.00	25.00
Bowl, 9½", vegetable		85.00
Creamer	8.00	18.00
Cup	4.00	17.50
Mayonnaise w/ladle	17.50	
Plate, 6" bread and butter	2.50	9.00
Plate, 8¼" luncheon	6.50	15.00
Plate, 9⅝" dinner	9.50	25.00
Plate, 11¼", sandwich	13.50	35.00
Saucer	1.50	5.00
Sugar	8.00	17.50

"DAISY, " NUMBER 620 INDIANA GLASS COMPANY

Colors: Crystal, 1933-40; fired-on red, late 30's; amber, 1940's; dark green and milk glass, 1960's, 1970's, 1980's.

	Crystal	Green	Red, Amber
Bowl, 4½" berry	4.00	5.00	8.00
Bowl, 4½" cream soup	4.00	5.00	10.00
Bowl, 6" cereal	9.00	11.00	25.00
Bowl, 7⅜" deep berry	7.00	8.00	12.50
Bowl, 9⅜" deep berry	12.00	15.00	27.50
Bowl, 10" oval vegetable	9.00	10.00	15.00
Creamer, footed	5.00	4.50	7.50
Cup	3.50	3.50	5.50
Plate, 6" sherbet	1.50	1.50	2.00
Plate, 7⅜" salad	3.00	3.00	6.50
Plate, 8⅜" luncheon	3.50	4.00	5.00
Plate, 9⅜" dinner	5.00	6.00	8.00
Plate, 10⅜" grill w/indent for cream soup		12.50	
Plate, 11½" cake or sandwich	6.00	7.00	12.00
Platter, 10¾"	7.00	8.00	12.50
Relish dish, 8⅜", 3 part	10.00		25.00
Saucer	1.00	1.00	1.50
Sherbet, footed	4.50	5.00	8.00
Sugar, footed	5.00	4.50	7.50
Tumbler, 9 oz. footed	9.00	9.00	17.50
Tumbler, 12 oz. footed	18.50	18.50	32.50

Please refer to Foreword for pricing information

FIRE-KING OVEN GLASS ANCHOR HOCKING GLASS CORPORATION, 1942-1950's

Colors: Sapphire blue, crystal; some Ivory and Jade-ite.

All Fire-King was made after 1940 and has been transferred to my newly released *Collectible Glassware from the 40's, 50's, 60's....*

	Ivory	Sapphire		Ivory	Sapphire
Baker, 1 pt., 4½" x 5"		5.00	Custard cup or baker, 5 oz.	2.50	3.00
Baker, 1 pt., round	3.00	4.50	Custard cup or baker, 6 oz.	3.00	3.50
Baker, 1 qt., round	4.50	6.00	Loaf pan, 9⅛" x 5⅛", deep	12.50	17.50
Baker, 1½ qt., round	5.50	11.00	Mug, coffee, 7 oz., 2 styles	*25.00	21.50
Baker, 2 qt., round	8.00	12.50	Nipple cover		125.00
Baker, 6 oz., individual	2.50	3.50	Nurser, 4 oz.		13.00
Bowl, 4⅜", individual pie plate		11.00	Nurser, 8 oz.		22.50
Bowl, 5⅜", cereal or deep dish pie plate	6.00	12.00	Percolator top, 2⅛"		4.50
Bowl, measuring, 16 oz.		22.50	Pie plate, 8⅜", 1½" deep		7.00
Cake pan (deep), 8¾" (½ roaster)		20.00	Pie plate, 9⅝", 1½" deep		9.00
Cake pan, 9"	12.50		Pie plate, 9", 1½" deep	6.50	8.00
Casserole, 1 pt., knob handle cover	8.00	11.00	Pie plate, 10⅜" juice saver	*50.00	65.00
Casserole, 1 qt., knob handle cover	9.50	12.00	Refrigerator jar & cover, 4½" x 5"	**7.50	10.00
Casserole, 1 qt., pie plate cover		16.00	Refrigerator jar & cover, 5⅛" x 9⅛"	**15.00	30.00
Casserole, 1½ qt., knob handle cover	11.00	12.50	Roaster, 8¾"		40.00
Casserole, 1½ qt., pie plate cover		16.00	Roaster, 10⅜"		60.00
Casserole, 2 qt., knob handle cover	13.00	18.00	Table server, tab handles (hot plate)	8.50	15.00
Casserole, 2 qt., pie plate cover		20.00	Utility bowl, 6⅞", 1 qt.		10.00
Casserole, individual, 10 oz.		12.50	Utility bowl, 8⅜", 1½ qt.		14.00
Cup, 8 oz. measuring, 1 spout		16.00	Utility bowl, 10⅛"		15.00
Cup, 8 oz., dry measure, no spout		150.00	Utility pan, 8⅛" x 12½", 2 qt.		30.00
Cup, 8 oz., measuring, 3 spout		18.00	Utility pan, 10½" x 2" deep	12.00	20.00

* Jade-ite w/embossed design
** Jade-ite

FIRE-KING OVEN WARE, TURQUOISE BLUE ANCHOR HOCKING GLASS CORPORATION, 1957-1958

Color: Turquoise blue.

	Blue		Blue
Ash tray, 3½"	6.00	Bowl, round, mixing, 3 qt.	10.00
Ash tray, 4⅝"	8.00	Bowl, round, mixing, 4 qt.	12.50
Ash tray, 5¾"	12.50	Creamer	5.00
Batter bowl w/spout	42.50	Cup	4.00
Bowl, 4½", berry	5.00	Egg plate, 9¾"	12.50
Bowl, 5", cereal	8.00	Mug, 8 oz.	8.00
Bowl, 6⅝", soup/salad	12.00	Plate, 6⅛"	8.00
Bowl, 8", vegetable	12.50	Plate, 7"	9.00
Bowl, tear, mixing, 1 pt.	9.00	Plate, 9"	6.50
Bowl, tear, mixing, 1 qt.	12.00	Plate, 9", w/cup indent	6.00
Bowl, tear, mixing, 2 qt.	15.00	Plate, 10"	22.50
Bowl, tear, mixing, 3 qt.	18.00	Relish, 3 part, 11⅛"	10.00
Bowl, round, mixing, 1 qt.	10.00	Saucer	1.00
Bowl, round, mixing, 2 qt.	8.00	Sugar	5.00

Please refer to Foreword for pricing information

FLORAGOLD, "LOUISA" JEANNETTE GLASS COMPANY, 1950's

Colors: Iridescent, some shell pink, ice blue and crystal.

	Iridescent		Iridescent
Ash tray/coaster, 4"	5.00	Creamer	8.50
Bowl, 4½" square	5.00	Cup	5.00
Bowl, 5½" round cereal	27.50	Pitcher, 64 oz.	30.00
Bowl, 5½" ruffled fruit	7.50	Plate or tray, 13½"	17.50
Bowl, 8½" square	12.50	Plate or tray, 13½", with indent	45.00
Bowl, 9½" deep salad	32.50	Plate, 5¼" sherbet	10.00
Bowl, 9½" ruffled	7.50	Plate, 8½" dinner	27.50
Bowl, 12" ruffled large fruit	6.50	Platter, 11¼"	17.50
Butter dish and cover, ¼ lb. oblong	22.50	* Salt and pepper, plastic tops	45.00
Butter dish and cover, round, 6¼" sq. base	37.50	Saucer, 5¼" (no ring)	10.00
Butter dish bottom	12.50	Sherbet, low, footed	12.00
Butter dish top	25.00	Sugar	6.00
Butter dish and cover, round, 5½" sq. base	600.00	Sugar lid	8.50
Candlesticks, double branch pr.	45.00	Tid-bit, wooden post	30.00
Candy dish, 1 handle	10.00	Tumbler, 10 oz. footed	17.50
Candy or cheese dish and cover, 6¾"	45.00	Tumbler, 11 oz. footed	17.50
Candy, 5¼" long, 4 feet	6.50	Tumbler, 15 oz. footed	65.00
Comport, 5¼", plain top	550.00	Vase or celery	325.00
Comport, 5¼", ruffled top	650.00		

* Tops $12.50 each included in price

FOREST GREEN ANCHOR HOCKING GLASS COMPANY CORPORATION, 1950-1967

Color: Forest Green.

	Green		Green
Ash tray, 3½", square	3.50	Sherbet, flat	6.00
Ash tray, 4⅝", square	4.50	* Stem, 3½ oz., cocktail	7.00
Ash tray, 5¾", square	6.50	* Stem, 4 oz., juice	9.00
Ash tray, 5¾", hexagonal	7.50	Stem, 4½ oz., cocktail	8.00
Batter bowl w/spout	12.50	Stem, 5½ oz., juice	10.00
Bowl, 4¾" dessert	5.00	Stem, 6 oz., sherbet	7.50
Bowl, 5¼" deep	8.00	* Stem, 6 oz., sherbet	7.00
Bowl, 6" soup	14.00	* Stem, 9 oz., goblet	12.00
Bowl, 6" mixing	8.50	Stem, 9½ oz., goblet	11.00
Bowl, 7⅜" salad	9.50	* Stem, 14 oz., iced tea	17.50
Bowl, 8½", oval vegetable	25.00	Sugar, flat	5.50
Creamer, flat	5.50	Tumbler, 5 oz., 3½"	3.00
Cup (square)	4.00	Tumbler, 7 oz.	3.50
Pitcher, 22 oz.	19.50	Tumbler, 9 oz, table	4.50
Pitcher, 36 oz.	22.50	Tumbler, 9 oz., fancy	5.00
Pitcher, 86 oz. round	25.00	Tumbler, 9½ oz., tall	6.00
Plate, 6¾" salad	3.00	Tumbler, 10 oz., ftd., 4½"	6.00
Plate, 6⅝", salad	3.00	Tumbler, 11 oz.	6.50
Plate, 8⅜" luncheon	5.00	Tumbler, 13 oz., iced tea	7.00
Plate, 10" dinner	20.00	Tumbler, 14 oz., 5"	7.00
Platter, 11", rectangular	25.00	Tumbler, 15 oz., long boy	8.00
Punch bowl	20.00	Tumbler, 19 oz., jumbo iced tea	12.00
Punch bowl stand	20.00	Vase, 4" ivy ball	3.00
Punch cup (round)	2.00	Vase, 6⅜"	4.00
Saucer, 5⅜"	1.00	Vase, 9"	6.00

*"Boopie"

Please refer to Foreword for pricing information

HARP JEANNETTE GLASS COMPANY, 1954-1957

Colors: Crystal, crystal with gold trim, and cake stands in Shell Pink, pink, white and ice blue.

	Crystal
Ash tray/coaster	4.50
Coaster	3.50
Cup	9.00
* Cake stand, 9"	20.00
Plate, 7"	8.50
Saucer	3.50
** Tray, 2-handled, rectangular	27.50
Vase, 7½"	15.00

 * Ice blue, white, pink or Shell Pink $25.00
** Shell Pink $45.00

HERITAGE FEDERAL GLASS COMPANY, 1940 -1955

Colors: Crystal, some pink, blue, green and cobalt.

	Crystal	Pink	Blue Green
Bowl, 5" berry	7.00	35.00	45.00
Bowl, 8½" large berry	25.00	95.00	150.00
Bowl, 10½" fruit	12.50		
Cup	6.00		
Creamer, footed	20.00		
Plate, 8" luncheon	7.50		
Plate, 9¼" dinner	10.00		
Plate, 12" sandwich	11.50		
Saucer	3.00		
Sugar, open, footed	15.00		

HOLIDAY, "BUTTONS AND BOWS" JEANNETTE GLASS COMPANY, 1947-mid 1950's

	Pink	Crystal	Iridescent
Bowl, 5⅛" berry	10.00		
Bowl, 7¾" soup	37.50		
Bowl, 8½" large berry	18.00		
Bowl, 9½" oval vegetable	15.00		
* Bowl, 10¾" console	85.00		
Butter dish and cover	32.50		
Butter dish bottom	10.00		
Butter dish top	22.50		
Cake Plate, 10½", 3 legged	80.00		
Candlesticks, 3" pr.	75.00		
Creamer, footed	9.00		
Cup, three sizes	6.00		
Pitcher, 4¾", 16 oz. milk	50.00	15.00	20.00
Pitcher, 6¾", 52 oz.	27.50		
Plate, 6" sherbet	4.00		
Plate, 9" dinner	14.00		
Plate, 13¾" chop	80.00		
Platter, 11⅜" oval	15.00		
Sandwich tray, 10½"	13.00		
Saucer, 3 styles	4.00		
Sherbet, 2 styles	5.50		
Sugar	8.00		
Sugar cover	12.00		
Tumbler, 4", 10 oz. flat	17.50		
Tumbler, 4" footed, 5 oz.	30.00		10.00
Tumbler, 4¼" footed, 5¼ oz.		7.50	
Tumbler, 6" footed	120.00		

*Shell Pink $35.00

MOONSTONE ANCHOR HOCKING GLASS CORPORATION, 1941-1946

Colors: Crystal with opalescent hobnails and some green with opalescent hobnails.

	Opalescent Hobnail		Opalescent Hobnail
Bowl, 5½" berry	15.00	Cup	7.00
Bowl, 5½" crimped dessert	8.00	Goblet, 10 oz.	17.50
Bowl, 6½" crimped handled	9.00	Heart bonbon, one handle	11.00
Bowl, 7¾" flat	11.00	Plate, 6¼" sherbet	5.00
Bowl, 7¾" divided relish	9.50	Plate, 8" luncheon	12.50
Bowl, 9½" crimped	17.50	Plate, 10" sandwich	20.00
Bowl, cloverleaf	12.00	Puff box and cover, 4¾" round	20.00
Candle holder, pr.	15.00	Saucer (same as sherbet plate)	5.00
Candy jar and cover, 6"	22.50	Sherbet, footed	6.50
Cigarette jar and cover	20.00	Sugar, footed	7.00
Creamer	7.00	Vase, 5½" bud	10.00

MOROCCAN AMETHYST HAZEL WARE, DIVISION OF CONTINENTAL CAN, 1960's

Color: Amethyst.

	Amethyst		Amethyst
Ash tray, ¾", triangular	5.00	Goblet, 4¼", 7½ oz., sherbet	7.00
Ash tray, 3¼", round	5.00	Goblet, 4⅜", 5½ oz., juice	8.50
Ash tray, 6⅞, triangular	9.00	Goblet, 5½", 9 oz., water	10.00
Ash tray, 8", square	12.00	Ice bucket, 6"	27.50
Bowl, 4¾, fruit, octagonal	6.00	Plate, 5¾",	4.00
Bowl, 5¾", deep, square	9.00	Plate, 7¼", salad	6.00
Bowl, 6", round	10.00	Plate, 9¾", dinner	7.50
Bowl, 7¾", oval	15.00	Plate, 10" , fan shaped, snack w/cup rest	7.50
Bowl, 7¾", rectangular	13.00	Plate, 12" , sandwich, w/metal /handle	10.00
Bowl, 7¾", rectangular w/ metal handle	14.00	Saucer	1.00
Bowl, 10¾"	25.00	Tumbler, 4 oz., juice, 2½"	7.50
Candy w/lid short	27.50	Tumbler, 8 oz., old fashion, 3¼",	12.50
Candy w/lid tall	27.50	Tumbler, 9 oz., water	10.00
Chip and dip, 10¾" & 5¾" bowls in metal holder	35.00	Tumbler, 11 oz., water, crinkled bottom, 4¼"	11.50
Cocktail w/stirrer, 6¼", 16 oz., w/lip	25.00	Tumbler, 11 oz., water, 4⅝"	11.00
Cocktail shaker w/lid	22.50	Tumbler,16 oz., iced tea, 6½"	15.00
Cup	5.00	Vase, 8½" ruffled	35.00
Goblet, 4", 4½ oz., wine	9.00		

"PRETZEL," No. 622 INDIANA GLASS COMPANY, Late 1930's-1980's

Colors: Crystal, teal and avocado with recent issues in amber and blue.

	Crystal
Bowl, 4½" fruit cup	4.00
Bowl, 7½" soup	9.00
Bowl, 9⅜" berry	15.00
Celery, 10¼" tray	1.50
Creamer	4.00
* Cup	5.00
Olive, 7", leaf shape	4.00
Pickle, 8½", two hndl.	5.00
Pitcher, 39 oz.	150.00
Plate, 6"	2.00
Plate, 6", tab hndl.	2.50
Plate, 7¼" square, indent	8.50
Plate, 7¼" square, indent 3-part	8.50
Plate, 8⅜" salad	5.00
Plate, 9⅜" dinner	8.00
Plate, 11½" sandwich	10.00
** Saucer	1.00
Sugar	4.00
Tumbler, 5 oz., 3½"	20.00
Tumbler, 9 oz., 4½"	22.00
Tumbler, 12 oz., 5½"	30.00

* Teal $30.00
** Teal $10.00

SANDWICH COLORS HOCKING GLASS COMPANY, 1939-1964

Colors: Desert Gold 1961-1964; Forest Green 1956-1960's; pink 1939-1940; Royal Ruby 1938-1939; Anchorwhite/Ivory (opaque) 1957-1960's.

	Desert Gold	Royal Ruby	Forest Green	Pink	Ivory White
Bowl, 4⁵⁄₁₆", smooth			3.00		
Bowl, 4⅞" smooth	3.00	15.00		3.50	
Bowl, 5¼" scalloped	6.00		18.00		
Bowl, 5¼", smooth				6.00	
Bowl, 6½" cereal	12.00				
Bowl, 6½" smooth	6.00				
Bowl, 6½" scalloped		25.00	35.00		
Bowl, 7" salad			50.00		
Bowl, 8" scalloped		35.00	60.00	15.00	
Bowl, 9" salad	27.50				
Cookie jar and cover	35.00		*17.50		
Creamer				20.00	
Cup, tea or coffee	3.50		17.00		
Pitcher, 6" juice			110.00		
Pitcher, ½ gal. ice lip			250.00		
Plate, 9" dinner	8.00		62.50		
Plate, 12" sandwich	12.50				
Punch bowl, 9¾"					15.00
Punch bowl stand					12.50
Punch cup					2.00
Saucer	3.00	10.50			
Sugar (no cover)			22.00		
Tumbler, 3⁹⁄₁₆" 5 oz. juice			3.50		
Tumbler, 9 oz. water			4.25		
Tumbler, 9 oz. footed	75.00				

* No cover

SANDWICH CRYSTAL HOCKING GLASS COMPANY, 1940-1964; 1977

Colors: Crystal 1940-1950's.

	Crystal		Crystal
Bowl, 4⁵⁄₁₆", smooth	5.00	Custard cup liner	12.50
Bowl, 4⅞", crimped dessert	12.50	Pitcher, 6" juice	50.00
Bowl, 4⅞" smooth	5.00	Pitcher, ½ gal. ice lip	60.00
Bowl, 5¼" scalloped	7.00	Plate, 7" dessert	9.00
Bowl, 6½" cereal	25.00	Plate, 8"	3.00
Bowl, 6½" smooth	7.00	Plate, 9" dinner	15.00
Bowl, 6½" scalloped	7.00	Plate, 9" indent for punch cup	4.00
Bowl, 7" salad	6.50	Plate, 12" sandwich	17.50
Bowl, 7¼" scalloped	7.50	Punch bowl, 9¾"	15.00
Bowl, 8" scalloped	7.50	Punch bowl stand	20.00
Bowl, 8¼" oval	6.50	Punch cup	2.00
Bowl, 9" salad	22.50	Saucer	1.00
Butter dish, low	37.50	Sherbet, footed	7.00
Butter dish bottom	20.00	Sugar	7.50
Butter dish top	17.50	Sugar cover	10.00
Cookie jar and cover	35.00	Tumbler, 3⅜" 3 oz. juice	12.00
Creamer	5.00	Tumbler, 3⁹⁄₁₆" 5 oz. juice	6.00
Cup, Tea or coffee	2.00	Tumbler, 9 oz. water	7.50
Custard cup	3.50		
Custard cup, crimped, 5 oz.	12.50		

REPRODUCTIONS

NEW "ADAM" PRIVATELY PRODUCED OUT OF KOREA THROUGH ST. LOUIS IMPORTING COMPANY
ONLY THE ADAM BUTTER DISH HAS BEEN REPRODUCED!

The new Adam butter is being offered at $6.00 wholesale. Identification of the new is easy.

Top: Notice the veins in the leaves.

New: Large leaf veins do not join or touch in center of leaf.

Old: Large leaf veins all touch or join center vein on the old.

A further note in the original Adam butter dish: the veins of all the leaves at the center of the design are very clear cut and precisely moulded: in the new, these center leaf veins are very indistinct – and almost invisible in one leaf of the center design.

Bottom: Place butter dish bottom upside down for observation.

New: Four (4) "Arrowhead-like" points line up in northwest, northeast, southeast and southwest directions of compass. There are very bad mould lines and a very glossy light pink color on the butter dishes I have examined; but these have been improved.

Old: Four (4) "Arrowhead-like" points line up in north, east, south and west directions of compass.

NEW "AVOCADO" INDIANA GLASS COMPANY Tiara Exclusives Line, 1974...

Colors: Pink, frosted pink, yellow, blue, red, amethyst and green.

In 1979 a green Avocado pitcher was produced. It is darker than the original green and was a limited hostess gift item. Yellow pieces that are beginning to show up are all new! Yellow was never made originally!

The original pink Indiana made was a delicate pretty pink. The new tends to be more orange than the original color. The other colors shown pose little threat since these colors were not made originally.

I understand that Tiara sales counselors told potential clientele that their newly made glass is collectible because it was made from old moulds. I don't share this view. I feel it's like saying that since you were married in your grandmother's wedding dress, you will have the same happy marriage for the fifty-seven years she did. All you can truly say is that you were married in her dress. I think all you can say about the new Avocado is that it was made from the old moulds. TIME, SCARCITY and PEOPLE'S WHIMS determine collectability in so far as I'm able to determine it. It's taken nearly fifty years or more for people to turn to collecting Depression Glass – and that's done, in part, because EVERYONE "remembers" it; they had some in their home at one time or another; it has universal appeal. Who is to say what will be collectible in the next hundred years. If we all knew, we could all get rich!

If you like the new Tiara products, then by all means buy them; but don't do so DEPENDING upon their being collectible just because they are made in the image of the old! You have an equal chance, I feel, of going to Las Vegas and DEPENDING upon getting rich at the blackjack table.

NEW "CAMEO"

Colors: Green, pink, cobalt blue (shakers); yellow, green and pink (child's dishes).

Although the photographer I left this shaker with opted to shoot the side without the dancing girl, I trust you can still see how very weak the pattern is on this reproduction. It was made by Mosser originally, but is now being made overseas. Also, you can see how much glass remains in the bottom of the shaker; and, of course, the new tops all make this easy to spot at the market. These were to be bought wholesale at around $6.00 but did not sell well. A new IMPORTER is making shakers in pink, cobalt blue and a terrible green color. These, too, are weakly patterned! They were never originally made in the blue, but **beware of PINK**!

Children's dishes in Cameo pose no problem to collectors since they were never made originally. These are "scale models" of the larger size. This type of production I have no quarrel with as they are not made to "dupe" anyone.

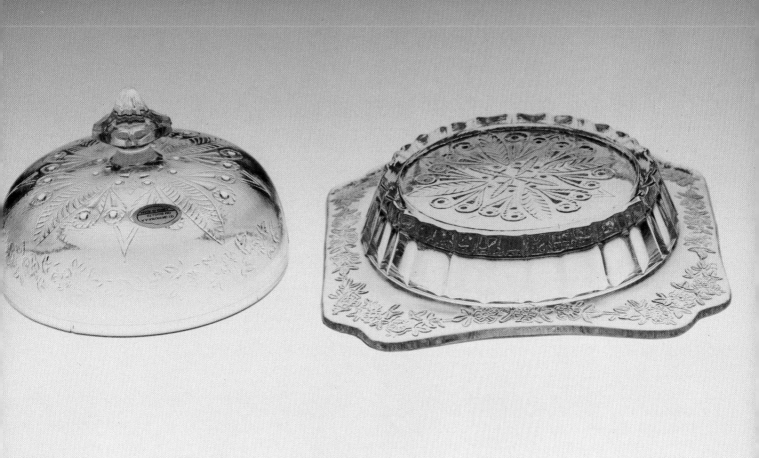

REPRODUCTIONS (Continued)

NEW "CHERRY BLOSSOM"

Colors: Pink, green, blue, delphite, cobalt, red and iridized colors.

Please use information provided only for the piece described. Do not apply information on tumbler for pitcher, etc.

Several different people have gotten into the act of making reproduction Cherry Blossom. We've even enjoyed some reproductions of those reproductions! All the items pictured on the next page are extremely easy to spot as reproductions once you know what to look for with the possible exception of the 13" divided platter pictured at the back. It's too heavy, weighing 2¾ pounds, and has a thick, ⅜" of glass in the bottom; but the design isn't too bad! The edges of the leaves aren't smooth; but neither are they serrated like old leaves.

There are many differences between old and new scalloped bottom, AOP Cherry pitchers. The easiest way to tell the difference is to turn the pitcher over. The branch crossing the bottom of my old Cherry pitchers LOOKS like a branch. It's knobby and gnarled and has several leaves and cherry stems directly attached to it. The new pitcher just has a bald strip of glass cutting the bottom of the pitcher in half. Further, the old Cherry pitchers have a plain glass background for the cherries and leaves in the bottom of the pitcher. In the new pitchers, there's a rough, filled in, straw-like background. You see no plain glass.

As for the new tumblers, the easiest way to tell old from new is to look at the ring dividing the patterned portion of the glass from the plain glass lip. The old tumblers have three indented rings dividing the pattern from the plain glass rim. The new has only one. Again, the pattern at the bottom of the new tumblers is brief and practically nonexistent in the center curve of the glass bottom. The pattern, what there is, on the new tumblers mostly hugs the center of the foot.

2 handled tray - old: 1⅞ lbs; ³⁄₁₆" glass in bottom; leaves and cherries east/west from north/south handles; leaves have real spine and serrated edges; cherry stems end in triangle of glass. **new:** 2⅛ lbs; ¼" glass in bottom; leaves and cherries north/south with the handles; canal type leaves (but uneven edges; cherry stem ends before cup shaped line).

cake plate - new: color too light pink, leaves have too many parallel veins which give them a "feathery" look; arches at plate edge don't line up with lines on inside of the rim to which the feet are attached.

8½" bowl - new: crude leaves with smooth edges; veins in parallel lines.

cereal bowl - new: wrong shape, looks like 8½" bowl, small 2" center. **old:** large center, 2½" inside ring, nearly 3½" if you count the outer rim before the sides turn up.

plate - new: center shown close up; smooth edged leaves, fish spine type center leaf portion; weighs 1 pound plus; feels thicker at edge with mould offset lines clearly visible. **old:** center leaves look like real leaves with spines, veins and serrated edges; weighs ¾ pound; clean edges; no mould offset.

cup - new: area in bottom left free of design; canal leaves; smooth, thick top to cup handle (old has triangle grasp point).

saucer - new: off set mould line edge; canal leaf center.

The Cherry child's cup (with a slightly lop-sided handle) having the cherries hanging upside down when the cup was held in the right hand appeared in 1973. After I reported this error, it was quickly corrected by re-inverting the inverted mould. These later cups were thus improved in design but slightly off color. The saucers tended to have slightly off center designs, too. Next came the "child's butter dish" which was never made by Jeannette. It was essentially the child's cup without a handle turned upside down over the saucer and having a little glob of glass added as a knob for lifting purposes. A blue one is pictured on bottom of page 217.

Pictured are some of the colors of butter dishes made so far. Shakers were begun in 1977 and some were dated '77 on the bottom. Shortly afterward, the non dated variety appeared. How can you tell new shakers from old – should you get the one in a million chance to do so?

First, look at the tops. New tops could indicate new shakers. Next, notice the protruding edges beneath the tops. In the new they are squared off juts rather than the nicely rounded scallops on the old (which are pictured under Cherry Blossom pattern). The design on the newer shakers is often weak in spots. Finally, notice how far up inside the shakers the solid glass (next to the foot) remains. The newer shakers have almost twice as much glass in that area. They appear to be ¼ full of glass before you ever add the salt!

In 1989, a new distributor began making reproduction glass in the Far East. He's making shakers in cobalt blue, pink, and an ugly green, that is no problem to spot! These shakers are similar in quality to those made before, but the present pink color is good; yet the quality and design of each batch could vary greatly. Realize that only two original pair of pink shakers have been found and those were discovered before any reproductions were made in 1977!

Butter dishes are naturally more deceptive in pink and green since those were the only original colors. The major flaw in the new butter is that there is one band encircling the bottom edge of the butter top; there are two bands very close together along the skirt of the old top.

REPRODUCTIONS (Continued)

NEW "MADRID" CALLED "RECOLLECTION" Currently being made.

I hope you have already read about Recollection Madrid on page 112. The current rage of Indiana Glass is to make Madrid in **blue, pink and crystal.** These colors are being sold through all kinds of outlets ranging from better department stores to discount catalogues. In the past few months we have received several ads stating that this is genuine Depression glass made from old moulds. None of this is made from old glass moulds unless you consider 1976 old. Most of the pieces are from moulds that were never made originally.

The blue is becoming a big seller for Indiana according to reports I am receiving around the country. It is a brighter, more florescent blue than the originally found color.

Look at the top picture! None of these items were ever made in the old pattern Madrid. The new grill plate has one division splitting the plate in half, but the old had three sections. A goblet or vase was never made. The vase is sold with a candle making it a "hurricane lamp." The heavy tumbler was placed on top of a candlestick to make this vase/hurricane lamp. That candlestick gets a workout. It was attached to a plate to make a pedestaled cake stand and to a butter dish to make a preserve stand. That's a clever idea, actually.

The shakers are short and heavy and you can see both original styles pictured on page 113. The latest item I have seen is a heavy 11 oz. flat tumbler being sold for $7.99 in a set of four or six called "On the Rocks." The biggest giveaway to this newer glass is the pale, washed out color. (It really looks washed out in the bottom photograph here. This is a little over done, but all the new is almost that bad.)

The bottom picture shows items that were originally made. The only concern in these pieces are the cups, saucers and oval vegetable bowl. These three pieces were made in pink in the 1930's. None of the others shown were ever made in the 1930's in pink; so realize that when you see the butter dish, dinner plate, soup bowl, or sugar and creamer. These are new items! Once you have learned what this washed-out pink looks like by seeing these items out for sale, the color will let know when you see other pieces. My suggestion is to avoid pink Madrid except for the pitcher and tumblers.

The most difficult piece for new collectors to tell new from old is the candlestick. The new ones all have raised ridges inside to hold the candle more firmly. All old ones do not have these ridges. You may even find new candlesticks in black.

NEW "MAYFAIR"

Colors: Pink, green, blue, cobalt (shot glasses), 1977... Pink, green, amethyst, cobalt blue, red (cookie jars), 1982... Cobalt blue, pink, amethyst and green (odd shade), shakers 1988...

Only the pink shot glass need cause any concern to collectors because the glass wasn't made in those other colors originally. At first glance the color of the newer shots is often too light pink or too orange. Dead giveaway is the stems of the flower design, however. In the old that stem branched to form a "A" shape; in the new, you have a single stem. Further, in the new design, the leaf is hollow with the veins molded in. In the old, the leaf is molded in and the veining is left hollow. In the center of the flower on the old, dots (anther) cluster entirely to one side and are rather distinct. Nothing like that occurs in the new design.

As for the cookie jars, at cursory glance the base of the cookie has a very indistinct design. It will feel smooth to the touch it's so faint. In the old cookie jars, there's a distinct pattern which feels like raised embossing to the touch. Next, turn the bottom upside down. The new bottom is perfectly smooth. The old bottom contains a **1¾" mold circle rim** that is raised enough to catch your fingernail in it. There are other distinctions as well; but that is the quickest way to tell old from new.

In the Mayfair cookie lid, the new design (parallel to the straight side of the lid) at the edge curves gracefully toward the center "V" shape (rather like bird wings in flight); in the old, that edge is a flat straight line going into the "V" (like airplane wings sticking straight out from the side of the plane as you face it head on).

The green color of the cookie, as you can see from the picture, is not the pretty, yellow/green color of true green Mayfair. It also doesn't "glow" under black light as the old green does.

The corner ridges on the old shaker rise ½ way to the top and then smooth out. The new shaker corner ridges rise to the top and are quite pronounced. The measurement differences are listed below, but the **diameter of the opening is the critical and easiest way to tell old from new!**

	OLD	NEW
Diameter of opening	¾"	⅝"
Diameter of lid	⅞"	¾"
Height	4 1/16"	4"

So, you see, none of these reproductions give us any trouble; they're all easily spotted by those of us now "in the know!"

REPRODUCTIONS (Continued)

NEW "MISS AMERICA"

Colors: Crystal, green, pink, ice blue, red amberina, cobalt blue.

The new butter dish in "Miss America" design is probably the best of the newer products; yet there are three distinct differences to be found between the original butter top and the newly made one. Since the value of the butter dish lies in the top, it seems more profitable to examine it. **There is a new importer who is making reproductions of the reproductions.** Unfortunately, these newer models vary greatly from one batch to the next. The only noticeable thing I have seen on these butters is how the top knob sticks up away from the butter caused by a longer than usual stem on the knob. All the other characteristics still hold true, but the paragraph in bold below is the best way to tell old from new!

In the new butter dishes pictured, notice that the panels reaching the edge of the butter bottom tend to have a pronounced curving, skirt-like edge. In the original dish, there is much less curving at the edge of these panels.

Second, pick up the top of the new dish and feel up inside it. If the butter top knob is filled with glass so that it is convex (curved outward), the dish is new; the old inside knob area is concave (curved inward).

Finally, from the underside, look through the top toward the knob. In the original butter dish you would see a perfectly formed multi-sided star; in the newer version, you see distorted rays with no visible points. Shakers have been made in green, pink, cobalt blue and crystal. The latest batch of **shakers are becoming more difficult to distinguish from the old!** The new distributor's copies are creating havoc with new collectors and dealers alike. The measurements given below for shakers **do not** hold true for **all** the latest reproductions. It is impossible to know which generation of shaker reproductions that you will find, so you have to be careful on these! Know your dealer and **if the price is too good to be true,** there is likely a good reason! **It's NEW!**

The shakers will have new tops; but since some old shakers have been given new tops, that isn't conclusive at all. Unscrew the lid. Old shakers have a very neatly formed ridge of glass on which to screw the lid. It overlaps a little and has rounded off ends. Old shakers stand 3⅜" tall without the lid. **Most new** ones stand 3¼" tall. Old shakers have almost a forefinger's depth inside (female finger) or a fraction shy of 2½". **Most new** shakers have an inside depth of 2", about the second digit bend of a female's finger. (I'm doing finger depths since most of you will have those with you at the flea market, rather than a tape measure). In men, the old shaker's depth covers my knuckle; the new shakers leaves my knuckle exposed. **Most** new shakers simply have more glass on the inside of the shaker – something you can spot from twelve feet away! The hobs are more rounded on the newer shaker, particularly near the stem and seams; in the old shaker these areas remained pointedly sharp!

New Miss America tumblers have ½" of glass in the bottom, have a smooth edge on the bottom of the glass with no mold rim and show only two distinct mold marks on the sides of the glass. Old tumblers have only ¼" of glass in the bottom, have a distinct mold line rimming the bottom of the tumbler and have four distinct mold marks up the sides of the tumbler. The new green tumbler doesn't "glow" under black light as did the old.

New Miss America pitchers (without ice lip only) are all perfectly smooth rimmed at the top edge above the handle. All old pitchers that I have seen have a "hump" in the top rim of the glass above the handle area, rather like a camel's hump. The very bottom diamonds next to the foot in the new pitchers "squash" into elongated diamonds. In the old pitchers, these get noticeably smaller, but they retain their diamond shape.

NEW "SHARON" Privately Produced 1976...(continued page 222)

Colors: Blue, dark green, light green, pink, cobalt blue, burnt umber.

A blue Sharon butter turned up in 1976 and turned my phone line to a liquid fire! The color is Mayfair blue – a fluke and dead giveaway as far as real Sharon is concerned.

When found in similar colors to the old, pink and green, you can immediately tell that the new version has more glass in the top where it changes from pattern to clear glass, a thick, defined ring of glass as opposed to a thin, barely defined ring of glass in the old. The knob of the new dish tends to stick up more. In the old butter dish there's barely room to fit your finger to grasp the knob. The new butter dish has a sharply defined ridge of glass in the bottom around which the top sits. The old butter has such a slight rim that the top easily scoots off the bottom.

In 1977 a "cheese dish" appeared having the same top as the butter and having all the flaws inherent in that top which were discussed in detail above. However, the bottom of this dish was all wrong. It's about half way between a flat plate and a butter dish bottom, **bowl** shaped; and it is over thick, giving it an awkward appearance. The real cheese bottom was a salad **plate** with a rim for holding the top. These "round bottom cheese dishes" are but a parody of the old and are easily spotted. We removed the top from one in the picture so you could see its heaviness and its bowl shape.

NEW "SHARON" (Continued)

Some of the latest reproductions in Sharon are a too-light pink creamer and sugar with lid. They are pictured with the "Made in Taiwan" label. These retail for around $15.00 for the pair and are also easy to spot as reproductions. I'll just mention the most obvious differences. Turn the creamer so you are looking directly at the spout. In the old creamer the mold line runs dead center of that spout; in the new, the mold line runs decidedly to the left of center spout.

On the sugar, the leaves and roses are "off" but not enough to DESCRIBE it to new collectors. Therefore, look at the center design, both sides, at the stars located at the very bottom of the motif. A thin leaf stem should run directly from that center star upward on BOTH sides. In this new sugar, the stem only runs from one; it stops way short of the star on one side; OR look inside the sugar bowl at where the handle attaches to the bottom of the bowl; in the new bowl, this attachment looks like a perfect circle; in the old, its an upside down "v" shaped tear drop.

As for the sugar lid, the knob of the new lid is perfectly smooth as you grasp its edges. The old knob has a mold seam running mid circumference. You could tell these two lids apart blind folded!

While there is a hair's difference between the height, mouth opening diameter, and inside depth of the old Sharon shakers and those newly produced, I won't attempt to upset you with those sixteenth and thirty seconds of a degree of difference. Suffice it to say that in physical shape, they are very close. However, as concerns design, they're miles apart.

The old shakers have true appearing roses. The flowers really LOOK like roses. On the new shakers, they look like poorly drawn circles with wobbly concentric rings. The leaves are not as clearly defined on the new shakers as the old. However, forgetting all that, in the old shakers, the first design you see below the lid is a ROSE BUD. It's angled like a rocket shooting off into outer space with three leaves at the base of the bud (where the rocket fuel would burn out). In the new shakers, this "bud" has become four paddles of a windmill. It's the difference between this ✾ and this ✻.

Candy dishes have been made in pink and green. These candy jars are among the easiest items to discern old from new. Pick up the lid and look from the bottom side. On the old there is a 2" circle knob ring; on the new the ring is only ½". This shows from the top also but it is difficult to measure with the knob in the center. There are other major differences but this one will not be mould corrected easily. The bottoms are also simple to distinguish. The base diameter of the old is 3¼" and the new only 3". On the example I have quality of the new is rough, poorly shaped and molded, but I do not know if that will hold true for all reproductions of the candy. **I hope so!**

A Publication I recommend:

Books By Gene Florence

Kitchen Glassware of the Depression Years, 4th Edition $19.95

Pocket Guide to Depression Glass, 7th Edition $9.95

Collector's Encyclopedia of Occupied Japan I $14.95

Collector's Encyclopedia of Occupied Japan II $14.95

Collector's Encyclopedia of Occupied Japan III...$14.95

Collector's Encyclopedia of Occupied Japan IV $14.95

Elegant Glassware of the Depression Era, IV $19.95

Very Rare Glassware of the Depression Years I $24.95

Very Rare Glassware of the Depression Years II...$24.95

Gene Florence's Standard Baseball Card Price Guide, 4th Edition $9.95

Collectible Glassware from the 40's, 50's & 60's...$19.95

Schroeder's Antiques Price Guide

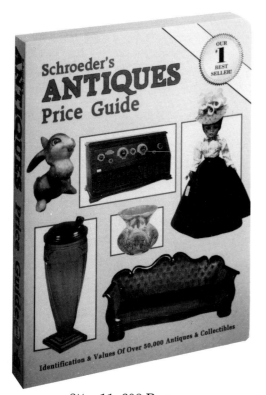

Schroeder's Antiques Price Guide has become THE household name in the antiques & collectibles field. Our team of editors works year around with more than 200 contributors to bring you our #1 best-selling book on antiques & collectibles.

With more than 50,000 items identified & priced, *Schroeder's* is a must for the collector & dealer alike. If it merits the interest of today's collector, you'll find it in *Schroeder's*. Each subject is represented with histories and background information. In addition, hundreds of sharp original photos are used each year to illustrate not only the rare and unusual, but the everyday "fun-type" collectibles as well – not postage stamp pictures, but large close-up shots that show important details clearly.

Our editors compile a new book each year. Never do we merely change prices. Each category is thoroughly checked to spot inconsistencies, listings that may not be entirely reflective of actual market dealings, and lines too vague to be of merit. Only the best of the lot remains for publication. You'll find *Schroeder's Antiques Price Guide* the one to buy for factual information and quality.

8½ x 11, 608 Pages $12.95

Collectible Glassware from the 40's, 50's, 60's...
by Gene Florence

Now that you have seen a copy of Gene Florence's popular *Collector's Encyclopedia of Depression Glass* you will be glad to know that now there is another book devoted to the newest glass collectible market since the ever popular Depression Glass! That is the glass made during the 40's, 50's & 60's. It is this glass that collectors are now turning toward. *Collectible Glassware from the 40's, 50's, 60's...* is formated in the same easy-to-use style as our *Collector's Encyclopedia of Depression Glass* with large color photographs, complete with prices and descriptions of thousands of pieces. Today's collectors are expanding their attention to glass made during the 40's, 50's & 60's. If this glass's popularity continues at its present trend, it will become the glass collectible of the 90's. This is the only book on the market today that deals exclusively with this field. Collectors and dealers will want this new title! It should quickly become the standard reference for this area of collectible and a bestseller in the field of antiques and collectibles. Having this new book will be like having a companion volume to the *Collector's Encyclopedia of Depression Glass*. This new volume picks up where the *Depression Glass* book leaves off. So get a copy and start buying the glass while it is still available and prices are low.

No dealer, glass collector or investor can afford not to own this book. It is available from your favorite bookseller for only $19.95. If you are unable to find this price guide in your area, it's available from Collector Books, P.O. Box 3009, Paducah, KY 42002-3009 @ $19.95 plus $2.00 postage & handling.

8½ x 11, 144 Pages $19.95